James Dean, Fairmount, Indiana & Farming

In 1955, Dennis Stock captured an apprehensive James Dean in front of Marcus Winslow Sr. on his tractor.

James Dean, Fairmount, Indiana & Farming

Conversations with
Marcus Winslow

Edited by Leith Adams

BearManorMedia.com

James Dean, Fairmount, Indiana & Farming: Conversations with Marcus Winslow
Edited by Leith Adams
Copyright © 2022 Marcus Winslow

Published in the USA by:
BearManor Media
1317 Edgewater Dr #110
Orlando, FL 32804
www.bearmanormedia.com

ISBN 978-1-62933-781-4
ISBN 978-1-62933-782-1 hardback

BearManor Media, Orlando, Florida
Printed in the United States of America

Book design by Adept Content Solutions, www.adeptcontentsolutions.com

Front cover photo by Dennis Stock/Magnum Photos © Dennis Stock/Magnum Photos
Back cover photos by Roy Schatt (left) and Frank Worth (right)
Both photos © Marcus Winslow

Contents

Introduction

James Dean and young Marcus's dog, Tuck, sit on the wall where Tuck would block
the boy from walking on the high parts of the wall.

In 1992, I was hired by Warner Bros. to create a Corporate Archive to preserve the studio's history, saving whatever I could find of historical interest that still existed in various departments, plus choosing props and costumes to save from current films and TV shows, a dream job.

One early focus was to plan an exhibit showcasing Warner Bros. history, mainly for employees, but also for visiting dignitaries, so they would know the hallowed ground of the studio where geniuses worked and classics were made.

As I finished a rough outline for that small exhibit, approval was suddenly given for a full-blown, two-story museum. The building was a jewel, brand new and empty, and attached to the Steven J. Ross Theater, which was named for the recently deceased and much beloved founder of Warner Communications and Time Warner Inc.

In 1995, a studio team led by my boss, Marisa O'Neil, interviewed museum exhibit designers. At one meeting, the presenters told us it would take three years to get from idea to opening. Marisa said, "We have one year."

Vincent Beggs and James Volkert looked at each other and they started discussing how an empty shell could be turned into a museum within a year. Their ideas flew back and forth and they got the job. Planning meetings were always invigorating. We all had our tasks with deadlines. It was an amazing year of working seven days a week.

Downstairs was "The Warner Brothers Years: 1915–1968," and upstairs was "Warner Bros. Animation." The first floor exhibits were Bogart and Bacall, Bette Davis, Musicals, the Oscar© Winners, the Warner Family (the four brothers: Harry, Jack, Sam, and Albert), and more. Those exhibits were displayed along the walls, but we still had to address the center of the floor.

James Dean! He would get the most space; it made sense. He starred in three WB films, all classics: *East of Eden* (1955), *Rebel Without a Cause* (1955), and *Giant* (1956). At filming's end, all costumes and props would be held in lock-up in case of re-shoots, eventually being put back into the Wardrobe & Property Departments upon the movie's release, available to be used in other films. So, between those two departments, we had artifacts from all of his films, costumes and props. Memos, scripts, set drawings, and daily production reports were at the University of Southern California's Warner Bros. Archives, and we could borrow some for the exhibit.

A museum in Fairmount, Indiana, where James Dean was raised, might have great items too. So, when I told Marisa I was soon going to my 30th high school reunion in Paris, Illinois, she said I should go to Fairmount and check out their museum.

"There's a problem," I said.

"What's the problem?"

I mentioned a lawsuit Warner Bros. had brought against the family a few years earlier claiming all rights to Dean's work and his image.

"Did we win?"

"No, Warner Bros. lost."

"Then you should go."

Paris, Illinois, is twelve miles from the Indiana border and thanks to Indiana newspapers trumpeting "Local Boy on TV," my family watched James Dean and his rise to television stardom. On a Sunday in 1955 *East of Eden* came to the Lincoln Theater, and at the age of eight, I went to see it by myself. None of my buddies wanted to go.

What I saw was so real, it was like being smacked in the face with a two-by-four. James Dean—furtive James Dean on the streets of Monterey looking for his mother; romantic James Dean on the Ferris wheel with Abra; angry James Dean fighting with his brother; anguished James Dean over his father's rejection of him and his birthday gift—the Lincoln was alive as it had never been before.

This movie wasn't monsters or cowboys or Martin and Lewis. This was real, so real I ran all the way home to tell Mom and Dad what I'd just seen. A few months later, James Dean was a headline in the October 1st *Indianapolis Star*: "Hoosier Film Star Killed in Smashup." I was devastated.

When *Rebel Without a Cause* came to the Lincoln, James Dean was alive again. A gunfighter comes to town, fights the bad guys, saves the girl, tries to rescue an outcast, and heals his family. I walked out of the theater feeling good, until I realized James Dean was dead. I was eight.

Over the years, I saw the films again and again, and there was always a dark cloud hanging over them. I programmed the first two at college screenings in 1968 and even with their Cinemascope images cropped for 16mm, they were powerful and still spoke to the hearts of the student audience. But the most memorable time was seeing *Rebel* in a Saigon neighborhood theater in 1971 when I was stationed there in the U.S. Air Force.

The Vietnamese audience was mostly young, probably students, and they reacted as I'd never seen before. When Dean beseeches his father to quit cleaning the rug and stand up like a man, then picks him up, shaking him and slamming him into a chair, a disapproving clicking sound began throughout the theater. The audience was expressing their shock at a son attacking his father by clicking their tongues off the roofs of their mouths. From 1955 to 1971, James Dean and *Rebel Without a Cause* were still relevant.

In 1978 I was put in charge of the Warner Bros. Collection of paper documents donated by the studio to USC's School of Cinema-Television. By that time, the cloud had lifted: *James Dean, what a loss!* had become for me, *James Dean, thank God he lived and left us three classic performances.* Books were crying out to be created from that collection, most especially from never-released photos of James Dean during the making of his three films. It seemed he never took a bad photograph.

After five years of having doors slammed in my face at WB, a kindly Consumer Products director signed a letter of intent, so I could pursue selling *James Dean: Behind the Scene.* An agent sold it immediately. Co-edited with a friend, the book also contained memos from the USC Collection on the making of the three films plus an "Introduction by

Dennis Hopper." It was in bookstores by Christmas 1990.

So, the plan was set: after my reunion in 1995, I would drive 150 miles to Fairmount and visit their Historical Museum and hopefully meet with Marcus Winslow. I felt I needed an introduction, so I called Gary and Sarah Legon who had made a documentary on Dean and filmed Marcus in Fairmount. They called him, and he said he'd try to meet me when I came to town.

It was a rainy day when I drove down Main Street and out to the Winslow Farm. Marcus had told me to come to the farm and he would take me to the Museum. Everything looked familiar thanks to Dennis Stock's photos for *Life* magazine of James Dean and his return home after finishing *Eden.* It was about 11:00 a.m. when I knocked on the Winslows' door. I'd expected to be in town only an hour or two, but I was drained when I left Fairmount at 7:00 p.m.

Some of the first words Marcus said to me I'll never forget. "That lawsuit...every morning I'd wake up, and it was like there was a death in the family hanging over me. I knew we hadn't done anything wrong, but if we lost the suit, we would have lost everything."

I couldn't answer. Even though I'd worked at USC when it happened, I felt some responsibility since the lawyer for Consumer Products who brought the lawsuit had called me in for meetings to discuss Dean. When the lawyer said the studio was suing, I told him, "Whatever you do, don't sue the family, because they raised him when his mother died." Needless to say, the studio sued the family.

My day with Marcus remains a blur, but I saw some incredible things. There was Dean's handwritten address book with Frank Mazzola's name. Frank played Crunch, a gang member in *Rebel,* and thanks to Bill Zavatsky, who was working on a book about the making of that film, Frank and his wife, Catherine, became friends.

Initially, Frank had been hired to teach Jimmie and Corey Allen about knife fights, since Frank had been in one when he was a member of Hollywood High's Athenians, a "social club." Frank also taught Jimmie about gang life to prepare him for *Rebel;* so that Jimmie could experience a gang up close, Frank called his members and told them they'd been challenged by an East L.A. gang, and they should meet him outside Miceli's in Hollywood. He thought only one or two guys would show, since it was such a quick notice, but they all came. Just inside the restaurant was Jimmie, watching them gather, whipping their chains and swinging their tire irons. They were so hot and angry, Frank knew he needed to calm them before they attacked the first person who walked by. In Jimmie's address book, "Frank Mazzola—scary" was written next to a phone number.

In the Fairmount Historical Museum was an 8-foot standee of Jimmie as Jett Rink from *Giant,* two rehearsal switchblades from *Rebel* that the studio gave to Jimmie's father after Jimmie died, Jimmie's Czech motorcycle, his high school sports ribbons, baby clothes, and Porsche racing mementos; but most impressive of all was his Triumph Trophy 500 motorcycle that Jack Warner had banned from the lot.

At day's end, I expressed interest in a few pieces, and Marcus said he would have to think about it. Eventually he okayed the standee, the switchblades, Jimmie's annotated script from *Giant,* plus the Triumph, which we put front and center in the Warner Bros. Museum, the first object you saw upon walking in. Needless to say, it was a "Wow!"

Over the years, Marcus and I became friends, so when Marylou, his wife and high school sweetheart, asked if I would write his biography, I was extremely honored and said I could do an oral history, so his story would be in his own words. They were both okay with that. As an aside, Marylou told me it wasn't until Martin Sheen came to town that Marcus was finally able to talk about Jimmie…that whenever someone asked about Dean, Marcus's jaw would tighten, and he would be sullen and depressed for days. The pain of losing his "big brother" hurt him that much.

But Marcus's story is also the story of the changes time has brought to small farming communities, changes I've seen happen to my own hometown. Mega-farming, Mega-stores, Mega-equipment, and Mega-more have changed the landscape and the world we small-town baby boomers knew and remember. So, *James Dean, Fairmount, Indiana & Farming: Conversations with Marcus Winslow* is Marcus's view of a life interrupted and the lives that must continue.

This book is for Marylou and Marcus and their sons Coy and Chuck and the Winslow Family. The interviews were conducted in Marcus's Car Barn at the Winslow Farm in 2016—April 3–5 and July 22–27 and 2017—May 8–12 and have been edited for brevity and clarity.

Leith Adams—June 2020

1

Jimmie's Death

Leith Adams: Your farm and your house are as famous as downtown Fairmount thanks to the James Dean photos Dennis Stock took here in 1955. James Dean was older than you, but would he play with you as a kid?

Marcus Winslow: Jimmie was already living in the house when I was born. He was nine years old in 1940 when his mother died and he came from California to live with us. I was born in late '43, so I remember him being here. He was a good athlete, played basketball and a lot of track. He did a lot of running on the track team and he did some high and low hurdles, they called it, and he used to pole vault some. My dad was very interested in athletics.

Jimmie set up a pole vault thing in the barnyard, just a couple of posts with little pegs in them to put a bar on, but he'd practice on that. He was pretty good in track. He won a lot of ribbons for pole vaulting and the high and low hurdles and, of course, basketball.

LA: Your sister, Joan (pronounced Jo Ann), was still in the house for the first couple of years after you were born?

MW: Yeah, but I don't remember her living here. I remember she visited a lot. It seems strange that I lived here and didn't know she was my sister, but she got married and left in 1946, so I was only two to three years old, though I do remember her coming back.

She and her husband lived just east of Fairmount, and I was always glad for her to be here. She had a son and he'd come over too and he and I would play or I would go over there, but it never registered to me that she was my sister for a long time.

(Marcus points to a framed piece on a table.) A friend of mine, Eric Plumb, gave me that right there and in it is a ticket and a program for the Sectional, which was when all the Grant County teams played basketball against each other, February 24, 25, 26, 1949; the games were always played at the Coliseum in Marion.

Here's a newspaper picture of Jimmie on the team. He was one of the better athletes. The Fairmount Quakers played Marion in the final game, and Marion won 41 to 36 or something. I'm going to put it in the Fairmount Historical Museum. Eric's aunt mentioned to him, "I went to that game and I still have the ticket and I still have the program for it," so he put them in this frame.

I've been trying to get a photograph to put in it because newspaper photos aren't real clear, especially when they're almost eighty years old. I would say it's a pretty rare thing really.

LA: Did you go to games as a kid?

MW: I'm sure I went to a lot of them, but I can't honestly say I remember them. I'm sure Mom and Dad went to all the games and I'm sure I had to tag along. *(laughs)*

LA: You don't remember cheering for Jimmie? He was like your older brother?

MW: No, I don't. I'd like to be able to say I did, but I don't really.

LA: How many of Jimmie's classmates are still alive?

MW: Not very many. Victor Hilton, he's dead, I know. (reading the caption) Bob Howell, I don't know him. Jim Grindle, he's still alive. Rex Bright, he died. Bob Roth is still going. Ray Turner and John Webster, I think they're both still alive. Paul Smith, he's deceased. I'd say over half have died, a lot of them just in the last two or three years.

Jim Folkerson, he died. He was one of the pallbearers during Jimmie's funeral and so was Paul Smith. Rex Bright also was one of the pallbearers. There aren't many left because… Well, they'd have to be in their mid-eighties now. Jim was born in '31, so he'd be eighty-five now and he could have been one of the younger ones in the class. Some of them are probably eighty-six, maybe eighty-seven, especially if they were held back a grade, so not many of them are left anymore. And the school…That's been torn down. It's kind of sad how time just goes on.

I remember Jimmie worked at Snider's, a canning factory in Fairmount, in the fall one or two years. When tomatoes were picked, they would bring them into this factory and process them, making ketchup or tomato sauce or whatever. I don't know what exactly he did, but a lot of Fairmount people worked at Snider's seasonally. Jimmie brought home a case of ketchup, and we had some of it in the basement up until just a few years ago, so I gave the bottles to the Historical Museum. They still had the Snider's label on them. Why we didn't use them, I don't know, but they were down in the basement.

LA: When you saw *East of Eden* (1955) the first time, was it in Fairmount?

MW: No, *East of Eden* was at the Indiana Theatre in Marion. The guy who managed it called up Mom and Dad when *East of Eden* was going to come in there. I don't know who all he called, but he had a private showing for the family and for some friends. I was in school, so I got out to go to it. Mom and Dad were there and Grandma and Grandpa Dean and Mrs. Adeline Nall, Jimmie's drama teacher. I don't remember who all else was there, probably Joan, my sister, but it was a private showing of *East of Eden.*

I didn't know what to expect, but, of course, right off the bat, Jimmie was on the screen. A lot of times when someone is in a movie, you don't see them until the movie is half over, but he was right there in the very first part of it and he was in most of the movie. I thought that was about the best movie I'd ever seen and I still feel that way. I really enjoyed *East of Eden.*

It took place in 1916 or '17. World War I was just starting and America was getting involved in it. I always enjoyed old cars and it had a lot of old cars in it, and I just liked the story. That night was when everybody got to go to it. A lot of people in Marion went to see it just because Jimmie was in it. It was always my favorite movie.

Jimmie had died when *Rebel Without a Cause* (1955) came out. I do remember going to see it a couple times. I saw it with Mom and Dad and then a few days later, a friend of mine who lived around the corner stopped by. He was driving, so he was probably sixteen. He asked if I wanted to go see *Rebel* with him, and I said, "Yeah," so I saw it again. *Rebel* was an awfully good movie, kind of a teenager type movie, but I didn't enjoy it as much as *East of Eden*. I think one reason was because I knew Jimmie was never going to be able to know how the public accepted it, the same as with *Giant* (1956).

Giant didn't come out for another year, and by that time Mom and Dad had given about a hundred interviews. It seemed like every time they turned around, some magazine was wanting to come and do an interview with them. I was in school, so I didn't have to deal with it much.

Giant was so long that when it was half over, the theater in Marion put in an intermission. Even though it's over three hours, Jimmie was in it only a little over thirty minutes, but he was what made that movie. I don't think there is any question about that. I enjoy *Giant* today. I guess I enjoy the memorabilia from it more than the other movies.

LA: Jimmie bought a motorcycle right down the road from the farm?

MW: Dad bought the motorcycle for Jimmie, a Czech, about a 1946 or '47 model. It was brand-new. Marvin Carter sold Indians, but they didn't build a real small cycle. I've been told several of the Indian dealers sold Czech motorcycles to customers who wanted a little bike. It really was built in Czechoslovakia.

Jimmie used to ride that thing to school. He rode it everywhere around. Even guys that had big motorcycles, he would go on rides with them.

Sometimes he'd take me down the road to a place that sold ice cream called the Dutch Mill. You could drive up to the window with that motorcycle and get an ice cream cone without getting off. He'd always put me straddling the fuel tank in front of him and then he'd put his arms up on the handlebars, steering, so I couldn't hardly fall off. He had that bike for several years.

When he went back to live with his dad in California after graduating high school, he wrote or called and told Mom and Dad he sure missed his cycle and would like to have it out there, so Dad shipped it out to him. I don't remember how, but he shipped that cycle to California.

Then one time when Mom and Dad were visiting Uncle Winton and Jimmie, he wanted to know if Dad could bring it back home, so they took the wheels off, took the fuel out and put it in the trunk of that '49 Ford, and Dad brought it home where it sat in our garage for a while.

Jimmie was here from New York one time and I don't remember him specifically trading the Czech in, but he must have. He bought a Royal Enfield and he wanted to ride it back. He had on these big heavy gloves with cuffs on them that went clear up your arms, so the air couldn't blow up them. They were more like mittens than they were gloves, no fingers on them, just a place for your thumb and then the rest of it was just like a mitten.

He had on a leather jacket and he had on a face mask that he put on clear over his head. It just had little slits cut in it, one slit for each eye and a slit for his nose and that was all. He had a little leather cap with a strap he put on, had wool and stuff inside of it, then he strapped it on.

The Indian Motorcycle shop where Jimmie's first motorcycle was purchased.

He rode that Enfield towards New York, but when he got to Pennsylvania, it broke down. It was on the Pennsylvania Turnpike, and someone came along and contacted an Indian dealer there. And this dealer came out and put Jimmie's bike in his pick-up truck and took him and the bike to the shop.

Jimmie ended up staying with this guy and his wife for three or four days. And from what I was told, the wife made real good spaghetti, and Jimmie just loved spaghetti. He finally ended up trading that Royal Enfield for an Indian, because the guy didn't know for sure what was wrong with the Enfield.

Jimmie called home because the title was still here. I don't know if it was in Dad's name or what the deal was, but I remember him calling and asking Dad to send the title to that motorcycle dealer. And then he called Jane Deacy, his agent in New York, to get an advancement on some money he had coming.

That's how he paid for the Indian, and then he rode it on to New York. I assume he sold it eventually. But I know Mom was really worried about him riding the motorcycle all the way back. It was in the winter and it was cold, you know, and he was all bundled up, but he didn't seem worried about it.

LA: So, this was when he was moving from California to New York?

MW: No, it was just one of the times he came back here from New York for a visit.

He came back at least once a year. One time he came back, and I didn't even know he was coming. This kid at school or maybe on the school bus said Jimmie was home. I didn't believe him because I hadn't heard anything about him coming home and, sure enough, when I got to the house, Jimmie was here.

Another time when he came home, Bill Bast and "Dizzy" Sheridan came with him, and Mom and Dad didn't know he was coming. One day, here they came, all three of them. Mom had arthritis real bad. I remember that. She had it so bad she could hardly dress herself. About that time, there was a place in Marion called Davis Clinic, and she started going to Davis Clinic at least once a week and they gave her something called "gold shots." I don't know what it consisted of, but it sure did help, and she got to where she was back in pretty good shape again.

Mom always did have trouble with her fingers. Her joints were swollen, but she got to where she could do what she wanted on her own. Anyway, Jimmie and Bill and "Dizzy" were here for, I'm going to say, three days, and Jimmie got a call from New York. They needed him to get back because he had a job on Broadway doing some play, so they took off and hitchhiked back to New York.

When they came here, a baseball player named Clyde McCullough, I think, had picked them up and brought them all the way, almost right to the door. They were real fortunate to have only one person bring them.

Going back to New York, I don't remember how they went. Knowing Mom and Dad, I wouldn't be surprised if they put them on a bus, but I really don't remember.

LA: Where did they stay? What room?

MW: We had a spare bedroom upstairs. Maybe there were two bedrooms. I'm not sure if we were using them both or not. I stayed in my room and nobody stayed with me. Apparently all three of them were in one room.

When Jimmie went back to California after high school, I took over his room. I had the same bedroom suite and everything he used. We've still got it. Right before Jimmie came here, Mom and Dad bought a maple bedroom suite. They bought it for themselves, but Jimmie liked it so well, they let him have it and we never got rid of it.

LA: Were the three of them fun to be around?

MW: Yeah, they were real talkative. I don't remember everything they did, but they were on the go all the time they were here.

LA: They didn't put on shows for you?

MW: No, I don't think so. That's about all I can remember about Liz Sheridan and Bill Bast being here.

LA: Did you meet them again later?

MW: I met Liz Sheridan a few years ago and then she came here once or twice in the past ten or fifteen years. She's a real nice person, seemed very close to Jimmie. Her most famous acting role came later in her life on TV on *Seinfeld* (1989–1998), when she played Jerry Seinfeld's mother.

Bill Bast, I met once since then, and it was at the Warner Bros. Museum opening in 1996. He was there and he introduced himself to me. After I saw him, I recognized him, but the only reason I recognized him was from photos I'd seen because he had aged a lot. When Mom passed away, somehow he found out about it, and he sent us a sympathy card, but I've never had any contact with him since.

LA: At the opening of the museum in Burbank, did he talk to you about coming back to Fairmount?

MW: I talked to him for maybe five minutes, and there was a lot of stuff going on and we really didn't talk about Jimmie, if I remember.

LA: Did you get to talk to Elizabeth Taylor at the museum?

MW: Yeah, I met her and Roddy McDowall, but I didn't get to have any conversations with her or anything.

LA: Did she react to you as Jimmie's cousin?

MW: Not especially. Of course, everybody was going up to her and shaking her hand. I think she hadn't been well, so I just introduced myself. Other people were wanting to talk to her, so I didn't try to have too much conversation with her. She was pretty much in demand. (*laughs*)

LA: Did your family have a television from the beginning?

MW: Mom and Dad had one of the earliest televisions in the area. And Dad used to watch ballgames, so neighbors would come

over, especially if it was the state tournament. This one neighbor in particular was a big basketball fan, and he had a couple of kids and they'd come over and we'd play and watch the state tournament on TV.

When Jimmie started to be on a few TV shows, he usually called Mom and Dad or sent them a postcard to tell them he was going to be on a certain show. Back then, you only had one TV and you had it in the living room, and you only had one phone and our phone was in the dining room, so whenever Jimmie would be on TV, why, the phone would start ringing. Other people in Fairmount had seen him and wanted us to be sure to see the show.

I think there were occasions when we didn't know he was going to be on, but usually we knew. We'd take turns getting up and going to answer the phone. As I look back on it, it was kind of a neat time seeing him on TV. It seemed like he usually played similar parts. He was always a thief or a gangster or something. I would never have guessed it, but he was in over thirty television shows. It was from people seeing him on TV, that's how he got even more parts.

There was a bar in New York he used to go to a lot and they had a television. And

Elizabeth Taylor with Roddy McDowall talks to Carole Bayer Sager near the James Dean Exhibit, June 1996, at the Warner Bros. Museum opening party.

6

they were watching this show, and Jimmie was sitting there drinking. He told the bartender, he said, "Keep your eye on that TV for the next half hour," and he left. And Jimmie was on the TV. He didn't tell the guy he was going to be on there. One reason he was drinking was to get himself psyched up for this character who was supposed to have been drinking too much.

It was always exciting to see him on TV, but we never dreamed he'd be in the movies. He got the opportunity when he was doing a Broadway play, *The Immoralist* (1954), at the time. The story is Elia Kazan had heard about Jimmie and went to see him. He asked him if he wanted to come do an audition and Jimmie quit *The Immoralist* and went to California and got the part in *East of Eden.*

He came back home with Dennis Stock in February of '55 and *East of Eden* hadn't been released yet. It was maybe within a couple weeks of being released, and then he went back and did *Rebel. Rebel* was released in October, only a couple of weeks after his death, but when we saw *East of Eden,* he was still alive. Like I said, that was pretty exciting to see him up on the big screen.

LA: Did your parents go see him in New York?

MW: No, I don't think they ever went to New York. Some writers claim they did in books and stuff they wrote, but I don't think they ever went to New York when Jimmie was there.

LA: But they did go to California when he was out there.

MW: They went out to visit Mom's brother, Jimmie's father, Uncle Winton. Dad and Mom would go to California one year for a vacation, and they'd be gone about a month. They always drove out. Then the next year, Uncle Winton and Aunt Ethel, Jimmie's stepmother, would come here and stay with Mom and Dad for one or two weeks, and then they'd drive back home. That had gone on since 1950 or 1951. Jimmie wasn't out there part of the time when they went out, and then part of the time, he was.

The last time Mom and Dad went out to stay with Uncle Winton was September 1955. They had left Los Angeles and were driving back when Jimmie was killed. They didn't even know it until they got home. I imagine, had Jimmie lived, they would have gone back more often, if he was going to stay out there. As it turned out, *East of Eden* was the only movie released before he died. It was always kind of sad to think he could have done so much more and wasn't able to, but he made three movies and he sure did make a name for himself.

LA: When he started appearing on TV, how did the townspeople react?

MW: Oh, they were excited about it. I remember when I'd get out of school in the evening, a lot of times Dad would pick me up and we'd go on uptown and he'd drink coffee and I'd get a Coke. People were always asking him, "What's Jimmie gonna be in next? What's he doing?"

At that time, a lot of people around town knew Jimmie. They could remember him from high school. He hadn't been out of high school only a year or two before he started getting into some TV shows, so they were always excited about what he was going to be in next.

Of course, when he made a movie, well, they were really excited about that. *East of Eden* turned out to be such a good movie, and they were all looking forward to what his next one was going to be. He was very popular around Fairmount at that time.

LA: When he returned to Fairmount one time, he went up to the high school?

MW: He usually went to the high school every time he came home. I don't know why, but he'd always go to the high school and at least visit Mrs. Nall's class. I remember one year one of the classes, had to either be a junior or senior class, was rehearsing for a play, and Mrs. Nall asked him if he would come back that evening and help with it, so he did. He kept them all there pretty late, rehearsing, and some of the parents got upset (*laughs*) because the kids were out until ten o'clock or later rehearsing for a play.

But Jimmie'd had a lot of experience in New York doing TV and plays, and he wanted them to get it right. The kids seemed to enjoy his visits. Of course, when he started getting on some TV shows, then they really enjoyed him coming back and helping them. It was kind of an interesting time.

LA: Did he ever drive here?

MW: No. The last time, he and Dennis Stock came on a train. I'm not sure if the train was out of New York or out of Chicago, but it was on a Saturday that he came in because I was out of school. We had had a lot of snow. Mom stayed home because she was going to cook up a big dinner. She always thought she had to entertain everybody by getting their dinners, so Dad had me go with him. We went down to Union Station in Indianapolis, and the train was late coming in.

I think we were there a couple hours or more waiting for him to get in. We probably got there early anyway, and the train was

at least an hour late. There were several stairways coming down from the platform up where the trains unloaded. We weren't too sure which one they'd use, but we just happened to be close to the right one, the one Jimmie and Dennis came down. Of course, we were glad to see Jimmie. We didn't know Dennis, but he was the photographer for *Life* magazine and he got pretty well acquainted with Mom and Dad. When Jimmie died, Dennis came back to the funeral. We hadn't seen Dennis since he was here with Jimmie. I don't even know if we had heard from him.

I was sitting on the front row at the funeral. The family was all in the front row, and I saw Dennis come in. He walked in front of me, and Mom and Dad were sitting over to the left. I think I was sitting with my sister. Dad was so glad to see Dennis. It was the first time I ever saw Dad cry in my life.

Mom said when Jimmie died that Dad had never shed any tears. And when Dad saw Dennis, he just started bawling like a baby. Dennis had a real affection for Mom and Dad, especially Dad, I think. I never knew for sure, but I always felt Dennis didn't have a real good life as a child and he looked up to Mom and Dad. Even though they didn't see each other hardly ever after that, there was still a close bond between them because of the circumstances of Dennis coming home with Jimmie the last time. It was a sad time for everybody then.

LA: When Jimmie was at the funeral home and you went there with your mom and dad, what do you remember?

MW: A lot of people were there, a lot of people. The funeral home used to have a big front porch that was open, but now it's enclosed. I remember being out on the front porch and it was crowded, a lot of flowers, a lot of people. They viewed the bodies at a different place in the funeral home then than they do now. It was quite an experience.

LA: Did your mom and dad view Jimmie's body?

MW: Dad did. Yeah, Dad told Mr. Hunt he'd like to see the body and he did. I was told his neck was probably broken. It had swollen an awful lot. Mr. Hunt said he could have done some things to make him viewable, but they didn't. That was back in 1955. They could do a whole lot more now than they could back then.

I think he was just dressed in a sport coat. Supposedly there were about three thousand people in town for the funeral. I know the church was full, and it was like a mob outside the church, so it was a pretty big deal at the time. To be honest about it, a lot of people there didn't know Jimmie. They just knew who he was and were curious as to what was going on and a lot of them were fans and really cared about him.

LA: Do you remember a lot of crying?

MW: Yeah, quite a bit, especially women, girls. Yeah, it was a sad occasion. Afterwards a lot of the people came back to the house. Nick Adams and Jack Simmons (actors in *Rebel Without a Cause*) came up to my room and Henry Ginsberg was here. He was one of the producers of *Giant* and he was downstairs talking to Mom and Dad and whoever else was there. I was just a little kid, but I do remember having a conversation with him. Mom and Dad commented he seemed like a real nice guy.

LA: So, Nick and Jack came up to your room and it had been Jimmie's. Were they talking to you about Jimmie?

MW: Not too much, not as I remember. They came all the way from California to get here, and they really didn't have any money. It was a sad time for them. I think they both felt close to Jimmie, but so did everybody that came from California.

Bob Middleton used to live across the field here and he stopped by for a while. He was one of Jimmie's pallbearers. Bob and his wife used to come and see Mom and Dad quite a bit. They lived in Marion for a few years, and then they finally got transferred to Fort Wayne, Indiana. They worked for the Indiana-Michigan Light Company. They were real close to Jimmie. Bob used to come over here when he was a kid and play with Jimmie. I think they'd swim together behind the barn and fish and just plain do what kids do. He was a good friend of Jimmie's.

Bob Pulley was also a pallbearer and a friend of Jimmie's from Fairmount. He worked for the telephone company and used to stop by quite often. He had a job where he had to drive around the country in a pickup truck, troubleshooting things, so if he got caught up on his work, he'd stop in and talk for a little bit, things like that.

Marvin Carter, Marvin and Mildred Carter, had the motorcycle shop down the road. I don't remember them coming here to see Mom and Dad that day, but they were very close to Jimmie. Dad and I would stop sometimes and talk to Marvin down there in the motorcycle shop. He was a good friend of Jimmie's, too.

Mildred and Marvin never had any children of their own, so they kind of took a special interest in Jimmie, especially since Jimmie's mother had died. They got pretty close to him and any time Jimmie'd come home for a visit, he'd always go visit Mildred and Marvin. I know they were pretty, pretty upset when he passed away.

LA: You've said your mom and dad never really got over it.

MW: No, they didn't.

LA: Could you feel it in the house all the time?

MW: Yeah, yeah. It's just they'd gotten awful close to Jimmie. When Jimmie's mother died, Mom and Dad took a special interest in him, raising him and all that. Jimmie apparently was different from a lot of kids. I mean he was just a fun-loving kid. He was a good athlete, a good artist. I don't think he ever caused Mom and Dad any trouble. I can't remember ever hearing anything about him getting in any kind of trouble. Kids back then, they didn't have all the stuff to deal with kids have today.

LA: Did Jimmie ever take the car out on the road when he wasn't supposed to or anything like that?

MW: Not to my knowledge. If he did, it wasn't a story I'd ever heard. I do remember something from Jimmie's senior year of high school. The first half would have been in 1948 and the second half would've been 1949 because that was when he graduated. It had to have been in November–December of '48. The Rexall Drugstore in Fairmount had a contest where when people came in and bought something, they'd give them a ticket, and they'd sign this ticket, and put whoever's name on it they wanted to win a prize.

One thing they were giving away, which was probably the main thing for boys, was an electric train set, a Lionel Electric Train. And Jimmie got everybody he knew, all his friends, to sign a ticket and put my name on it, and I won the electric train. I still have it. I can remember Jimmie down on the living room floor with me,

helping me put the track together and putting all the cars and engines and so forth on the track. I remember that real well.

He was just like an older brother. Thinking back on it, it was pretty amazing that he was able to get enough people to sign my name on their tickets. I'm guessing that contest probably started November 1, or it could even have been October 1, for people to vote. It was a way for the drugstore to get people to come in and buy stuff. I don't remember what all they gave away.

I did see a newspaper article not too long ago. Someone had done some research at the library in Fairmount. A lot of the old Fairmount newspapers are printed out or are on a disk there, and they found that contest and made a copy and gave it to me. I've got it somewhere, but it told all the winners and I was the winner of the electric train and that was pretty neat.

LA: Did Jimmie ever talk about his mother to you?

MW: No. I've heard Mom and Dad say that Jimmie never mentioned his mother. Never. I'm sure he missed his mother. I mean, any kid would, but he seemed to accept it or adjusted well to it from what Mom and Dad both said. I heard them say they never, never heard Jimmie mention his mother.

Jimmie used to call my Mom, "Mom," and he'd call Dad, "Mark" or "Rack." Rack. R-A-C-K. That was a nickname my dad had. All his old friends, or people that knew Dad when he was young, they always called him "Rack," and Jimmie liked that name. He wanted people to call him "Rack." I don't think anybody did, to speak of, but I know there are several places in people's yearbooks where he signed, "Jim (Rack) Dean," so he liked that name Rack.

LA: Did your dad get it because of pool, the game of pool?

MW: No, he got it from playing tennis.

LA: Because of the tennis racket...?

MW: Yeah.

LA: He must have been good.

MW: Evidently when he was young, he played a lot of tennis and he got that nickname. It is kind of a neat name. I've never heard anybody else called that really.

But I still have that Lionel train, still as good as new, because I only get it out about once a year and play with it for a while. It took up a lot of room. We'd set it up usually in the winter and play with it, and then we'd get tired of it and tear it apart and put it in the box. It's pretty easy to take apart and put back together.

LA: Lew Bracker was there at the funeral?

MW: Yeah, Lew was there. He came out to the house. Dad and Lew Bracker, I don't remember whether Dennis Stock went with them or not, but they got in the car and just went for a ride. Since Lew was such a good friend, Dad wanted to know all about Jimmie and what he'd been doing.

There were two ministers at the funeral. One of them was Xen (pronounced "Zen") Harvey. He was a local guy. The other was James DeWeerd. He had a brand-new '55 Thunderbird, a black one. They were pretty fancy cars when they first came out. We were here at the farm and he asked me, "Do you want to go for a ride in the Thunderbird?" Of course I did and I got in and we got about a mile from home and Jim DeWeerd stopped the car and started to get out.

He said, "You come around and drive it." I said, "Are you sure?" And he said, "Yeah." I wasn't even twelve years old yet, but I knew how to drive. I'd never driven a Thunderbird, but I got out and went around and got in and he said, "You've got to put your foot on the brake to put it into gear."

I did and I pushed a button on the gearshift handle. That's how you moved from one gear to the other, by pushing this button down to unlock it and putting it in drive, and away we went. That was an exciting experience for me. I didn't drive very far, maybe half a mile or maybe even a mile, I don't know.

Jim DeWeerd was a good friend of Jimmie's and he had kind of helped Jimmie when Jimmie was younger, when he was living here with Mom and Dad. They wanted him to do the funeral and also Xen Harvey who was a good friend of the family. He was the pastor at the Fairmount Friends Church at that time. That's where the funeral was.

I told you it was a huge funeral. The church was totally full, and they had the windows open. They put speakers up in the windows, so the people outside could hear. There were people all around the church. It was really a big deal for Fairmount.

Everybody thought there would be a bunch of movie stars and there wasn't. Elizabeth Taylor sent flowers. There were yellow flowers at the funeral home from her. Nick Adams, I guess he told someone at Warner Bros., "I'm going to Indiana to the funeral."

He didn't even have the money to fly out, but he was going to hitchhike or whatever he had to do. As I understand it, the studio advanced him the money to come to the funeral and he didn't have a suit, so they gave him a suit out of the Wardrobe Department to wear.

Jimmie, Nick Adams and Perry Lopez reveal their inner Brando on the set of *Rebel Without a Cause*.

After the funeral when Nick and Jack came out to the house and I took them upstairs to see Jimmie's bedroom, Nick had been smoking a cigarette and he dropped some cigarette ashes on that suit and burned a hole in it and, God, he was worried. He was really worried (*laughs*) what Warner Bros. was going to say when he got back. That's something I always remembered.

LA: Did Jimmie's father come back for the funeral?

MW: Oh, yeah, Uncle Winton was back. Yep. Jimmie's father and stepmother came back. Oh, they were here for just a couple of days. The funeral was on a Saturday. I was out of school. Saturday, October 8. I think they went back to California on Monday or something. That's the way I remember it.

Winton had a lot of stuff to do, had to get Jimmie's house cleaned out and a lot of loose ends were still hanging, so they weren't here too long after the funeral. They were originally going to bury Jimmie over in Marion where his mother is. Mom and Dad wanted to know if Uncle Winton would go along with burying him here in Fairmount because they felt they would be the ones that would have to look after the grave and take care of it. It would be a lot easier for them to do it here than it would be in Marion, so that's what they ended up doing.

LA: Do you remember where you were exactly when you heard Jimmie had been killed?

MW: Yeah. Whenever Mom and Dad would go to California, they'd be gone for four weeks and I'd stay with my sister, so I was staying with her. Reece was her son's name, and he and I were about like brothers. I'd sleep upstairs with him, and I remember the phone rang and it was late at night. I hadn't had much sleep yet. I could tell from what little I could hear of the phone conversation that something had happened to somebody and I didn't know who. I didn't get up and ask. I thought maybe something happened to Mom and Dad, but I didn't know.

The next morning, I went downstairs and my sister was gone and my brother-in-law's mother, she just lived next door almost, she was there watching us. She's the one who told me. She said she had some bad news and that Jimmie had been killed in a car wreck and nobody knew too much about it. They knew someone had turned in front of him and that was about all. They didn't know where it happened or what he was driving or

anything. That was on a Saturday, Saturday morning. I know they tried to get ahold of Mom and Dad somehow, but there wasn't any way to do that.

I think they had the state police looking for them. Dad always said he had the car radio on and he heard the guy on the radio talking, saying a young, aspiring movie actor had been killed in a car wreck. And he just kind of had a gut feeling it was Jimmie and he reached over and turned the radio off. Mom didn't notice it, and he made a point not to have the radio on after that. He made it a point not to buy any newspapers. He made it a point to drive right back home, straight on through then. It was on the Saturday when he heard it and even then, he didn't know if it was Jimmie for sure, but he had this feeling. Jimmie had died Friday, September 30.

The neighbors over here near us, Bob Middleton's family, they saw the lights come on in the house late Sunday night. They called my sister and told her, and she came over and told Mom and Dad. I don't remember whether I came over on Monday or if it was on Tuesday. They let me ride the school bus home, and I remember Mom was in the dining room sitting in that chair. Jimmie had bought a red chair for them the last time he was home, a tilt-back chair, a La-Z-Boy-type chair. It had red plastic covering on it like artificial leather. It was a nice chair.

She was sitting in that chair, and her face was just as red as one of those flowers down there (Marcus points) on that rug from crying. Of course, she was glad to see me, but I didn't stay that night. I don't think I stayed here with Mom and Dad until after the funeral was over. My sister kept me over there.

Mom and Dad never did get over Jimmie's death. I don't think Uncle Winton ever did either. It was just kind of one of those things where people wouldn't let you forget it. They continually had people asking this or asking that or wanting an interview.

Jimmie's dad and stepmother, they were a little different. They were used to moving a lot. They always did move a lot. They got so they didn't want anyone to know who they were. They'd move and if they suspected a neighbor knew who they were, they'd have to move again. They lived down in Florida for probably seven or eight years in a housing addition and nobody ever knew. Nobody knew they were Jimmie's mom and dad because they didn't want anybody to know it.

My mom and dad, they lived here on the farm, and the farm had been Dad's life. They couldn't just pull up and move, not that they wanted to. I'm sure there were times when they wished they could, but they were always very nice to the fans. They felt they owed it to them, I think, because the fans liked Jimmie so well.

They would even let people into the house. They'd show them scrapbooks, and if fans wrote letters, Mom and Dad would write them letters back. I have to admit, I've tried to be nice to the fans, but I don't very often answer a letter. Maybe that's a bad trait I have, but I just don't. Mom and Dad felt it was their responsibility, since Jimmie wasn't here, to be nice to everybody. I've met a lot of nice people over the years, and Mom and Dad made some good friends, too. People have started out as fans of Jimmie's and turned out to just be good friends, period. I know I've met some that way. It's been quite an experience.

LA: That week before the funeral, did you go back to school?

MW: Yeah, yeah, I went back to school. He was killed on a Friday, and I went back to school the next week and... (silence)

LA: How did the kids act?

MW: They talked about it some. I remember them talking about it, that he'd been killed. I don't remember too much about what happened then, but I do remember some of the kids talked about it. Everybody hated it.

LA: His drama teacher, Adeline Nall, did she talk to you?

MW: Adeline Nall wasn't here. Adeline Nall, if there was ever a person that was interested in theatrical stuff, it was her. Especially after Jimmie made a movie, she really wanted to get into theater then. Jimmie told her to move to New York, and he'd try to get her some breaks, talk to some people. She took a leave of absence from her job here at school and moved to New York City. It seems to me she got a job in a hotel or something there, but then Jimmie was killed and, of course, had she known he was going to be killed, she never would have moved to New York in the first place, but she stayed for a couple years. Then she came back to Fairmount and went back to teaching school, but she wasn't in Fairmount when he was killed.

As I remember, I don't think she came back for the funeral. Of course, it wasn't as easy to do things like that then, as it is today. A lot of people don't realize you couldn't just pick up the telephone and call anywhere. Oh, you could, but people just didn't do it. You just didn't pick up the phone and call California and talk to someone. You'd send them a letter, but you didn't call them.

I remember when Jonesboro was long distance. Marion was long distance. The only people you could talk to on a regular phone call were people right here in Fairmount.

I remember when we still had operators. They had an operator when Jimmie was killed because Uncle Winton called and told Joan that Jimmie had been killed, and this lady who was the operator, I think she told everybody in Fairmount before the next morning and (*laughs*) that's just the way it was.

We had what was called a "party line." People down the road from us were on the line. It seemed we were more fortunate than some others who had three or four houses on the line with them. We only had one other family, but they had kids and they were always getting on the phone and leaving the phone off the hook or not getting it laid back down all the way and finally Dad would go down and ask them if their phone was off the hook. "No, no, it's..." But when he came back home, it would be okay. (*laughs*) You knew it was off the hook, but that's just the way it used to be. I'm sure everybody on a party line had those experiences.

LA: As a kid, you weren't using the phone that much though?

MW: No, I might call a friend of mine occasionally, but you didn't use the phone then like you do now. These kids today, the telephone is the most important thing they have. If they don't have a phone to chatter on, why, it's the end of the world. You sit there and try to have a conversation with them, and they're texting somebody or going through reading texts that have been sent to them and talking to you at the same time. Really, it's pretty rude, but that's just the way it is. (*laughs*)

James Dean: Searching.

2

Jimmie in Fairmount

Leith Adams: When Jimmie came to town at the age of nine, where did he go to school?

Marcus Winslow: For grade school, he went to the West Ward School. That's where farm kids mostly went. Junior high was held in the high school building, so he went there for both junior high and high school. I was born in '43, and that's probably when he started junior high, so I wasn't even a year old yet when he went to the high school building.

LA: Did they have Jimmie's picture on the wall at the high school as part of the basketball team or for track when you were there?

MW: Well, they always had the senior pictures for every year hanging in the hallway.

LA: So, his picture was there?

MW: It was there from 1949, yeah. There was a big trophy case in the old high school, and I'm guessing there were pictures in it of some of the old teams, but I don't know for sure. A lot of the old yearbooks show pictures of the teams Jimmie was on. Matter of fact, I think a lot of the pictures in books and magazines have been taken out of the yearbooks.

LA: Can you talk about some of Jimmie's teachers?

MW: Mrs. Nall was a very theatrical type person. She was his speech teacher. She probably saw, not only in Jimmie, but in other students, too, things that most kids don't have. And she really saw a lot in Jimmie. I think she encouraged him to pursue an acting career, and she was thrilled to death when he did. I can't say she's the sole reason he got to where he got. Jimmie just seemed to have this inner thing about him. He seemed to take his characters from people he had known in the past or experiences he'd had in the past and rolled them all up into the part, but I can't give you an honest answer on how Fairmount influenced him like that.

LA: Maybe it has something to do with Indiana. He read the poet James Whitcomb Riley. Was that your parents' influence? Did they read James Whitcomb Riley?

MW: Not that I know of. My folks had a lot of books, but I never did see them read hardly. The books were mostly the ones that had been in the house from back at the turn of the century until 1940 or so, but Jimmie...

Marcus tries to pull Jimmie in a wagon at the farm.

I think some people are born with a talent for certain things and never do develop that talent. They go through life doing something else, but Jimmie wanted to be an actor and he apparently was able to bring out his personal feelings in his characters. He was very determined. He always told Mom, he said, "If I could just get a break, I know I could make it."

He always had confidence in himself. I don't think he ever thought he was going to fail. He always thought he was going to be famous someday. Why he had that feeling, I don't know, but that's just the way he was.

He was just very, very confident in himself. I suppose he kind of showed that in some of the ways they say he was. During the making of something, he was very serious about every part and tried to make his character stand out a little bit from the rest. And he did a pretty good job of it apparently.

My sister, Joan, had a going-away dinner for Jimmie before he left to live with his dad. Grandma and Grandpa Dean were there, Mom and Dad, and me and Uncle Nolan and Aunt Mildred, and their three kids. At that time, Joan had had Reece and Jane Ann too. Jane Ann was just a baby then.

I've heard Joan say she never dreamed Jimmie would get into the movies or anything, but she said as they were leaving her house to come home after his going-away party, Jimmie rolled down the back window and kind of hung out and said, "Well, see you in Hollywood," and waved at Joan, and she said, "I never forgot that."

LA: Do you remember him reading at home?

MW: No, I don't. I know he read a lot because I've seen most of the books he had in his New York apartment. A lot of them are acting books and some of them are bullfighting books. And in some of them, he's made little notes or drew a line under a word, so apparently, he wasn't just glancing through them. He was really trying to get something out of them.

LA: In George Perry's book *James Dean* (Palazzo Editions, 2005), Jimmie and another student were in competition and they got into a fight?

MW: It was in Mrs. Nall's class. Her class was upstairs at the school, and this kid was apparently making fun of Jimmie when he was giving some kind of a report in front of the class. When it was over, the stairway was right there and they were going down the stairway, and they got into a fight and were sent to the principal's office and he kicked them out of school for three days.

Apparently, Jimmie told Dad what happened and Dad said, "Well, you can help me here at the farm." (*laughs*) Now, if that had been me, I'd probably have gotten my hind end burned, but not Jimmie. "Yeah, you can help me here on the farm." (*laughs*) I don't mean anything bad about that, but Jimmie could get by with anything.

LA: The kid Jimmie had a fight with, do you know who he was?

MW: Yeah, it was Dave Fox.

LA: Did they compete for parts and stuff?

MW: I couldn't tell you. Dave was a little bit younger, maybe a year younger than Jimmie. I don't know if they were bitter about each other after that or if it was just a one-time deal.

LA: Another one of the things I read in George Perry's book was when Jimmie won the speech award here in Indiana for "The Madman," he exceeded the time limit for the speech.

MW: Yeah, that's what they say.

LA: Did you know about that when it happened?

MW: I knew about it. Apparently, Mrs. Nall had told him, "Now, you're going to have to cut that down to a certain time limit," and he said he didn't do it because he felt if he cut it down, it was going to ruin the presentation. He knew they'd disqualify him or mark his score down if he went over the time, but he felt it was more important to do it the way he thought it needed to be done, instead of ending it sooner. But they didn't mark him down in Indiana.

LA: In Indiana, he won the State Contest, even though he went over the time limit, but he lost the Nationals in Colorado. George Perry quotes Adeline Nall that Jimmie was really upset when he lost. Did you ever talk to Mrs. Nall about Jimmie?

MW: A little, but not a lot. I probably should have, but she was really obsessed with

Jimmie. She just talked about Jimmie all the time. When I was a kid, I guess I have to say I got tired of hearing it. (*laughs*) That doesn't sound very nice, but that's just the way it was.

Jimmie, there's no doubt about it, was very talented in speech and, if he didn't do it in the amount of time he had, apparently, he was just bound and determined he was going to do it right, rather than win the award. You have to give him credit for that. I think Mrs. Nall was probably honked off at him because he didn't do what he was supposed to do, because she had spent quite a bit of time with him on it.

I don't know that I ever talked to Mrs. Nall about it personally. She may have told me about it. I don't know. She talked so much about Jimmie at the time...and I'd already heard plenty at home... (*laughs*) ... after a while, you have to shut some of that stuff out.

I remember Grandma and Grandpa Dean—Grandma really—Dad used to get so disgusted with her because in their house she had Jimmie's pictures hanging all over the walls and in frames sitting on shelves. People sent her pictures or would bring her pictures in a frame, and then there'd be one single picture of us grandkids. Dad never thought that was right. She was old, and Jimmie was special. There is no way around it.

Jimmie's grandparents, Charlie and Emma Dean, with some of the fan mail they received after Jimmie's death.

I've told you that if he wanted something, he was going to get it. It was the same way here at home. He wanted something, he was going to get it, somehow or other. If he wanted to do something and Mom and Dad said, "No," he'd keep pestering them until they finally gave in. (*laughs*) Of course, I was very young at the time, but as I've gotten older, I've seen how great a mind he had. It's just too bad it got wiped out so soon, though I don't think he could have gotten any more popular if he'd lived to seventy or eighty.

LA: When he came back one time, he recorded his grandfather?

MW: Uh-huh. Well, see the character Jimmie played in his first movie was Cal Trask, and Jimmie's great-grandfather's name was Cal Dean. He thought it was kind of neat he was playing a character who had the same first name as his great-grandfather, and Cal is not a real common name. Also, his great-grandfather was one of the best auctioneers around at the time. He was busy every day crying auctions.

There used to be a lot of farm auctions and auctions of livestock and other things back at the turn of the century up until 1940 or so. Cal Dean was very much in demand as an auctioneer, and Jimmie was fascinated with that. It takes talent to get up in front of people and auction stuff and get a decent price out of it. At times, no one is bidding or even acts like they want something, so you have to coax them into getting started on buying something and you kind of have to know what stuff is worth. He was very good at that.

Jimmie asked his Grandfather Dean, Charlie Dean, to tell him some family history. Jimmie seemed to be interested in where he came from and where the Deans were from

and what his past ancestors had done for a living. Of course, Grandpa didn't know he was being recorded.

Jimmie had a little tape recorder. It had a battery pack with a clip on it you carried in your shirt pocket and he had a wire that ran down his sleeve to what looked like a watch. That watch was a microphone and Jimmie let his arm lay on the table, so no one knew he was recording. He got quite a bit of information from Grandpa Dean about the Dean Family. Grandma Dean was there, and she'd have to pop in every now and then and say something, but it was pretty interesting.

LA: Do you have the whole tape?

MW: I have most of it. Years ago, someone sent Mom and Dad a record, and it had part of the tape on it. Some of it wasn't on the record, so I don't have it all, but I have several minutes of it. At the time, we heard Nick Adams had gotten the tape from Jimmie, but I really don't know what happened to the original. I feel fortunate to have what I have. I wish I had it all, but I don't.

Some of it was used in *The James Dean Story* (1957), and I know how things get lost when you loan them out to people. Some of it may have gotten lost in the shuffle when they were making *The James Dean Story*. Where it came from, I don't know. Like I say, I've heard rumors that Nick Adams had it, but I don't know if he did or not.

LA: The speeches...do you remember Jimmie practicing in his room?

MW: No, I was too little for anything like that. When Jimmie was a junior or senior, the years he was developing himself as a speaker, I was only four or five, so I wouldn't have paid any attention to it.

LA: The other thing he was doing at the time was drawing and painting.

MW: Yeah, he was very good at anything to do with the arts. He was such a good artist, always sketching, drawing pictures of things. He was a good photographer. He just had an eye for everything. It's just like on the set

of *Giant*. You see him taking photos all the time. He was interested in learning everything he could about acting and directing a movie.

Jimmie could just take a piece of paper and sketch out something. He painted with charcoal, which I imagine he had done in his art class in school. He painted with watercolor some and he painted with oil. I don't think

Frank Worth documented Jimmie shooting footage on location for *Giant* as George Stevens Jr. watches on horseback.

he was ever satisfied with just settling on one thing. He wanted to be able to do it all. He even did some sculpturing. Jimmie was just very talented at anything in the way of the arts.

I think a lot of our family is good at drawing pictures and sketching things. I used to be fairly good. I could sit with a piece of paper and draw a scene that I could see. I was never good at dreaming up a scene, but I could see something and draw it pretty good. As I got older and got married, life goes on and you don't have time to do all that stuff. Since then, sometimes I have thought I ought to take up oil paints, but I just never have. Probably never will.

My mom used to be a good oil painter. She was probably sixty years old when she started taking lessons. She'd go every week to a class where she and some other women went out and they'd paint a covered bridge or something. The teacher would show them what to do. I guess you could consider her an amateur artist, but she did a pretty good job considering she started so late in life. All she did were oil paints. Now my Grandmother Winslow, she was a real good watercolor painter. Jimmie even mentions in this recording that his Grandmother Winslow was a good artist who used to paint. Of course, Grandmother Winslow wasn't really blood relation, but he may have considered her that.

LA: Did he paint the farm at all?

MW: Not to my knowledge, no. He liked to do abstract stuff. I've seen some paintings of his that were of flowers or weeds or something, and they were pretty "abstracty." There is a pencil drawing he did I have up at the house that Uncle Winton had. It's sort of a controversial drawing, I think. That's the reason I've never displayed it. It shows a life mask lying on a table, so it must have been

done late in his life for that life mask to be there, maybe during *Giant*. He has a candle burning and there's a wolf sitting with its eyes kind of beaming out at something. It's a spooky-looking drawing, and I think it could very easily be taken in the wrong context. It is kind of neat though. All the drawings on display in the Museum are scenery drawings, the sun going down over a big body of water, silos by a barn, things like that.

LA: He never did drawings of New York City?

MW: I have seen some little drawings of city buildings, but not really serious drawings of the city with people or the streets or anything.

LA: Do you have his report cards from the colleges in Los Angeles that would show the classes he took?

MW: I might have a copy of one. Somebody went to UCLA, and UCLA let them copy the records. It told what classes he took, but I couldn't put my hands on it right now.

LA: Didn't he take classes at Santa Monica College, too?

MW: Yeah, he did some "behind-the-scenes" work on plays, painting scenery and things like that. He was busy, that's for sure.

LA: Now the sculpting, did he sculpt here in Fairmount or was that when he got to New York?

MW: He did some here and did some in California. Apparently, the photographer Sanford Roth introduced him to an artist that did some sculpturing. Jimmie was working on a bust of himself when he died. Sanford Roth or someone got ahold of Jimmie's dad and told him he needed to take that somewhere and have it fired, so Uncle Winton did. It's not a finished bust, but you can tell who it is.

LA: Is that in the Museum?

MW: That's in the Museum, yeah. Also, he did a little sculpture. It was a little character he called "Self." It's a guy sitting with his legs crossed and he has his arm up. He probably copied it from somewhere, but it's pretty good. It's still soft clay. It's not the kind of clay you'd fire or anything. I remember it from when I was a kid…that little "Self" thing. When Jimmie died, one of the newspapers had a photograph of it, and I always wondered what had happened to it.

Probably in the early 1990s, I got a call from someone who visited James DeWeerd's widow, and she had it. Mr. and Mrs. DeWeerd didn't have any children, so this little clay bust had always sat up in a cupboard, and there were no kids to bother it.

This guy wanted to know if Mrs. DeWeerd would consider loaning it to the Museum, and she said she didn't know. She said she'd have to think about it. And then he mentioned, "Well, what about giving it to Marcus Winslow," and she said she'd be interested in doing that. He gave me her phone number and I called and had a conversation with her. It was the first time I'd ever talked to her.

I said, "Would you want to sell it or what do you want to do with it?" She said, "Why don't you just take it and make a donation to…" It was some kind of a children's home down in Kentucky, I believe. She and Jim DeWeerd had been big supporters of this children's home, and she said, "Why don't you just donate some money to them and that would do it?" So, I made an arrangement to visit, and she and I had a nice visit. She

gave me this little bust, and I made a pretty generous donation to her children's home.

I kept that little bust here at home for quite a while. I had it up at the house in our china cupboard and then I finally thought, *There's no point in keeping this here where people can't see it*, and so I put it in the Historical Museum. It's pretty nice. I feel fortunate to have it, but you have to be careful how you handle it. It's still soft.

LA: It didn't dry out?

MW: No.

LA: And that is a sculpture he did here?

MW: He did it in high school and gave it to Mr. DeWeerd. Mr. DeWeerd apparently influenced Jimmie in some ways, maybe in Dramatics and he was interested in bullfighting, Mr. DeWeerd was. He kind of introduced Jimmie to bullfighting. Jimmie never actually fought a bull, but he had a bullfighter's cape and a set of bullhorns.

He was home one time and brought that cape with him, and he got a big kick out of someone charging that cape. He'd act like he was a bullfighter. I don't know if he would ever have actually done that or not, but I've read he went to Mexico, right across the border, to a bullfight. I can't really see him actually fighting a bull, though. I'm not saying he wouldn't, but with the profession he was in, he had to be awful careful.

LA: Did he have the bullhorns when he was here, or did he get those in New York?

MW: He got those in New York apparently, because in some Roy Schatt pictures, you can see them hanging on the wall in his New York apartment—the bullhorns and the cape.

In New York, while learning photography from Roy Schatt, Jimmie shot this photo of Martin Landau.

Roy Schatt photographed Dean posing with his bull horns in Jimmie's New York apartment.

Jimmie's dad kept those. That's some of what he kept. They're on display in the Museum.

LA: That little film Jimmie made was a bull-fight film.

MW: Mm-hmm. Yeah, he made a little bullfighter film, taking the characters and moving them a fraction. Then he apparently shot a clip of film, then moved them all again. It only lasts a few seconds, the film does. The characters are moving all around, and it is kind of neat to see.

LA: Did he make those little figures of the bullfighter and the bull and the others?

MW: No, they look to me like they were bought somewhere because they're real tiny.

They're not very big. I would assume he bought them in New York.

LA: It's interesting if he made his first film in New York. I mean, everyone knows he took home movies on *Giant* with his camera in Texas.

MW: It could have been made in Los Angeles; I suppose.

LA: But the figures would have been in Los Angeles I would have thought.

MW: Where were those figures when Jimmie died? I'm trying to think. I have an itemized list of everything that was in New York and everything that was in California and I don't remember at which place they were. The bullfighter's cape and the horns, I'm pretty sure were in New York, but the little bullfight figures he made the film with, I'm not sure where they were.

LA: Now…you sent Jimmie a drawing you'd done, and he wrote you back?

MW: Jimmie had written a letter to Mom and Dad and told Mom and Dad to have me send him some pictures, so I drew a castle and sent it to him. I think Jimmie thought it was a prison. You know how a castle and a prison both have gun turrets and bars on the windows and all that?

Well, he thought it was a prison and he wrote me back right away and said, "Don't draw things of confinement like jails and prisons. Draw things created by God like mountains and animals and trees." I took his letter okay. I appreciate it a lot more now than I did then because at the time, I felt like I had been criticized (*laughs*), but I fully understand what he meant.

Like I say, Jimmie was…could draw. One time when Jimmie came home from New York, he had a couple of false front teeth and he was having some trouble with them. I have the letter he wrote to his dad wanting to know if Uncle Winton could meet him here because a couple of teeth were causing him a problem.

Jimmie even drew his front teeth in this letter. His dad was a dental technician, not a dentist, but he made false teeth. Uncle Winton came back, and I assume he made Jimmie some new teeth. Jimmie was staying here, and I think Uncle Winton was staying over at Grandma and Grandpa Dean's.

Jimmie was getting ready to leave, because he had to get back to New York. He used to draw this little bull's head. You've probably seen it before. He drew it when he was here that time, but I mostly remember Jimmie asking Uncle Winton to show me how to draw something. I don't remember what it was now, but Uncle Winton was pretty good, too. Maybe Jimmie inherited some of that

In April 1953, Jimmie asked Marcus's parents to have their son send Jimmie some "art work."

from him, I don't know. Mom was good, but Dad wasn't a drawer or a painter. He couldn't draw flies. He just wasn't an artist, but I was pretty good.

LA: Did you continue to send Jimmie drawings?

MW: I don't remember whether I did or not.

LA: You never got any more letters about your drawings?

MW: (*laughs*) I might not have sent him any more after that. I really do think it was a nice letter, especially as I've gotten older. It means a lot more to me now than it did at the time, but that's the way Jimmie was. He was fairly intelligent. It has always amazed me that somebody could leave a little town like Fairmount and end up in New York City. I mean, that's a jungle. He made friends with people and stayed wherever he could. I know he really struggled.

MUrray Hill 2-7464   BETWEEN FIFTH AND SIXTH AVENUES

HOTEL IROQUOIS
49 WEST 44th STREET
NEW YORK 36, N. Y.

Dear Marcus Jr.

First I want to thank you for the fine pictures.

I feel the urgent need to warn you about something. Anyone at all can draw ~~soldiers~~, guns, and barred gates with locks on them. Why? because there are a lot of those things to see. That shouldn't mean that they are good things to draw. We live in a world where these things became very important. And that is bad. You should be aware of that because you don't have to see too many of these things because you live on land that is

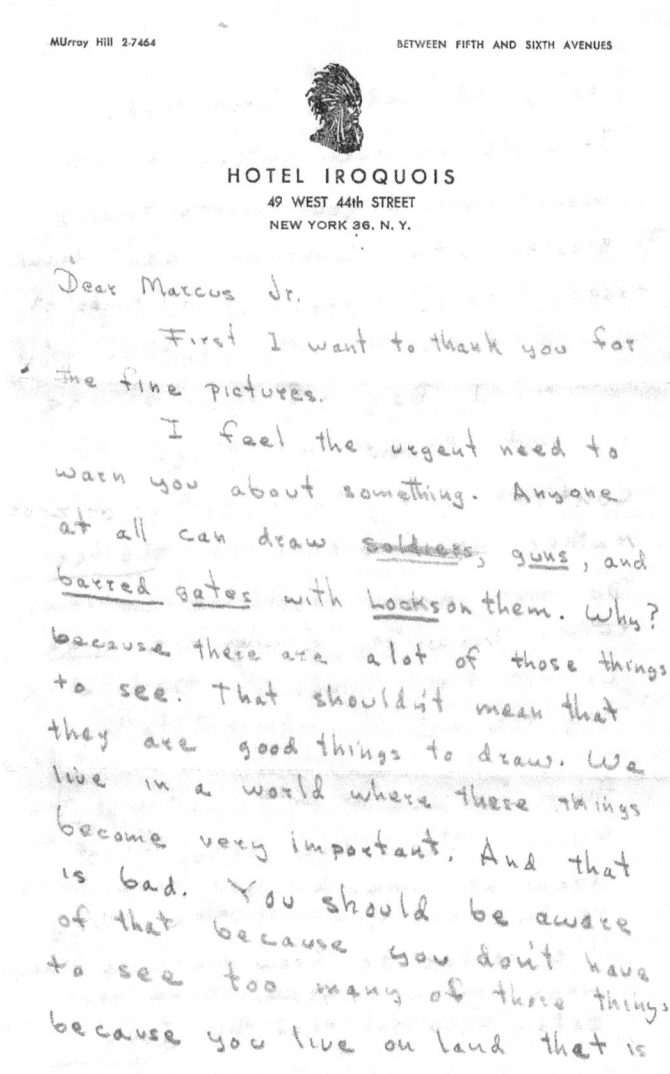

Later in April '53, Jimmie writes Marcus after receiving the art work.

I do have letters Jimmie wrote to his dad asking if he could send him some money. In one letter to Mom and Dad, he said Christmas was coming up and he always appreciated presents at Christmas, but he would much rather have cash because, you know, he needed money to just exist. I know he had a hard time until he started getting some TV work and started getting a halfway steady income. He really had a hard time making ends meet.

I'm sure back when Mom and Dad and Uncle Winton sent him money, it helped a lot. I know Mom and Dad; they'd send him money even if they didn't have it. It's just the way they were. They used to talk about, and I'm not mad, I'm not jealous, I don't want to leave that impression, but they said Jimmie could do no wrong in their eyes.

LA: Ever?

greatly blessed by Lord God.

It would be much better if you would spread your talents toward the greater arts. Everyone can't draw trees, clouds, sheep, dogs, all kinds of animals, the earth, hills, mountains, seas oceans. I Beg of you please Do not draw buildings of confindment, Jails, castles or zoos rather draw places of shelter. Do not draw people in onifocus, rather draw people who are free Do not draw things of Destruction, they are not so important to the good + true artist that he must draw them – rather draw tool, things that build. There are many things to draw at home. All you have to do is look and you will see. They Are harder to draw because they were harder to grow. Have your Daddy help you read this Love Jim

MW: No. (*laughs*)

LA: Is there a list of every TV show he did?

MW: There is of everything that they know. Michael Sheridan (director of *James Dean: Forever Young* (2005)) did the research and just came out with a new DVD set of TV shows that have been digitized and restored, and they're pretty interesting to see. (Note: *James Dean: The Lost Television Legacy* (2015)) They are from Jimmie's early career up to the TV show he did between *East of Eden* and *Rebel Without a Cause*, *The Unlighted Road* (1955) is what it was called, so he apparently enjoyed doing that type of work, too.

If it was a live show, they'd film it off a TV screen as they were doing it in New York, and then they'd send that film to Los Angeles and show it in California a week or so later. At that time, the thought was, once a show had been on, well, that was the end of it. They didn't make any attempt to keep a lot of that stuff like they should have.

Michael Sheridan has spent a big share of his life, whenever he had the time, tracking down films. If it wasn't for him making *James Dean: Forever Young*, I think a lot of the TV shows would be lost. They just didn't make an attempt to store them or keep them. Of course, that was before anyone thought about reruns.

LA: In the documents Uncle Winton had, were there pay stubs for the shows he did?

MW: Yeah.

LA: Are there pay stubs for the Broadway plays he did...*See the Jaguar* (1952) and *The Immoralist*?

MW: I don't know whether those two are there or not. There are pay stubs for different things, but the ones I'm familiar with are mostly TV shows. *See the Jaguar* and *The Immoralist*? I don't remember seeing anything like that.

LA: He never kept a diary, did he?

MW: No, but he had one little notebook where he wrote a lot of stuff down. It seems he had so much going on, it felt like he had to write it down to remember what he was supposed to be doing. I wouldn't call it a diary. It's kind of a daily ledger. He would write down when he was supposed to meet somebody or go to a studio, and he did put down some thoughts. Apparently, at least for a while, he thought he was out of his comfort zone in Los Angeles. He liked New York.

LA: You mean when he went to work on *East of Eden*?

MW: Yeah. He made some notes about: "Why did I ever leave New York?", things like that, and some personal notes. He mentioned some of the people we're familiar with, Dennis Stock, Martin Landau and, oh, I don't know. It has been so long since I've read them, I don't remember who all he mentions.

LA: James Whitmore seems to be the guy that recommended Jimmie go to New York.

MW: That's what they say. He writes about James Whitmore in some letters I have. Apparently, Whitmore saw his talent and told him he ought to go to New York. At the time, Broadway plays and about all of the TV work were coming out of New York, so he did go. Apparently, Jimmie liked to perform live. It's hard for me to imagine, but most of those shows he did were live on television.

Jimmie got so busy in New York that sometimes he'd be in a show one night and

1951   1.

WEST SIDE BRANCH
YOUNG MEN'S CHRISTIAN ASSOCIATION
5 WEST 63RD STREET
NEW YORK 23, N. Y.
TELEPHONE SUsquehanna 7-4400

MEMBER'S CORRESPONDENCE

Dear Mom & Dad,

Just received your nice letter. It makes me feel very happy and wanted when I find a letter in my box.

It looks like I may be in New York for Christmas. I don't like spending Xmas away from home; but if I can find a good friend to spend it with, here, things wont be so bad. I hate being alone, especially on Christmas.

Boy! is it cold. Mom, do you think you could find my light tan scarf and my gloves, my hands get awfully

–over–

YOU ARE CORDIALLY INVITED TO VISIT

ONE OF THE FINEST YMCA BUILDINGS IN AMERICA.

JUST WEST OF CENTRAL PARK.

5 WEST 63rd STREET.

In early December 1951, Jimmie writes his father and stepmother with news and has a couple of requests.

30

cold.

Thanks you very much for the money. I needed it so very bad. I have to get pictures taken for agents & files. This will take money I didn't count on. The pictures are a necessity; you can not do anything without them.

I met a man who is very interested in me, as an actor. (Notice I qualified the word interested.) He knew of a situation where the juvenille actor was being drafted and couldn't keep his role. The Show is "Mama" on T.V. I met the casting director today. She was very impressed. I then met the producer and she gave me a couple of scripts, which I am to prepare for an audition next week in front of the director. It looks very, very good. If I get it, I'll probably start to work around Dec. 1 or 15. Keep your fingers crossed.

2.

WEST SIDE BRANCH

YOUNG MEN'S CHRISTIAN ASSOCIATION

5 WEST 63RD STREET

NEW YORK 23, N. Y.

TELEPHONE SUsquehanna 7-4400

MEMBER'S CORRESPONDENCE

There are many, many people to meet yet. So far, I have gotten very good reactions + results. I think I'll make it all right.

New York is just great. So easy to get around in. Plenty of good, fast transportation with no hassle. It is nothing like L.A. or Chicago, they're horrible.

I think it would be wise to keep in touch with Ted Avery at NO-13360 in case the draft-board tries to get me at the old place. Best time to call is in the morning about 9:00.

Dad, tell the fellows at work that I'm doing just great, also say hello for me. Say hello to Johnny + Dorothy for me too.

over

YOU ARE CORDIALLY INVITED TO VISIT

ONE OF THE FINEST YMCA BUILDINGS IN AMERICA.

JUST WEST OF CENTRAL PARK.

5 WEST 63rd STREET.

Re: 1759
WA 1759
Draesemer

8272 Sunset Bl
LA 46, Calif,

You can do me a great
favor by calling my agent for me
and getting her mailing address. —
Isabelle Draesemer HI-1282 if that
busy try GR-1472: Don't call until after
4:30 or 4:45. Tell her nothing is
forgotten and that I'm sorry that
I had to run off like ▬▬ I did.
We'll make monkeys of them when
I get back. Give her my love.

Whose name was it I got in
the Christmas drawing. I forgot.
Tell the people not to send present—
m o n e y! It's not that I don't
like opening packages. It's more
fun to eat once in awhile.

With Love

Jim

P.S. Call James Whitmore or
his wife and get his mailing
address   EX-45790

maybe the next day, he would do another show. How in the world he could memorize his lines and not get them mixed up from one show to another, I don't know, but he didn't.

LA: Jimmie never owned a car here in Fairmount, did he?

MW: Nope. All he ever had was that Czech motorcycle. Dad let him drive that '49 Ford occasionally. It was brand-new then. I know he drove it to the Senior Prom and I assume he might have driven it to high school a little.

When he moved to New York and would come back home, that would be the car he would always drive. Dad traded it off in '54 for a new Dodge and, of course, when Jimmie and Dennis Stock were here in February of '55, they drove that Dodge, but Jimmie never had a car when he was here.

I'll always remember one time; Paul Marvin Smith came out to the farm to visit Jimmie when he was back. He and Jimmie used to pal around together a lot when they were kids. Marvin had a brand-new '55 Buick and Jimmie had Dad's '54 Dodge, and as we were driving to Fairmount for something, we were running about eighty miles an hour past the cemetery. That road has a pretty sharp turn there at the cemetery, and Jimmie and Marvin went around that curve running about eighty and Marvin was following us so close you couldn't even see the bumper on his car. (*laughs*) He and Jimmie both were pretty wild drivers, and they were both killed in car wrecks. You know Jimmie was, but Marvin was too, up by Wabash, I would say around 1972.

He was one of the pallbearers at Jimmie's funeral, a year or so older than Jimmie, but they were good friends. I imagine he graduated in '47 or '48 because Jimmie graduated in '49. The Smiths lived real close by, and Jimmie

would go over there and Marvin would come over here and play. Larry, Marvin's brother, according to him, Jimmie used to sneak out of the house at night and come over to their house and do stuff, probably things they shouldn't have. (*laughs*)

LA: And then sneak back in?

MW: Yeah, sneak back in.

LA: So, your mom and dad never knew?

MW: If they did, they never said anything, but Jimmie never got in any serious trouble that I heard of. I think he was kind of mischievous, but as far as I knew, he never got in any serious trouble. Maybe he would have if he had gotten caught, I don't know.

He used to ride that cycle pretty wild. I'd see him run by here on purpose coming from Fairmount. He'd go up there to the corner and turn around and come back by, lying down on the cycle and letting his feet stick straight out the back and just running as fast as that little cycle would go. Mom would just throw a fit. She was afraid he was going to get hurt.

I don't think Dad ever thought too much about it. Jimmie was pretty fortunate. He never ever had any bad accidents with it or hurt himself here on the farm. I remember Dad making the comment, "Maybe if he'd broken his leg or something here, been in something, maybe he wouldn't have gotten killed in that car," but he just never got hurt doing anything.

LA: Did your dad have him driving the tractor at a young age too?

MW: Yeah, Jimmie used to drive the tractor. This old Bill Burwick, he used to work here and he'd get disgusted. He'd tell me, "Jimmie would drive the tractor and he'd be back there in the field, but then here he'd come, walking up to the house because it was too cold." (*laughs*)

Dad never said a thing about it. Jimmie liked the farm, but I don't think he cared about farming. He'd help Dad. If Dad was baling hay or baling straw, why, he'd tell Jimmie to get some kids from town and come out and help. I can remember that.

Now about Jimmie's cars, when he got to California, I guess his dad bought him some kind of an old Chevy. I never did see a picture of it. I've read somewhere it was a '41 or '42 Chevy, something like that, but I don't think he had it very long. Then he moved to New York, and he didn't have any cars in New York.

When he went back to California to make *East of Eden*, he bought an MG. I don't know if it was new or used. That car he either traded in or sold, I don't know which, for the Porsche Speedster. It was a brand-new car. And then he bought that Porsche Spyder, and it was also brand-new.

There was only one thing of Jimmie's that I've really tried to find and I can't find it and neither can a lot of other people. That's Jimmie's '55 Ford station wagon, a Country Squire. We've traced it to the mid-1960s, and then it just kind of falls off the earth. He got it to pull the trailer for the Spyder, so evidently, he must have bought it the last month or so he lived. I don't know what happened to it. It could have gotten wrecked.

The serial number on it was a fairly low one for that year, and the license plate is a lot lower than the license plate for the Spyder. It also makes me wonder if it was a used, brand-new car that had been traded back in, but anyway, it was a nice car. The Country Squire had wood grain siding on it and an all-red interior. It was pretty.

LA: It doesn't show up on any insurance document or anything like that?

MW: No. We've checked the license bureaus over the years. It doesn't show up in California, and it doesn't show up in any of the neighboring states. It's been run through a nationwide search at least once, but it didn't show up, so it's hard to say. You go out to California, and there are an awful lot of vehicles just sitting behind people's houses and in their driveways, and they've been there for years and years and years.

Some people have bought collections of cars, and they have a big old warehouse they park them in and the cars just sit there. Something like that could've happened to it. Uncle Winton sold it to a guy, according to the estate papers, by the name of Robert F. Braun, and I think he was a preacher from what I can find out. He may have been some relation to Ethel because going through some of their papers, I found Braun's name mentioned.

A guy told Lee Raskin (author of *James Dean at Speed* (David Bull Publishing, 2005) and *James Dean: On the Road to Salinas* (Stance and Speed, 2015)) that he bought the car in the early Sixties, like 1963 or '64. He said he bought it off the guy who got it from Jimmie's dad. He said the guy was a preacher. He told Lee he had it for a while, maybe six months to a year, and that, when he went into the service, his folks sold it. He had no idea where it went, because his parents didn't know who they sold it to or anything. That's about all we can find out about it. It could have been taken off the road almost immediately. Several years ago, I had someone try to run it through the Department of Motor Vehicles, and it didn't show up. He ran it through every DMV in America, and it still didn't show up.

WEST SIDE BRANCH
YOUNG MEN'S CHRISTIAN ASSOCIATION
5 WEST 63RD STREET
NEW YORK 23, N. Y.
TELEPHONE SUsquehanna 7-4400

MEMBER'S CORRESPONDENCE

[handwritten letter]

Dear Mom and Dad,

After sending my gloves and such a sweet letter, you have not only warmed my hands a great deal but my heart. I thank you so much. I have so much to thank you for. The black, leather jacket as you know is one of my great loves. It has taken me through rain, snow, mud and everything else, so it is a great comfort to have it with me again.

Isn't J. Whitmore a great guy. It wasn't nearly as hard as you thought it would be, was it? Calling him, I mean. Now, don't confess, it's a virtue to be shy.

You will find Isabel equally nice. Above everything, do not sign a document, contract or

YOU ARE CORDIALLY INVITED TO VISIT
"over"
ONE OF THE FINEST YMCA BUILDINGS IN AMERICA.

JUST WEST OF CENTRAL PARK.

5 WEST 63rd STREET.

In early March '52, Jimmie sends his thanks, asks for some money and for the first time lets his father know that his dental plate may need some work.

anything she might put before you concerning me. I am now under 3 year exclusive contract to the Louis Shurr Agency. Mark has signed them to make it legal. Isabelle tyeup with me was not notarized or signed by my guardians and I was not of age. I am not sure of the conflict this would have upon either agency, possibly none. Nevertheless, don't say anything as yet. Ok? Please take her to dinner, she is a wonderful gal.

I have been working my tail off for the last 2 weeks. I may have some excellent news for you after tomorrow. I'm expecting a call that will give me the lead in the next "Studio One" production. Keep your fingers crossed. I also have a reading for "Lux" tomorrow. Also waiting for the outcome of a reading I did for "Armstrong Theater". I tell you, I am dying of anxiety and nervous strain. You can't possibly conceive the torment an actor goes through. I'm rooming with a fellow now and my rent is cut in half. Nevertheless I could use some money. Dad, could I have about 10 or 15.

WEST SIDE BRANCH

YOUNG MEN'S CHRISTIAN ASSOCIATION
5 WEST 63RD STREET

NEW YORK 23, N. Y. .

TELEPHONE SUsquehanna 7-4400

MEMBER'S CORRESPONDENCE

Mark wrote me a letter and told me about a couple of girls who went to Indianapolis. They went to a movie there and saw me in it. They're all excited, aren't they crazy.

If you feel that you can't send the money just now, that's O.K. I can borrow some from somebody until I can get set again.

Tell Bob and Judy ~~hello~~ hello for me, will you? Hey! Daddy you know that right lateral, well I'm starting to get a blister on the gum and my plate doesn't fit ~~so~~ good. I almost lost it yesterday. Gee! I might have to come and see you before I expected to.

With all my love

Jim

P.S.
Write soon,

YOU ARE CORDIALLY INVITED TO VISIT
ONE OF THE FINEST YMCA BUILDINGS IN AMERICA.

JUST WEST OF CENTRAL PARK.

5 WEST 63rd STREET.

38

LA: It could've been used for parts.

MW: That's possible, although it was a pretty good car. It is very desirable today, one of those wood grain station wagons. It wasn't really wood. It was fiberglass, but it looked like wood. In 1955 Ford quit using wood on their station wagons and started using decals and fiberglass that looked like wood. It was a pretty good likeness.

Anyway, I've hunted for years trying to find it. Either someone has it and they don't know it was Jimmie's, or whoever his folks sold it to knows whose car it was and they've just parked it somewhere. It could have gone to Mexico. As close as Mexico is, someone might have bought it and driven it down there.

Mark Roesler (Chairman and CEO of Curtis Management Group) hired a private detective who was supposed to be checking it out, but he never came up with anything. You really have to be devoted to something to dig in and find it. If you stop and think, it happened sixty years ago. It doesn't seem like it. It just seems like maybe ten years ago, but it has been sixty years since Jimmie had his accident, so that's a long time for that car to deteriorate and get out of circulation.

Jimmie's Speedster, Lee Raskin printed its serial number in his book ten years ago thinking someone would read it and come forward with it, but nobody ever has. A guy in France claims he has it, but Lee says it's not the right one.

I'm not interested in hunting that Speedster, because they're too expensive. My God, I remember when you could buy a decent Speedster, and it hasn't been too many years ago, for $40,000. I thought, *Man, $40,000 for a car that's thirty years old?* Now those cars are bringing from a quarter to a half a million dollars. Speedsters. That

Spyder Jimmie was driving, one of those just sold recently. Seinfeld had one and he sold it. It brought five point something million dollars, so they've gotten to be worth a lot of money. I wouldn't even make an attempt to hunt the Speedster. Couldn't afford it, if I found it. That's too much expense to just park and have sitting here in the Car Barn.

LA: Did you know Jimmie had a horse?

MW: I knew he had a horse and named him Cisco. Of course, he had one and then he didn't have one. According to Lew Bracker, Jimmie bought the horse, but then didn't know what to do with it. That sounds like Jimmie, to buy something and then not know what he was going to do with it. That's kind of the way he was.

LA: Do you remember other incidents where he'd do that?

MW: I think it was just sort of his nature that if he had a dollar in his pocket, he was going to spend it. Of course, he liked horses. I don't know what the circumstances were for him buying this horse, but according to Lew, he didn't have anywhere to keep it after he bought it.

Lew's family had a ranch up near Santa Barbara. I don't think it was a large ranch, but he told Jimmie if he wanted to, he could bring Cisco up and leave him there so that is what he did. Lew said he never did come up to see it. It was just kind of an impulse thing. He saw it, wanted it, and then once he got it, he didn't know what he was going to do with it, and then Lew gave Jimmie an out and he was happy. Just recently Lew got a letter from someone who sent him a color picture of a horse that was supposed to be Cisco and Lew said it definitely is Cisco.

LA: Did Jimmie ride horses here in town?

MW: He may have ridden some with friends of his, I really don't know. When I was a kid, some of my friends had horses, but they wouldn't have been the same friends Jimmie had, so I don't know if he rode any horses here or not.

LA: When you would ride, where would you ride?

MW: I never did ride much. Some of my friends would ride horses out in the country. At that time there were more side roads than there are now. Now the roads are so doggone busy, and they're all paved. Back then, a lot of the roads were still gravel roads, and most of the kids that had horses lived on farms, so there might have been places on the farm where they could ride. That's probably where they rode them. But I never had a horse, so I rode theirs a little, not a lot, but some.

LA: Do you remember going out on the road?

MW: No, it was all on the farm. It was all new to me. You have to be careful with horses. If you don't know what you're doing, they can run away with you. I never did have any do that, but I know it's a possibility.

LA: You never wanted a horse?

MW: I said something to Dad about it one time and he said, "I had to farm with horses and I had to walk behind horses, and there are not going to be any more horses here on the farm." (*laughs*) "O-kay," and I didn't argue about it. So that's the horse story.

3

Childhood & Meeting Marylou

Marcus Winslow: I heard Mom and Dad talk about when my sister was out at the barn. Joan was pretty small then and she got behind the milk truck and the milk truck backed up and smashed her head between the barn and the truck and just scalped her, peeled her scalp all the way back. They took her to the hospital and sewed her up, so you can't tell it today, but I guess it was an awful thing to see. If she had been just another inch or two taller, it would have crushed her head. Dad eventually got rid of the milk cows around '50 or '51, somewhere right in there.

Leith Adams: Do you think it was because of the accident?

MW: It was not because of the accident. That would have happened in the late Thirties or the early Forties because Joan was born in '26 or '27. She would have been about thirteen years old in 1940. It was just one of those things that can happen on a farm.

LA: Were you ever in an accident?

MW: Nope, I was always pretty careful. I did get hurt a lot of times, but not from farming, mainly from falling down or off this wall up by the house.

Once I was walking around on the wall and got clear up on the highest part near the end and I fell off onto the driveway. Hit my head on a rock. Cut a big gash in the back of my head. That was when they didn't run you to the hospital for every little thing, so they just bandaged it up and went on.

I cut it pretty good. My hair was full of blood and I will always remember, right when it happened, I didn't know if I was dead or not because I could feel myself floating. I was just kind of floating in the air. I was up above the wall looking down.

Evidently it knocked me out, but I got into the house and Mom and Dad washed the blood out of my hair. Today they'd have taken me to the hospital and put some stitches in it, but I've had that scar forever back there.

In grade school at West Ward, I was playing with some kids outside at recess, and it had rained. There was a sand pit in the ground where you landed when you pole vaulted. It still had sand in it, but rain stood there too. We were running by, throwing brickbats that were lying around, splashing each other, and I remember thinking to myself as I ran along, *I hope nobody throws a brickbat while I'm running here.*

About that time, WHAM! I got hit in the head. (*laughs*) Well, the brickbat put another big scar on the back of my head, and I had that scar for years. It may still be there, I don't know. Those are the two times I got hit hard in the head with something. They had a nurse at West Ward, and I had to go up to her office and she dressed it up.

LA: Did you play in the barn? Up in the haymow?

MW: I used to play in the haymow a lot. We'd keep straw in one part of the barn and hay in another part and we'd make tunnels up there in the hay. We'd take out a bunch of bales and restack them, so there'd be tunnels to crawl down. We'd make a little room back in there and we'd take a flashlight with us and sit back there. We really thought we were hidden. I had a lot of fun playing in the barn.

LA: Did you have a rope in the barn hooked up, so you could swing on it?

MW: Not when I played, but there used to be one because Mom and Dad talked about Jimmie swinging up there. He fell or jumped and knocked a couple teeth out. That's why his two front teeth were artificial.

We also had two basketball hoops at the barn. There was one right inside the doors, just as you went in the barn, and one at the "tramp shed." It was what you might call a "lean-to" built on the side of the big barn, so the cattle could go into it during the winter. The cattle would tramp around in there, otherwise they'd be outside. Cattle mostly like to be outside, unless it's too hot.

I liked the basketball hoop at the tramp shed the best, but the only one left is the one

in the barn up there by the doors. It's still there. Jimmie used to play at both of them, probably got in a lot of practice from playing out here at the barn. I used to play some ball, but I was never on the team like Jimmie was.

LA: So, you don't ever remember any of the basketball games Jimmie played in?

MW: I'm sure I had to go with Mom and Dad some, but there were some times they just left me at Grandma and Grandpa Dean's. They only lived four or five blocks from the high school. It's one of those things where if you knew what the future was going to be, you'd do things a lot different. I had no way of knowing Jimmie was going to be famous one day. He was just another family member to me. My memories are of him coming home from school.

LA: Did your dad have time to take the family on vacations?

MW: Mom and Dad would take a couple of days off, now and then. One time they went up to the Wisconsin Dells, but I stayed at Grandma and Grandpa Dean's while they were gone.

Grandpa and I were sitting out on the front porch and boy, a big strike of lightning hit. We both jumped, and then he said, "Oh, I'm going inside," so I came in the house with him. It wasn't but five minutes later that the phone rang and his barn was on fire. That strike of lighting was the lightning hitting the barn.

They'd just built it ten years before. Real nice barn and that lightning burned it clear down to the ground. Some wagons in it were burnt up. It happened that he left his tractor just sitting outside by the barn and neighbors shoved it out to the road before it caught on fire.

It sure broke Grandma and Grandpa's hearts that their barn burnt down. He didn't

Marcus Winslow views his world from the Winslow Barn...1956.

get it all rebuilt, just some of it. I don't think he had enough insurance money to build a barn back like what he had.

Mom and Dad, other than going to California every other year, didn't go on a lot of vacations, and they didn't take me on any vacations. I don't think I ever went on a vacation with them.

LA: Never did?

MW: Well, to Canada, to Quebec one time and to California for *The James Dean Story.*

LA: How did you meet Marylou?

MW: We were in school together starting from seventh grade. Fairmount High School is where the junior high was, so we met there.

Jimmie used to go with Marylou's sister, Joyce, and when Jimmie was leaving for California, she had a surprise going-away party for him. I remember we parked our car over at Grandma and Grandpa Dean's and walked down two blocks to their house. It wasn't very far.

Jimmie came and, of course, he was surprised that everyone was there. A little grocery store was just down the street, and I remember walking to it with three or four girls. I didn't know who they were. I was six, so it was probably between the first grade and second grade. One of the girls was Marylou, but I didn't know it at the time. The first time I really noticed her was when we both started going to junior high, but we didn't date until I was a junior in high school.

LA: Jimmie took Marylou's sister to the prom?

MW: Mm-hmm, Joyce Wigner. Jimmie used to write her letters for a while after he left and went back to California. Eventually they both went their separate ways, but she always had fond memories of Jimmie.

LA: Did she ever talk to you about him?

MW: Not especially. You know she'd gotten married and had a family, and when I was around her, I didn't think it was appropriate to be asking about Jimmie. She'd mention him now and then, say something about him.

Jimmie had given her a coat, and she had that coat for years and years. Marylou's mother had a quilting machine, and so she gave that coat to Marylou's mother and had her make her a quilt out of it that she kept. Actually, Joyce was Marylou's half-sister. Marylou's mother had been married before and her husband was killed. Marylou was quite a bit younger than Joyce.

LA: So, Marylou probably never really had contact with Jimmie?

The West Ward School patrol boys circa '53-'54." Back row (l-r): Jim Titus, Kenneth Vetor, Doug Mann, Mr. Cloud, Doug Woolen, Jay Buffington, Roland Hollenbeck, Denny Craven. Front row (l-r): Phil Hoke, Marcus Winslow, Philbert Scott, Jack Ratliff, Steve Thomas, Gilbert Sullivan, Gary Parsons.

MW: Not a lot. She remembers Jimmie. We're the same age, so she remembers Jimmie coming to the house and taking Joyce places. There would've been eleven or twelve years difference between Marylou and Joyce. She married a guy from La Fontaine, Indiana and she had a good life. Like I said, she and Jimmie kind of went their separate ways.

Marylou did have several sisters who were around, but I was almost an only child. I told you my sister got married in 1946, and I was born in November of '43, so I don't remember her being here hardly. Jimmie didn't leave till '49, so I remember him being here, but as to my growing up years from first grade on, they were both gone.

Living in the country was a good life. I can look back on it now and see that it was a lot better than what I realized. At the time, I envied the town kids because they always had friends to play with, and it didn't matter whether it was evenings or daytime or what, they had things they could do, whereas country kids didn't have anything to do and didn't have any friends to play with and usually had to work, but I think it turned out to be the better.

LA: When you were growing up did you have a best buddy you hung around with?

MW: Yeah. I had a friend named Jay Buffington. He lived at the west edge of Fairmount. It really was in the country but right at the edge of town. He and I were best friends and a guy by the name of Doug Mann. We were close friends and a boy by the name of Jack Ratliffe. He lived in town. He and I were pretty good friends, too. Jay joined the Air Force and had a good career, and he and his wife, Judi, moved back here from Texas.

Usually every Friday, Jay and some church friends from the Fairmount Methodist Church come to the Outpost Restaurant for breakfast, so I still see Jay about twice a week. Sometimes he and Judi will come over and Marylou and I will go out with them for supper. He's probably my best, best friend from high school, but I've made so many friends through Jimmie. People come here because of Jimmie, and we'll get acquainted with them.

I guess I've had kind of a strange life, kind of two lives. There's my life here in Fairmount, and then I've had a life of Jimmie's friends or people that were interested in Jimmie. They came to Fairmount, too. I've met a lot of nice people over the years. I feel very fortunate. Sometimes it's a hassle, but overall, it has been very rewarding. I've seen some things and done some things that I wouldn't have done if it had not been for Jimmie. I'm kind of a homebody anyway, so to get me out and get me doing something has probably been good for me.

I did take the Army physical. I got my notice to report to Indianapolis, so what we did was go to Marion to some parking lot and they picked us up and took a whole bunch of guys down to Indianapolis for physicals. Then they brought us back home.

Max Engle, another kid I knew, was a year or two younger than me; I think he'd just gotten out of high school. Anyway, he was wanting to go into the service, and his plan was to take the physical the same time I did and go right on down to Fort Knox, Kentucky for basic training. It just happened that it was a time when they were starting to draft a lot of younger guys. For several years, the people they were drafting were older, like twenty-three, twenty-four. When I went down, they were starting to draft them a lot younger, and I think they had more people than they knew what to do with.

I used to have heart trouble when I was a kid. I had a heart murmur. This guy comes along with this stethoscope and listened to your heart. I saw him and I thought, *Well hell, he can't even hardly tell if you're dead or alive,* you know, because he didn't stop to listen, but when he put that on my chest, he did stop. He stood there a few seconds and listened to it and said, "Go get dressed." (*laughs*) That was the end of that.

It made me pretty happy because Vietnam was beginning to start up and whether I'd have had to go to Vietnam or not, who knows? I was probably nineteen when I took my physical, and Marylou and I got married when I was twenty. And I never heard from the Army again.

And Max Engle, he'd already sold his car and everything. He thought he'd be leaving from Indianapolis and going right down to Fort Knox, but they claimed his hearing wasn't good enough. He still doesn't have hearing aids today. I don't think it took anything hardly for them to turn him down. I guess, in a way, I look at it as a lucky thing and in other ways, I wonder if I would have been better off if I had gone in, but I didn't.

4

The Aftermath

Leith Adams: Did your mom and dad ever talk to you specifically about Jimmie's death?

Marcus Winslow: No, not really. It was different in that Jimmie was killed in California and we were living here in Indiana, and it was a few days before we even realized how the accident had happened. We knew a car had turned in front of him, but we didn't know any of the details or anything.

It's always been kind of tough on that part. Mom and Dad always considered Jimmie just like their own son. They more or less raised him. When he was killed, he had a hundred-thousand-dollar insurance policy, life insurance policy, and his dad never mentioned sharing it with anyone. I blame a lot of that on Ethel, but whatever.

It was just a tough time. People were coming here, fans mostly, but writers too, wanting to know this and wanting to know that, wanting to know all about Jimmie and taking pictures and wanting to borrow photographs. Mom and Dad were really good people. They loved Jimmie just like my sister and me, and they felt an obligation to be nice to Jimmie's fans because they thought that's what Jimmie would've wanted. They

never turned anybody away, didn't matter what time of day or night.

If someone came to the door, they would talk to them and invite them into the house. It's a wonder they didn't have some disastrous results from it, but back then there wasn't the crime we have today. There was crime, just not the way it is today. People would come in and they'd get the scrapbooks out and it might be, if we were getting ready to eat, they would have them stay for dinner or supper. Mom and Dad made a lot of friends over the years, but when stuff like that is going on all the time, you never have a chance to get over the death because you're continually reminded of it.

Jimmie's dad and stepmother, they lived in California, didn't have any children and weren't going to have any, so they could just move at the drop of a hat. Even before Jimmie died, Winton and Ethel moved a lot, but after, they didn't want to deal with anyone and they'd just up and move. They didn't want anybody here to give out their address. It wasn't easy for them. I'm sure Jimmie's death really affected his dad's mental state, but he also didn't have to deal with the fans, didn't deal with any of the magazine or book writers or any of that stuff.

Mom and Dad finally got to the point where they cut off all the magazine and book writers, too. They said they didn't want to talk to them, because a lot of times they'd say stuff Mom and Dad said, but then they would add other things from someone else making it sound like Mom and Dad endorsed it, you know.

Times were a lot simpler back in the late Fifties and Sixties. If Mom and Dad could see some of what's been printed about different celebrities in the last twenty years they would turn over in their graves, but it was a different time back then. Like I say, they loved Jimmie just like he was their own.

Matter of fact, I'm not jealous or anything, but I would imagine they probably spoiled him. He probably got more than my sister and I did, but they were good parents. I never heard an unkind word out of them. If they ever fought, they did it quietly because you never heard any dissension between them. They were really good, good people. Jimmie or I or Joan couldn't have had better parents than what they were. They weren't wealthy. They didn't have a lot of money. Dad always worked and Mom used to work when she was younger.

After Jimmie died, there was a lot of commotion in Fairmount for quite a while. People were coming in, strangers, and some said, "You ought to set up a museum for Jimmie," and even local people wanted to get involved. Dad didn't mind being behind-the-scenes. He didn't want to be one of the spokesmen for the James Dean Memorial Foundation, but it turned out he had to.

It was supposed to be a nonprofit deal. No one was supposed to make any money off it, but it cost money just to keep the doors open on the nonprofit. You have to pay rent for the building, and you have to pay someone to manage it and run it and one or two secretaries to answer the phones and so forth.

Uncle Winton was kind enough to loan Jimmie's clothing and trophies and some other things to display, but he didn't put any money into it. He made it clear right off the bat he didn't want to have any investment in it, financial investment.

Dad hadn't planned on putting any money into it either. He wasn't supposed to, but as time went on… (pause) …He never talked about it much, but I think he got himself pretty much in debt, borrowing money to feed to the James Dean Memorial Foundation to keep the doors open. After the Foundation closed, I don't know how long it was, four years or so, there was no chance of getting any of his money back. I feel Dad and Mom got a raw deal from the word "go" on Jimmie's death, but that's just life. I guess that's about all I can say about that.

LA: Where was this exhibit located?

MW: In downtown Fairmount, across from what used to be a grocery store. It's a Helping Hands store now, but it was right in downtown Fairmount.

LA: On the ground floor?

MW: It was on the ground floor, yeah. They had the personal effects of Jimmie's on display. Kenneth Kendall, the artist, loaned them a painting he'd done, a big oil painting. He also made this big bust of Jimmie he gave to them and they had it on display there.

LA: Would you work in there?

MW: No, I didn't work in there, but I was in there quite a bit.

LA: Would your dad go in?

MW: Yeah, he would go in some. If he went in, that's when I went in.

LA: Were any scholarships ever given?

MW: Yeah. I think they gave them out one or two years. They also had some theater productions here in town two summers in a row. They put on plays up at the Fairmount High School and they had a school too because the kids who were in the plays, most of them, were also going to this school.

LA: It was an acting school? In town?

MW: Yeah, it was in the high school, but the high school didn't have anything to do with it. Like I said, they put on plays. I was in a couple of them. The first year they did *Our Town*, and I played the paperboy. Joe, I think, was the character's name. They had another play that same year, and then the next year they did a couple of other plays. I was in one of them, *Our Hearts Were Young and Gay*. It gave the kids going to the school some experience.

LA: Did any of the kids go to New York or Los Angeles and try to make it?

MW: Some of them did. I don't know if any of them made it as actors, but some were sort of involved in the movie industry or the theater. One of them in particular, Larry Smith, who I was acquainted with, went to work for a company called Samuel French.

LA: Oh sure. They publish plays.

MW: I think he turned out to be one of the main people at Samuel French after a few years. He was in New York last time I heard. He's probably retired by now or maybe even deceased. I hate to say that, but he was older than me by a few years. I lost contact with him years and years ago. Another guy, Coy Bronson, was the one that directed the plays. He stayed here at the house with us all the time. I remember that.

LA: When he came to town?

MW: Yeah, mm-hmm. Both years, he directed the plays. I imagine he was probably even one of the teachers at the school. He worked for Samuel French. I think it was when he retired that this other fellow moved up to his position because Coy had been in New York for several years. I think he knew the lady that owned Samuel French very well.

LA: Was Coy an Indiana guy?

MW: No. I don't remember how we got acquainted with him, but he supposedly was a friend of Jimmie's. As time went on, years went on, and we got to talking to a lot of people who knew Jimmie, nobody ever knew Coy, so I don't know. I never thought any less of him, but I have my doubts as to whether he knew Jimmie.

We even went to the Indiana Theater in Marion with one of the plays and put it on. Evidently, sometimes they had something besides movies there. I think it was at the Indiana, after Jimmie died, they had this thing where Jimmie was going to come back to life. They used to advertise that stuff. You've probably seen it in movie magazines.

LA: A séance?

MW: Yeah, they were going to bring him back to life.

LA: You're kidding? In Marion?

MW: Yeah, I never went; it kind of turned me off.

LA: Do you know what they'd do in the theater?

MW: No, I don't know what they did, but I remember their advertising. I'd see ads in movie magazines, too, something similar to it. He was going to come back to life and he was going to be there. I don't know what they did. I never went and never talked to anybody who did.

LA: That was when your parents were still alive?

MW: Oh, yeah. It would have been a year or two after he died. I was just a kid, but I know I kind of looked down on the theater for doing it. Anyway, that's just the way it was.

LA: When you acted in those plays, do you remember hearing the applause?

Typical ad for a 1958 James Dean Spook Show such as the one that came to Marion, Indiana.

MW: Yep. In the summer plays, yeah. I had more of a bit part in *Our Hearts Were Young and Gay* than the part in *Our Town*, but there were several kids in that one, so it was fun.

Since Coy Bronson was staying here with Mom and Dad, I'd always ride up there with him and ride home with him. A lot of times after practicing a play, we'd go over to Marion to the drive-in for supper. One of the guys would drive over.

There used to be a place called Moon's Drive-In. It's gone now, but we'd go there quite a bit, and they showed "B" movies for free. You'd park your car and watch these "B" movies. Of course, those guys were all older than me, but Mom and Dad always let me go.

One time they did a play in Richmond, Indiana at Earlham College. I think it was a Quaker school. They did a play over there and some of the people who were in it stayed in dormitories, maybe just one or two nights. I wanted to stay, but Mom and Dad wouldn't let me. I was so upset. When I look back on it, I can understand why. I was just a little kid and these kids were all older. That's the only time Mom and Dad ever told me no, I think. (*laughs*) They wouldn't let me do that.

LA: You had to come back home every night?

MW: Yeah. It was probably *Our Hearts Were Young and Gay.* It seems to me it was in the second year. As I look back on it, I enjoyed it. At the time I didn't think it was all that great, but I can see I had a good time.

LA: You didn't have stage fright?

MW: Oh, yeah, I had stage fright. (*laughs*) That's what I didn't like about it, I reckon. Hey, after you practice and practice and practice, you get to where you're not as afraid. Still you have some stage fright.

LA: Did you ever forget your lines?

MW: No. I always remembered my lines, even in school plays. I was in some of those, too. I always knew my lines. I might not have said them with the feeling I should have, but I always remembered them. (*laughs*) I always studied. Remember your lines. I always wondered how movie actors remembered their lines. It's probably good for you to do that. Helps your memory.

LA: Was Marylou in plays?

MW: I don't think so. She doesn't like to get up in front of people.

LA: But didn't she sing with her sisters?

MW: When she had to. (*laughs*)
In our Senior class play, I was Andy Hardy, the main character. Whether I earned

it or not or whether Mrs. Nall just gave it to me because of who I was, I don't know. We'd do the play two or three times at least, on different nights. I think I was in the Junior play too and probably the Sophomore play. I don't remember what I played. I don't know how I ever got the nerve to do that, but I did.

LA: And your parents came to the plays, right?

MW: Oh, yeah. They'd come to the plays. During the day you'd put on the play for the school. Then at night, you'd do the play for your folks or whoever else wanted to come. They'd usually do it again another night, too.

LA: So, your son, Coy, is named after the director of the James Dean Foundation plays?

MW: Yeah.

LA: Did you keep in touch with him?

MW: Oh, somewhat. As I look back on it, Coy was a strange bird. He had a personality that just—everybody liked Coy. He was living with us, and it seemed he'd always been here. He really went over well with people in town. He came to our wedding, but he just kind of became unconnected. I don't know how to say that. I didn't call him much. I don't remember that he called here or anything or not, but if you'd ever talk to him, he'd just act like he was tickled to death. You called and on and on and on… "I'm going to come back this summer," and this 'n that. Never saw anything of him.
One time I was in New York, I called him and, oh, he wanted me to go to plays. We went to two Broadway plays—*Cats* and that one where they rode roller skates around, *Starlight Express.* We went to both and we

went out to supper. Talked about Mom a lot. He asked about Uncle Winton. "I'm going to be home this summer." And I said, "Well, you'd better make it quick. Mom's going to die." "Oh, I'll be there." Never heard another word from him. I don't know what was the matter with him.

LA: Where was he from?

MW: He was from North Carolina. Matter of fact, one time Marylou and I and the kids went to Florida and we stopped there either on the way down or coming back. He lived way back between these mountains. The mountains came down both sides. It seemed to me a mountain was in the back, too. And he had a general store down there. We stopped and had to ask some questions to find out where he was.

The first place we stopped at was a car repair shop, and I said, "Do you know a guy named Coy Bronson?" "Oh, yeah." "Well, do you know how to get to his house?" "Right down the road. You're on the right road."

We got down there, found this little general store, seems to me like it was temporarily closed for the day or half day or something, so we started back. Someone had told us to stop at this one house and we did and that's where Coy's sister lived. She said, "Oh, Coy is going to be so disappointed that he didn't get to see you guys." He had talked to her about us. She knew who we were and everything. Matter of fact, she just insisted we stay for dinner. She cooked up a big dinner. She was a good cook.

Coy had gone to Florida to help somebody move. She said, "He'll probably call you just as soon as he gets back." Never heard a word from him. That's just the way he was. Anytime you'd finally find him, oh, he's just

all over you and you thought he was your long lost friend, but he'd never carry through on anything.

I always wondered if it was because he didn't know Jimmie and Coy knew that we found it out. I don't know, but that's what I always wondered. It didn't make any difference to us. We didn't think a bit less of him when we had those doubts than we did when we thought he was a good friend of Jimmie. It didn't make any difference to us, but anyway, that's the way it was.

LA: And he worked at Samuel French?

MW: Yeah, he worked at Samuel French in New York first and then supposedly this old lady who he said owned Samuel French, she took a liking to him and ended up making him president of the company. She wanted him to come to New York and run that office and he finally did, but he didn't like it because it was cold there in the winter. He liked it out in California where it was warm.

He used to talk about another old lady, Ethel Waters. Coy had a Volkswagen and he'd go pick her up and take her to a performance that she was supposed to do. She sang a lot of religious songs, beautiful, beautiful singer. Coy used to tell stories about her. As you look back on it, you have to wonder if they were true or not, but we thought they were at the time. (*laughs*) He was quite a character. Everybody fell in love with him.

LA: And the Foundation hired him to direct the plays?

MW: Yeah, I don't know if he was paid or not. I don't know the details about that. It was something he wanted to do. He must have been paid something. He must have had some kind of living expenses even though he stayed with us. He was just like a brother, too. The first time he was here, he was here all summer and then he had to go back and it was really sad for me because I was used to having him here. Everywhere he went, I went with him.

LA: So, he returned to Los Angeles?

MW: Yeah. As a matter of fact, when I got out of high school, Dad tried to get me to go to California just to visit him for a few days. I didn't do it.

LA: What happened to the James Dean Foundation?

MW: It just folded up. Didn't have enough money to keep it up. After it closed, Kenneth Kendall wanted his oil painting back, which was only natural. The Foundation didn't have any money to return it, so Dad had it packaged and he paid to have it sent to California just because that was the right thing to do. I don't know what could have been done any different.

I imagine Uncle Winton didn't get involved because he felt it was going to be a no profit deal. Dad didn't intend to get involved in it like that, but when you're living right here, what are you going to do? So, he would borrow money and give it to the Foundation. They were probably supposed to pay it back, but they couldn't.

That bust of Jimmie was put at the cemetery, one of those big bronze Kenneth Kendall busts, and the Foundation built a brick structure to mount it on. It was pretty nice looking, but it wasn't there two or three weeks before somebody stole it, went in with a hacksaw and sawed the neck off.

Kenneth Kendall made busts later with a big neck, so you couldn't easily saw them off. They didn't just have a little shaft for a neck

In conjunction with the World Premiere of *The James Dean Story* in Marion, Nick Adams, Ortense and Marcus Winslow Sr., with Chicago Disk Jockey Howard Miller, unveil artist Kenneth Kendall's prototype of the monument for Jimmie at Park Cemetery, Fairmount, Indiana, August 13, 1957.

anymore. I remember coming home from school one day and Dad said he had some bad news, and I thought maybe someone died. He told me somebody had stolen the bust at the cemetery and he was very upset over it. They never did find it. I think it was done out of meanness. I don't think a fan did it. Whoever did it wasn't mature enough to realize the damage they were doing. We've heard stories about them burying it and one thing or another, but who knows what's true and what's not?

Jimmie's tombstone disappeared a couple times. The last time it was stolen was in the late 1970s or early 80s. I called Winton and Ethel and told them. I figured I'd better tell them before they read it in the newspaper, and Ethel said, "Well, we're not buying another one. They just keep vandalizing it and stealing it, and we're not going to pay for another one."

Then the local tombstone place came along and said the stone was bought from them originally. They offered to replace it with one exactly like the original. Of course, they wanted the publicity from it. I wasn't too crazy about that, but I called Ethel back and told her. I didn't want to do it without her okay. "That's all right," she said, "We weren't going to pay for it, so if they do it, that's all right."

The company was generous enough to replace it and they also did something special with the letters in the stone. They aren't cut sharp deep like normal. If you look close at the letters and rub your fingers over them, they're kind of little rounded out places in the stone, and that's so someone can't take a chisel or something and cut out pieces as keepsakes. The tombstone has been there several years and the stone still looks pretty good.

Even this stone was stolen once, but it was found in Vincennes. That's a college town and again, I think somebody just wanted to be ornery and they happened to know Jimmie was from Indiana and that there was a headstone and they were going to try to steal it and they did.

LA: Wasn't it found on a road?

MW: Yeah, a police car ran over it.

LA: Oh, it was in the middle of the road?

MW: Yeah, we were told it tore the transmission out of the police car, but it

didn't hurt the stone any. It might have put a little scratch in it, but it did some damage to the underneath of the police car.

When we put the tombstone back, we had holes drilled up through the stone and down through the base with steel rods and then a special glue. No one has bothered it since, or if they tried, they haven't been able to get it loose.

Things like that happen and it upsets you, but you have to believe it's someone doing it for a prank, somebody who didn't know anything about Jimmie because I don't think his fans would do anything like that.

The fans have been awfully good over the years. We've had a good relationship with them. Even so, you get tired of dealing with it sometimes, but they've all been very nice to us and very respectful. It's just a good group of people.

LA: Who was in charge of the James Dean Foundation? Do you remember?

MW: A guy by the name of Les Johnson from Marion. I always liked Les, but a lot of people, locally at least, didn't like him. I thought he was really a go-getter, a good publicity man. He got the job of being the manager, and considering what they started with and the fact they didn't know anybody, I thought he did a pretty decent job.

I do know that when they closed up, there were a lot of unpaid bills. Like I say, my dad paid a lot of bills out of his own pocket just to keep the doors open for a while. I think Dad was invested pretty deep with the Foundation pretty quick.

LA: So, it shut down probably in '59?

MW: Sounds about right to me. It was open a couple years, at least. *The James Dean Story* was supposed to contribute some money from theaters back to the Foundation, but nothing ever came of it. Maybe it didn't make any money. You know how it is, movies never make any money and it might not have. I just know the Foundation didn't get anything out of it.

LA: *The James Dean Story* was filmed in Fairmount?

MW: After Jimmie died, some people wanted to make a documentary about him. Let's see, Robert Altman and a guy named George W. George. I remember George W. George real well, but Robert Altman, I'm not sure I remember him.

There was a private showing of it in California in 1957, and they had Mom and Dad and me come out. We saw Winton and

George W. George directs Marcus Winslow Sr. as he's filmed by Lou Stoumen, cameraman and production designer of *The James Dean Story*.

Ethel when we were out there. Seems to me Mom and Dad just called them and told them we were out there, and they came and got us and drove around Hollywood for a while.

They didn't have anything to do with *The James Dean Story*. That was when Uncle Winton was disgusted with all the press and he didn't want anything to do with anything. The story I always heard was Mom and Dad went along with *The James Dean Story* and helped them all they could because they were supposed to give some of the profits off of it to the James Dean Memorial Foundation. I don't remember what percentage the Foundation was supposed to get, but it would have helped with the scholarships.

I think documentaries in movie theaters were pretty new then, so how well it went over, I don't know. When they first talked about it, it was supposed to be shown in between the regular movies...like a fifteen or twenty minute short. It turned out to be a full-length movie. Probably more copies of it have been sold in the past twenty-five years than people ever went to see it in a theater. It's more popular now than it was at the time.

LA: Are you interviewed in it?

MW: I'm in it. I don't know if I'm interviewed or not, but there are some scenes with me. Robert Altman went on to do some pretty big stuff, but what George W. George did after this, I don't know. He was a nice guy. I have some pictures of him here at the farm in albums up at the house, photos people took when they were filming.

When we went to California, Jimmie's house had burnt just a month or so before we arrived. Someone had a newspaper clipping they'd saved and gave to Mom and Dad, and it showed a picture of it. The house wasn't burnt clear down, but it had to be demolished.

It was a small house that resembled a log cabin, had a little front porch on it. Jimmie had always lived in an apartment and he really enjoyed this house. There was a loft in it and I assume that was the bedroom. Sanford Roth took several pictures of Jimmie inside it.

Jimmie used to go to a restaurant called the Villa Capri there in Hollywood, and this fellow who owned the house worked at the Villa Capri. Somehow, he and Jimmie got together on this house and Jimmie moved in. I don't think he lived there more than a couple months before he died.

Sanford Roth's pictures show a big eagle. It might have been made out of cast iron, but a pretty huge eagle always sat in there. A bearskin rug was on the floor. I don't think that was Jimmie's. The owner must have left some stuff in it of his own.

Jimmie had just put a speaker system in. They say the speakers were kind of cone-shaped and he had them in the corners of the room. I guess he was really proud of the system. He'd listen to a lot of music, a lot of classical music. I wish I could have seen the house, as I look back on it, but I was still pretty small when it burnt down.

That house is gone and the house beside it too, both torn down. A great big fancy house was built there with gates out front and so forth. People still come by just to see the property. Another place Jimmie lived was an apartment over a garage and people still drive up there to see that.

LA: Have you seen that place?

MW: Yeah, I've seen it. Can't tell you where it is. The address has been published several times, so it's no secret. It's kind of up on a hill. It wasn't a very big apartment and you had a long driveway you drove up to get back to it, but it's still there.

LA: When you went to see *The James Dean Story,* did they show it at Warner Bros.? Is that where you went?

MW: I don't know where it was. It was at a theater somewhere. I was too young to even think about where it was. I remember we went to Stewart Stern's place, where he lived. Stewart Stern wrote *Rebel Without a Cause* and *The James Dean Story* and he picked us up at the airport. That was in 1957, and he had a '56 Ford convertible. He hadn't had it very long. It was all black, as I remember.

And we went up to his house. I can't tell you the address, but I remember the house. It was on a hill and had a garage under it on the right side. A big long deck went across the whole front of the house. You had to go up these steps to get up to this deck to go inside. It was a neat house.

There was kind of a partition going down the center and on one side was a living room and the other side of that was probably a kitchen. Clear at the end of the room was a balcony where you walked up some steps to get to the bedrooms and the restroom up there.

Joe Hyams came up to Stewart's house for a little while. Joe had inherited a Mercedes Benz from Humphrey Bogart. I don't know the connection, but it was a neat car, kind of a coupe-type car. He and I went in that Mercedes to a little store to pick up milk or something. That's one experience I always remembered.

One of the most memorable experiences was going up in the hills of this housing addition. You went round and around, around and around and around to get to the top. Stewart Stern's cousin was Arthur Loew Jr. and this is where Arthur Loew Jr. lived. You'd turn into the drive and there were walls on both sides, but the walls were the sides of the mountain.

As you got close to the house, the drive opened up. It wasn't a long ways back, but it was kind of private. It wasn't a large house, but it was a nice home. It had a swimming pool over on the left side. The backyard, you could go out the rear of the house and walk out to the backyard and there was a little wall that went around it and if you looked over that wall, you were looking right down on top of the houses below.

At night, it was just beautiful. Los Angeles…those lights just went on forever. It was really a memorable experience for me. I'd love to have had that house. It's probably changed so much now, you wouldn't even recognize it, but it was a neat place, not real fancy, but it was nice.

LA: So, Stewart Stern took you and your parents to Loew's house?

MW: Stewart Stern. I've always liked '56 Fords, like this one right here in the Car Barn and Stewart's all black '56 Ford convertible is what he took us around in. It was just a car to him, but I was pretty impressed with it.

We stayed at the Hollywood Roosevelt. We were at the front because you could look out the window and across the street was the Chinese Theater with the handprints and stuff. I thought that was pretty fascinating. It wasn't very far from there to the Villa Capri, the restaurant Jimmie liked, because we walked down the street and up a hill to it. Stewart walked us up there and we had supper with Lew Bracker. I don't know if we had spaghetti or what, but Stewart and Lew said that's where Jimmie used to hang out. We did a lot of walking.

LA: Did you get a tour of Warner Bros. Studios this time?

MW: I don't remember having a tour of that studio, but we went to it because I remember eating in the cafeteria and there was a photograph of Jimmie hanging on the wall. We also went to Walt Disney Studios and we did get to tour around there. Disney was making *Old Yeller* (1957) then, and we got to see them get ready to do it. I also met Annette Funicello and another Mouseketeer named Cheryl. (Note: Cheryl Holdridge) As a matter of fact, they came over and ate with us in the Disney Commissary. It was quite an experience for a little kid. I suppose I was not over fourteen at the time.

LA: It was you, your mom, and dad. Was anyone else with you that showed you around?

MW: There was a guy from Warner Bros., an older guy. He kind of took us under his wing. He had just retired or was retiring, but really a nice old guy. He did show us around the studio come to think of it, the back lot where it looked like a city. Seems like we might have gone down to the western part of it too. We saw what looked like an old western town.

LA: Did you meet a TV cowboy there?

MW: No, but we went to the Brown Derby Restaurant with Stewart, the old one. It looked more like a hat than the new one. All the walls were covered with sketches of famous people. Caricatures.

Hugh O'Brian came in. He played Wyatt Earp, and they pointed him out to me. At the time we couldn't get that show on television. We're out here in the country, and back then, the only thing we had were TV aerials. We could get about two or three different stations, so when they pointed him out, I didn't know who he was. After we got back home, it was not

very long until Channel 13 became available on our television and I saw *Wyatt Earp. (Life and Legend of Wyatt Earp*, 1955–1961).

LA: So that means you weren't getting *The Mickey Mouse Club* (1955–1958) either?

MW: No.

LA: Did you know who Annette was?

MW: I knew who she was. I don't know how I knew it, but I knew she was one of the main Mouseketeers. They were real nice. Annette was real nice. The other Mouseketeer, Cheryl, she seemed to be a real nice person.

LA: Stewart Stern treated you and your family very well.

MW: He was here at the farm quite a bit when they were filming *The James Dean Story*.

LA: So, he must've liked Jimmie a lot?

MW: He and Jimmie probably met on *Rebel* and became good friends. I have a letter from Stewart asking Jimmie for his advice on a script he'd sent him. When the writer of *Rebel Without a Cause* asks for advice from a new actor, that tells you something.

I don't think he was at the funeral, but I remember real well him being here helping make *The James Dean Story*. I always liked Stewart. I know my dad thought an awful lot of him. Stewart was a good writer. He wrote Dad letters too, and Dad thought enough of those letters that he put them in his lockbox. He didn't want to lose them. Stewart had a way of saying things that was different from the average person.

LA: Do you have those letters?

MW: Yep.

LA: Great. So where did the filmmakers for *The James Dean Story* stay?

MW: I imagine they stayed at the Spencer Hotel in Marion. The Spencer Hotel isn't there anymore. It's been turned into a county building, but at that time it was a pretty busy place. It was a regular hotel like a lot of towns used to have. There also used to be the Crossroads Cafe out here at the intersection of State Road 22 and State Road 9. They had a little motel, but I don't think any of those people stayed there. I imagine they stayed in Marion.

LA: Joe Hyams probably had interviewed Jimmie for newspapers. Did he talk about Jimmie?

MW: No, I don't know too much about Joe Hyams, I don't know why we even met him in California, but we did. Oh, I remember now…Joe came to Fairmount not too long after Jimmie died. That's what it was. Joe came here and wrote a story for *Redbook* magazine. He was around here for a couple days, and I think Mom and Dad got pretty acquainted with him. And that's the reason we saw him in California.

He claimed to be a friend of Jimmie's, and Jimmie has a little book where he wrote things to do, kind of a date book. He mentions Joe Hyams in there a couple times, so apparently he and Joe were acquainted. Joe wrote a book about Jimmie that I didn't appreciate very much (*Little Boy Lost*, Thomas & Mercer, 1993), but that's just my personal opinion.

LA: I think Joe Hyams also hung out at the Villa Capri, so he probably knew Jimmie from there.

MW: He might have.

LA: Did you like the documentary *The James Dean Story?*

MW: I enjoy it more now than I did then, because it has a lot of people in it and just about everybody is gone. They interviewed Mom and Dad and they had pictures of the farm here in it and some people around Fairmount. They even interviewed the guy in New York at a bar where Jimmie went quite a bit. "Jerry's," I think, was the name of it. They interviewed that guy. As you look back on it, it's pretty interesting, but at the time it wasn't as interesting. Documentaries were a pretty new thing then.

Since then you see a lot of documentaries, especially on television, but like I say, I don't think it was real successful. That could be the reason the Foundation didn't get anything out of it. Mom and Dad went along with it and tried to help however they could. It did document a lot of history. I have to give it credit for that. I still see it advertised on eBay all the time.

I'll never forget, when we saw it in California, there was a scene at Jimmie's grave with this kid, a Fairmount High School kid. He had on a black leather jacket and the boots and all that, which is the way a lot of the kids dressed. They had him coming up to the grave. I don't remember what he did, whether he bowed down or what, but there he was on the screen at the very end.

He asked me when I got back home, "Did they cut my part out or not?" And I said, "No, it was in there. You're right there at the very end," and he was so happy. But when the movie came out, it wasn't there. They showed it in Marion at the Paramount Theater, kind of their premiere. I remember going and I sat there and watched it and,

"Oh, my God, they cut that kid's part out." I felt bad because he saw me the next day.

"I thought you said I was in there?"

I told him I didn't know they were going to cut him out. I don't know why they did it. What we had seen was supposed to be the finished product, but anyway they cut out his part. It probably meant a lot to him. Nothing I could do about it; you know?

LA: How long were you out there that time, do you remember?

MW: I'm thinking three or four days. A day or two before we went to California, I had been down to the basement of the house and I started back up the stairway and I fell somehow. I'm pretty sure I broke a couple of toes. Those toes turned black and blue and I couldn't walk without a crutch and I didn't think I was going to go to California because my toes were hurting so bad.

It went on for a couple days and they began to feel better, so I got to go. I remember I was very careful how I stepped around because… oh…my toes hurt. There's not much you can do for broken toes. I don't know if they were or not, but they sure were black and blue.

It was quite an experience. We flew on one of those TWA Constellations, sat in front of the engines, so you could look out of the window and right there were the engines and the wing. My God that thing was noisy. You could hardly talk to the person beside you, it made so much noise.

When we came back home, it was at night and it wasn't even a direct flight. It seems like we had to land in Las Vegas, but I was able

Ortense, Marcus and Marcus Sr. say goodbye to their stewardesses after their 1957 arrival in Los Angeles to see a special screening of *The James Dean Story*.

to sleep because it was dark. There wasn't anything to see anyway. Those big Constellations were state-of-the-art at the time.

LA: Now, you've done more traveling thanks to Brian Jamieson (former Vice President of Promotions and Special Events, Warner Home Video), haven't you?

MW: The first trip he sent me on was in 2003 down to Marfa, Texas. Warner Bros. was going to show *Giant* at the old Paisano Hotel where a lot of the cast stayed. They had just digitized and restored the movie. The hotel had kind of a courtyard, and they showed it outside on a big screen.

It was pretty neat. It was full of people, the courtyard was. Can't tell you how many it held, but it was full. They charged the people something to get in. I don't remember what now. It wasn't a whole lot. And then Brian Jamieson and Kirby Warnock (West Texas native and documentary filmmaker of *Return to "Giant"* (2003) and *When Dallas Rocked* (2012) who assisted Brian in making the screening possible) gave the money to the library in Marfa, which was really nice. That's what Brian wanted to do here in Marion for the 50th Anniversary. He wanted to have a celebration in Jimmie's name and make some money and give it to some organization here, but it never worked out. (The event happened in Marion, but it was not a financial success.)

It was interesting to see outside of town where the big Reata house used to sit and to see the town too. I don't think Marfa was actually in the movie, but a lot of people who lived there were extras. It's very interesting. There's nothing around Marfa, it's just a big bunch of nothing.

There's a big courthouse in Marfa. I was surprised to see that. I wondered why they have such a big courthouse in such a little town, but it's probably the only courthouse for miles around. I was really impressed with the town. It was suffering a lot from stores that had closed up and hadn't reopened, but years before I went there, someone had come to Marfa and opened up some kind of a store with paintings and sculptures that they'd done. (Note: Artist Donald Judd moved to Marfa in the Seventies and through him, his Chinati Foundation, the Judd Foundation, and their museums, the town has become a magnet for artists, galleries, and fans of minimalist art.)

People said more artists were going to come in, and I've found out since that they have. It's gotten to be an artsy-type town. You also hear about the Marfa lights, and that's interesting too. Marfa is kind of like Fairmount in a way. A lot of Marfa's old buildings, you'll see them in the background in some photos of Jimmie. The buildings are still there and a big old movie theater even had its marquee, but it wasn't a movie theater anymore.

There is a building right beside the hotel, and there're two or three pictures of Jimmie getting some ice at it. Seems like a sign was on the side of the building that said "Ice Company." You don't see that sign anymore, but the building's still there.

LA: Did people in Marfa talk to you about Jimmie?

MW: Yeah, there were a couple of women who had been girls of thirteen or fourteen when *Giant* was made, and they said, "You know Jimmie would come out every night and talk to the people that were in town." They said you couldn't get some of the others to do that. They wanted to stay in their rooms or in their trailers or whatever, but they said Jimmie was always very, very polite and always gave autographs and would let them take pictures with him. It's something they've always remembered and as far as they're concerned, Jimmie was *Giant*.

LA: The story I'll never forget was from a Warner Bros. retiree, Ken Taylor, who worked as an electrician on the fair scene in *East of Eden*. He said when they were shooting at night on the Warner's backlot, it was really cold.

MW: Mm-hmm.

LA: And Jimmie saw him and said, "Why don't you go into my trailer. There's something in there." It was a little flask of whiskey and Ken went in and took a shot of whiskey and it warmed him up and he went back out and worked. He said Jimmie was the star of the movie and noticed how cold he was and offered him a chance to warm up and that was something stars of movies just didn't do.

MW: Jimmie could see the common guy, you know, the little guy, and their problems and their lives. He wasn't too good to talk to them, be friends with them. Most of what I've read of the people in Marfa, Texas, was about how he made a lot of friends down there and got pretty acquainted with the people in the town. I think Jimmie enjoyed the different lifestyles of the Mexicans and the townspeople of Marfa, which was something different from what he'd ever been around.

When we were down there, we went out to the ranch, Evans Ranch, and from the road you can't see anything. Then you turn at this big entrance and you drive onto the ranch. We drove for three miles before we got to the house where the stuff is. The Evans Family lives just to the left of where the old Reata house was built for *Giant*, but you can't see the Evans house in the movie. Warner Bros. was careful when they filmed it. The movie didn't show any of the original Evans Ranch buildings or the older house that was there when *Giant* was made or the newer home the family was building at that time.

There were a few horses and a few cattle when I was there, but they had a drought in Texas for years, and there wasn't anything for animals to eat. The pasture was just brown. You'd see some deer and some antelope running around, but there weren't hardly any cattle.

It's changed some since then. They started getting rain. I don't know how it is today, but a few years after we were there, someone said they got quite a bit of rain and that everything was green again, but when I was there, all the way from Marfa to the airport, there was just a lot of nothing, just brown country.

LA: So, the Evans Family was still in the house?

MW: Yes, yep.

LA: Did they remember the making of the movie?

MW: Oh, yeah. They were real nice people. Kirby Warnock, he had something to do with the visit. He and Brian made arrangements with the family for us to come back there where the house had been, so we could look at it.

When we got there, the only thing standing was just a post from the side of the big Reata house. After *Giant* was made, Warner Bros. sold the windows out of the house to someone and they just left the house and within a couple of years a big, strong wind came along and blew much of it down.

Pieces from the side of the house were on the ground, plastering they'd made for the house. Mr. Evans, the old man, told us to pick up anything we wanted, and I picked up some plaster and some bolts. It's part of a corner off a block and I put it in the Historical Museum. Then Mr. Evans, he drove out in his pickup truck and invited us up to their house and he and his wife had coffee and ice tea for us.

It was a typical ranch-style house, a nice place, nothing real, real fancy, but it was "homey." They had a lot of stuffed animal heads on the walls, deer, antelope, things that had been killed on the ranch. You know, wild animals. I always thought it was awfully nice of them to open up their home for everybody, and everybody had a good time. We were probably in their house for a half an hour or forty-five minutes.

They had had one son who played a part in the movie. I don't remember what, probably just an extra, and he had been killed. They had a picture on the wall of their son in a rodeo, riding a bucking bronco horse. He was killed not too long after that picture was taken. I think it was the only child they had and it was kind of sad to see that.

I guess that pretty much killed the old man and when they showed *Giant* outside there at the hotel, Mr. and Mrs. Evans both came, but they left early. Someone said that she kept a pretty close eye on him because he got to drinking pretty heavy. I guess his son being killed just about ruined him. I forgot how he was killed, but I think it was in a car accident.

LA: So, the father and mother were there when the movie was made?

MW: Mr. Evans, he was a young guy when *Giant* was made, and I heard he even dressed up in clothing to look like Mercedes McCambridge in some of the shots with the horse. He did some of her stunt work.

He had a script from *Giant* just like the one I have that was Jimmie's. Big thick yellow script laying there on the table, so evidently the movie meant something to him since he kept that script out all those years.

LA: Was Jane Withers with you?

MW: Mm-hmm. Jane Withers and Earl Holliman were both there. He seemed like an awful nice guy, Earl Holliman did. I talked to him quite a bit. Of course, Earl Holliman and Jane Withers both came here for the 50th, and you know Jane Withers is really a nice person too.

LA: Yeah, she gets emotional when she talks about Jimmie.

MW: Yeah, she acts like she and Jimmie were very close friends. She says Jimmie used to come over to her house and read the Bible. Like you say, she gets pretty emotional when you start talking about Jimmie. She used to have a big collection, a lot of clothing and things from the movies, but I don't know whatever happened to all of it. I've heard that water damaged some of it one time. She's pretty proud of the shirt she had that used to be Jimmie's. I heard it got stolen. I don't know.

LA: That's what I heard too. So, Jimmie would read the Bible at her house in Marfa?

MW: That's what she says.

LA: I know she's very, very religious.

MW: Yeah, she said she'd invite him in to read the Bible. Kind of interesting.

LA: Uh-huh. Was Jimmie that religious here?

MW: I don't know. I was too little to know about that. I know the Back Creek Church gave him a Bible when he graduated from high school. His name was engraved on it, and he still had it there in California. I put it in the Museum.

LA: Did you go to Sunday school?

MW: I used to go when I was a little kid. Mom would always insist we go to Sunday school and church. We went to the Back Creek Church. As I got older, it got so I didn't go to Sunday school. I'd just go to church. Then I went for a long time without going, not that I'd forgotten about it. Life just goes on, you know?

Marylou and I have tried to get in the habit of going back to church again. I guess everybody should. As you get older, you think more and more about the future and death and so forth. When you're young like Jimmie, there's still no excuse not to be going to church like you should, but a lot of young people don't. Life is so hectic anymore. You have so many things going on and even though you have the best intentions in the world, you don't always get things done like you should.

I'd like to think that Jimmie was a Christian and truly believed in God. I think he did from the way it looks with him saving his Bible and the way Jane Withers talks about him coming to her house and reading Bible verses, but he was only twenty-four and his life was wiped out in a split second. You certainly hope that in the future you're going to see your family again.

LA: In Marfa, did you all see the Little Reata, Jimmie's ranch in *Giant*?

MW: Yeah, the Little Reata was at a whole different location. That was on another ranch.

LA: Oh, it wasn't on the Evans Ranch?

MW: No, it was before you got to the Evans Ranch, just right along the road. There was a pretty wide ditch between the road and the fence. You could park your car along the side, no problem. We parked there and jumped over the fence and I looked for someone to come run us off all the time, but they never did. (*laughs*)

The thing is still there where the Little Reata sign used to hang. Two big posts, those are still there and the windmill was still there. It was kind of up on a ridge. Matter of fact I think a couple windmills were up there. One of them Jimmie climbed up on and it was in bad shape, but it was still there.

LA: It was a working windmill?

MW: It was at one time, but I don't think it was when we saw it. At the start of *Giant*, you see a bunch of cattle drinking water out of a big pond. Well, that pond is still there, but it doesn't have any water in it. Apparently, it wasn't a natural pond. It was just a low place, and they saw it could be a pond.

I guess they filled it with water for the movie, but it doesn't have water standing in it all the time like you would think. It was amazing everything was still there. It appears that in Texas the stuff gets so dry that nothing ever rots out hardly and that old windmill, even though it looked pretty ragged in *Giant*, it was still there and that was fifty years later.

LA: What was the best of the trips Home Video sent you on?

MW: Oh, they were all very interesting. Brian and I went to France and we went to England and went to Japan and I enjoyed seeing all those countries, but I enjoyed Marfa more than any of them.

James Dean waits to film one of his most iconic moments in *Giant*.

LA: What did you do in France?

MW: In 2005, they were showing *James Dean: Forever Young* at the Cannes Film Festival. It premiered there and it was pretty interesting. We gave a lot of interviews to people, and there was a guy that lived close by, Pierre Cardin, clothes designer.

We went to his house for dinner. He lived in a very, very unusual house. (Note: *Palais Bulles*, "Bubble Palace.") It was a bunch of round rooms all kind of hooked together, but it was a nice home, tastefully done.

One room would overlap into the other one a little bit and that's how you'd go from one room to another. It's pretty unusual and when it was being built, a lot of people there in Cannes were objecting to it, wanted to stop it because it was so different from everything else, but now that it's built, they don't want anybody to do anything to it.

It's a work of art now. It has a theater, an outdoor theater with seats and a cover over it and people sit there and watch the entertainment. If he has a band or something, why you look out over the ocean and over Cannes. It's at a very good location up on a hill. I enjoyed it. I mean, it was interesting.

England, or London, I enjoyed London. I got a kick out of seeing the buildings. A lot of them were old, old buildings and then right beside them would be a brand-new building. It was because the old building had been bombed out during the war. That's the reason the new building was there. Germany bombed them so bad that... (pause) ...it was an interesting experience.

Japan was nice, the only thing I didn't like was I didn't know what anybody was saying. I always felt uncomfortable not knowing, but where we were, in the hotels and other places, they all spoke English.

LA: And Brian was with you all the time?

MW: He was with us most of the time. Mark Roesler of CMG and I went on our own to see Seita Ohnishi. (Note: A Japanese fan of Jimmie's who built a memorial to him near the site of his deadly accident and who also purchased Sanford Roth's photos and negatives of Dean.) The last time I was in Japan, the only reason Mark and I went, was to see Ohnishi.

Tokyo is very interesting. The streets are very clean and their lifestyle is just so much different from ours. They seem to use a lot of different cartoon characters for decorations everywhere. The people are neat. They were all very nice. I was really impressed, the last

time I was there, with the kindness and the courteousness of the Japanese people.

You go into a store and they just bend over backwards to try to help you and they carry your stuff to the door and then we got back to the Los Angeles Airport and that was a whole different ballgame. Clerks act like they wish you weren't even there because they're having to do something, you know.

I thought at the time it would be nice if our people who work in commercial stores had to go to Japan and live for a couple years and see how they operate because they make you feel welcome. Like I say, they grab the bag right out of your hand and carry it to the door for you. It's sure not that way in the United States. Here, a lot of clerks act like they're upset, because you're bothering them.

LA: So, the first time you went to Japan, was it for *James Dean: Forever Young*?

MW: Mm-hmm.

LA: And who was in the audience? Was it critics or was it the public?

MW: It was the public. There may have been some critics too, but as far as I know, it was mostly the public.

LA: And you would answer questions after?

MW: Yeah. Let's see, it was in London they had us get onstage before they showed the movie and answer a lot of questions and after it was over with, a lot of people came by where we were sitting and asked more questions. In France, they had it set up where writers were sitting around different tables, round tables, and about every seven or eight minutes, they'd say, "Change tables." And you'd go over to another table and the person who was sitting there would go to another table and they'd ask questions, wanting to know this or that and it got to be work after a while, but that's a part of keeping Jimmie's memory alive.

LA: Who else was there?

MW: Dennis Stock was there and Phil Stern was there because of their photos of James Dean, and Frank Mazzola was there who acted in *Rebel Without a Cause*.

LA: He was in France? Or England?

MW: He was at one of those places. I can't remember for sure, it's been so long ago, but there were people who had something to do with Jimmie's movies, yeah.

LA: Was Carroll Baker ever at anything?

MW: Carroll Baker was at the James Dean Stamp Ceremony in '96 at Warner Bros. She was there, but I've never seen her any other time.

LA: That Stamp Ceremony was really nice.

The James Dean Stamp Ceremony...June 24, 1996 at Warner Bros. Studios, Burbank, California. (left to right: Honorable Tirso del Junco, Chairman, Board of Governors: USPO, Carroll Baker (*Giant*), Frank Mazzola (*Rebel Without a Cause*), Robert A. Daly, Chairman and Co-CEO, Warner Bros. Inc., Jean Picker Firstenberg, Director and CEO, American Film Institute, Marvin Runyon, Postmaster General and CEO, USPO, Lois Smith (*East of Eden*), Marcus Winslow, President, James Dean, Inc.)

MW: Very nice, very nice. Whoever organized that did a wonderful, wonderful job.

LA: It was neat because Lois Smith spoke about Jimmie working on *East of Eden* and Carroll Baker spoke for *Giant* and Frank spoke for *Rebel Without a Cause.*

MW: You sent me that big roll of photos of Jimmie that were real tall that you had hanging all around the studio.

LA: Mm-hmm, yeah.

MW: Well, I didn't open that for a long time and finally one day I thought I better open it. The end of it had been knocked off and I was afraid maybe mice or something had gotten in there, but they hadn't. They hadn't bothered it at all. And what was a big surprise was once I unrolled it there was a bunch of other big pictures inside of it.

LA: Oh, we'd rolled up everything that we could find. We gave Frank one from outside the police station.

MW: Is that right?

LA: Yeah, we hid it in a bush and then when Frank was leaving the studio, he put it in the trunk of his car and so he's got a big picture of himself. It was when Jimmie was going up the steps to the police station and he…

MW: They were standing there on the steps.

LA: Yeah.

MW: There was a big picture?

LA: Yeah, yeah, we put pictures around the locations where everything was filmed. Yeah, that was a really good time.

MW: It was. It was very nice. I don't know how Warner Bros. happened to get involved in it.

LA: Well, it was the Post Office. I think probably it started when Warner Bros. tried to get, and they did, they got Bugs Bunny a stamp. Then somehow the Post Office got the idea or somebody got the idea to do a James Dean stamp, and I think they had a postmark here in Fairmount and then they had a postmark in Burbank.

MW: Yeah, the first day was in Burbank and the second day was in Fairmount.

LA: Is that how they did it?

MW: They wouldn't let them do a first day in Fairmount.

LA: Yeah, because they wanted the celebrities to…

MW: Yeah.

LA: …call attention.

MW: Yeah, and they did get a lot of attention to it out there, seemed like to me.

LA: Oh, yeah. The studio had never done anything like that before. You know…that big stage and…that was the thing about Bob Daly and Terry Semel, they loved the history…they literally loved the history of the studio and, boy, I couldn't have been there at a better time. It just…that was fun stuff…that and the opening of the Warner Bros. Museum, you know, were just fun stuff. Now you brought Chuck to the opening, right? Or was that Coy?

MW: Coy went to the opening of the museum and Chuck came to the stamp ceremony, which was only about two weeks later.

LA: At the stamp ceremony, for your speech you read that letter Jimmie wrote you when you were a kid. It's a pretty incredible letter, especially considering how young you were at the time.

MW: I haven't made a lot of speeches because I don't like to, but I guess one of the first ones that really meant anything was that one at the stamp ceremony.

LA: Really, before that you hadn't made many speeches?

MW: Not very many, no, and I thought about that one quite a while. I really didn't know what to say because here is little me from a little town in Indiana and you've got all these actors that are used to getting in front of people and you know they're going to get up and say something, too. I had to think quite a while about what to talk about, but it turned out okay. I've had some little deals where some little group would want me to kind of talk about Jimmie or something, but as a rule, I don't. That's not really me.

LA: Since you wrote Jimmie letters, did you write him after you'd see him on TV?

MW: I don't remember referring in any letters to a TV show. I think maybe Mom wrote him and told him we'd seen him on this or that, but I don't think I ever did.

LA: Do you have any other letters Jimmie wrote to you?

MW: Yeah, I have some other letters. I guess I thought that one was the most important one. The others are just "letter" letters. I mean, they're nice, but this one had a story behind it because he wrote to Mom and Dad and told them to tell me to send him some drawings.

As time went on, I realized what he was saying. When he wrote me that letter, I was almost too little to comprehend. He even says in the letter, "Have Mark or somebody help you read this."

LA: Did he write you from California, too?

MW: No, just New York.

LA: He was probably too busy in California.

MW: That'd be my guess. He may have written Mom and Dad. I don't know. Jimmie got awful busy, and I'm sure he wasn't able to do everything he wanted to do. He tried to make the most out of every minute, I think. He was always doing something.

LA: When you went to the Cannes Film Festival, do you remember any questions they asked that you thought were really interesting…that you'd never heard before?

MW: I think I've heard them all.

LA: Which question do you get the most tired answering?

MW: "What kind of a guy was he, really?" and that type of stuff. I didn't know Jimmie as a movie star. I knew him as an older brother who lived here with us. It's hard to talk to people about it because they are looking at him as a movie star, as a character in one of the movies, and that's not the Jimmie I knew. My memories and experiences aren't of a movie star. I am very aware of his talent and everything and I know he is a movie star, but that's not how I remember him. It's very unusual for someone to be as young as he was and only make three movies and sixty years later, he's still pretty well known.

Johnny von Neumann, owner of Competition Motors, shows Jimmie a Ferrari Mondial
before the Santa Barbara Road Race, May 1955.

LA: You said that you thought Jimmie in *East of Eden* was the most like you remember him.

MW: Yeah, to me. I couldn't get over it. The first time I watched him in the film I thought, *Man, he's not acting. That's just him.* It was really amazing. *East of Eden* was a good movie. It was very well written and very well

played by the actors. It was a good show and even still fits in today, I think.

LA: Marylou said that you couldn't talk about Jimmie for a long time.

MW: It was hard to talk about him. I saw a documentary on him one time. In it was a clip of a race and Jimmie was walking around at the race and, boy, that just tore me up to see that. As time got on, I got to where I can talk about him, but I didn't used to talk about him to speak of.

LA: Was it seeing him alive at a race and knowing how much he loved to race?

MW: I think so, yeah. He was having such a good time and you could just see the smile on his face. He was walking around the pits there and it really touched me. That film still exists. It's been shown in several documentaries, but that was the first time I'd seen it. I forget which one it was now. I don't remember if it was *James Dean: The First American Teenager* (1976) or what. There was another one. I don't remember a whole lot about it, but I remember the guy that used to play Jimmy Olson in *The Adventures of Superman* (1952–1958) was interviewed.

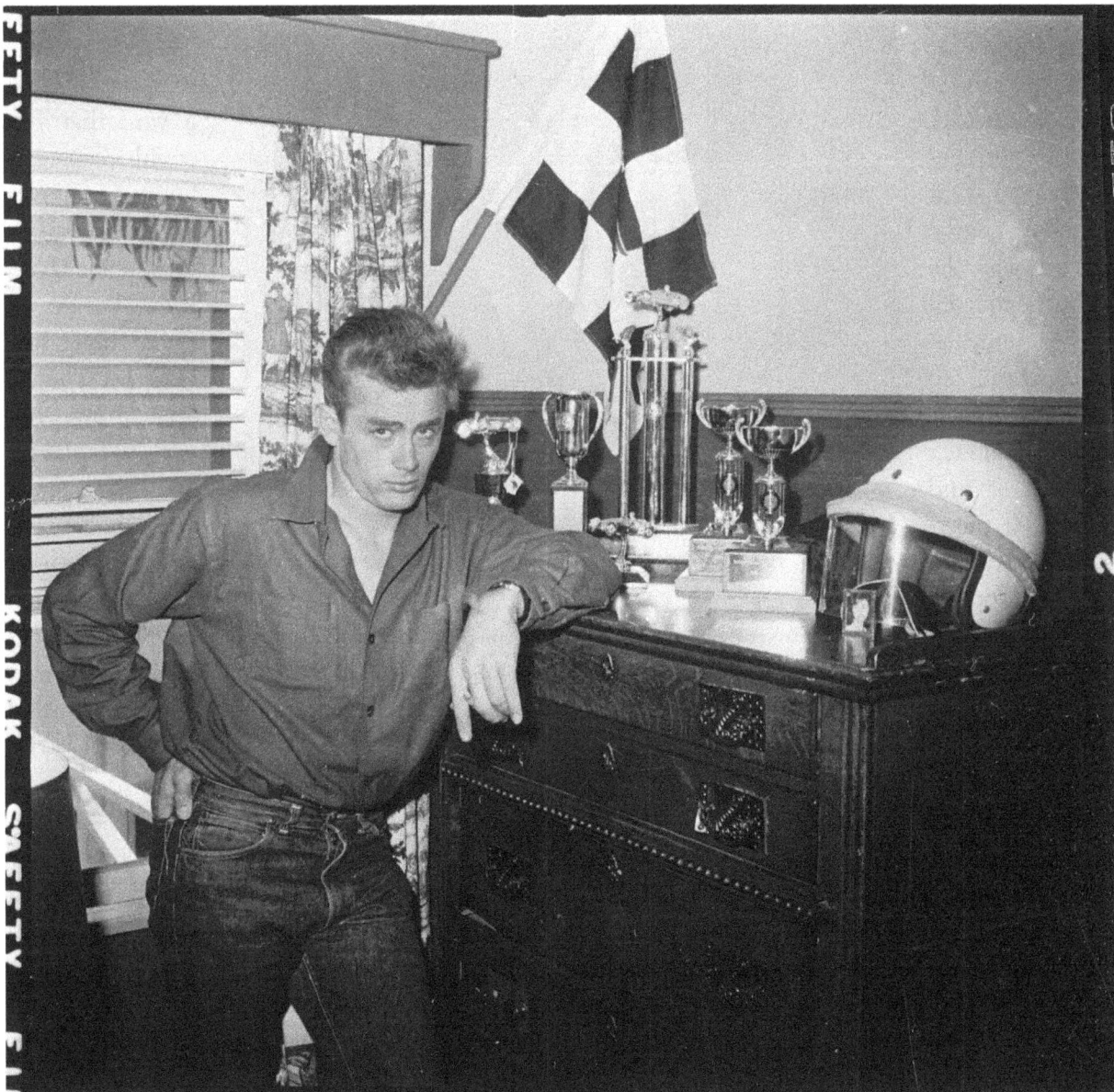

Jimmie and his racing trophies with Pier Angeli's photo in front of his helmet.

LA: Jack Larson.

MW: Yeah. And he didn't think too much of Jimmie. He didn't understand what the big deal was. I guess that always stuck with me all these years.

LA: Have you ever been up to where *East of Eden* was made?

MW: Up in Mendocino, yeah.

LA: How'd you go up there?

MW: My friend, Charlie Bridenfield, and I went up there. Charlie had a car he wanted to sell in Monterey at an auction, so we took the car to Monterey and left it and the trailer there, then drove on up to Mendocino. It's very nice up there, right on the ocean.

Someone told us, and we hadn't noticed it, but they'd taken down all the overhead electrical wires and buried them. There were no telephone poles sticking up in the town. I didn't realize it, but a lot of movies are made in Mendocino. When we were there, it was getting so commercialized a lot of the houses were now shops where people sell stuff. I don't know how much longer they can keep using it as a movie set.

Some guy put out a book called *James Dean in Mendocino*. (Compiled and Edited by Bruce Levene, Pacific Transcriptions, 2001) He lived there and got a lot of photos from people who took pictures during the making of *East of Eden* and put them in a little book. We were able to walk around and take that book and compare it with places where the movie was made.

The little hill Jimmie walked down in one of the scenes is a blacktop now. It wasn't a blacktop when the movie was made. There is a fence that goes around a yard that you could recognize. Some downtown buildings in the movie have been torn down, right along the water. They're gone now, but the buildings across the street are still very recognizable, especially if you have that book to compare them.

I was glad we got to go up there because I enjoyed Mendocino, right on the ocean with the water splashing up. Down the road from the town a little ways, a hotel (Note: Little River Inn) where a lot of the cast stayed is still there. We stopped in, didn't stay there or anything, but I was glad I could go there. If you're a fan, it's a good place to see.

Rebel Without a Cause was mostly made at Warner Bros. and a lot of the sets are still

(l-r) Bill Tunstall, Jimmie's friend who assisted him in a couple of races, unknown girl, Kathy Case and boy friend, Steve Rowland, before Jimmie's Santa Barbara Road Race.

Jimmie with his Speedster after it blew a piston in Santa Barbara.

there, but it's nice to be able to go outside the studio and see the real locations.

LA: Did anyone ever take you around Los Angeles to some of the locations where *Rebel* was shot?

MW: *Rebel,* no. I do know there's one place they call "Rebel Alley," which is behind the

house where Jimmie parked his car. At the James Dean Gallery, David Loehr has part of the fence that was there. It's a cement block wall now, but David just happened to be in L. A. when they were tearing the old wall down.

LA: You've never been to Santa Monica High School?

MW: I never stopped, but it sort of seems like we went by it and someone pointed it out, but I didn't go up to it. I wasn't up on the sidewalk or anything.

LA: And the planetarium?

MW: Yeah, I've been there. I just saw a commercial the other day using the plan-etarium. It was a night shot and you could see the back of it where you come out and you're up high overlooking the city. A couple of shots later showed the front of it, too, just for a few seconds. I don't think the planetarium has ever changed much.

LA: I know you liked Marfa the best, but what was the most memorable place you've

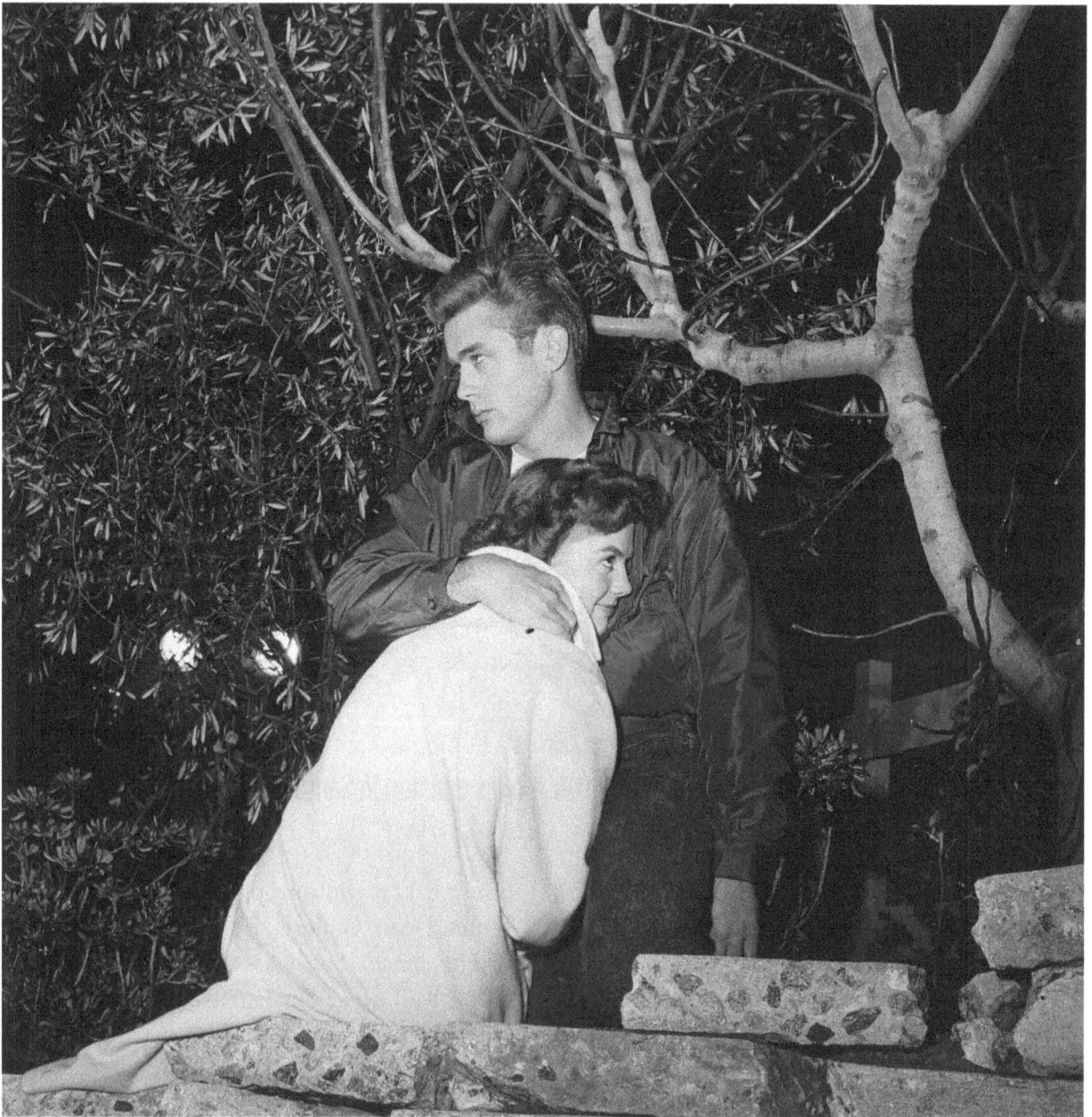

James Dean warms Natalie Wood during a *Rebel* night shoot.

Jimmie loved cars so much that just backing his Speedster out of his driveway makes him smile.

seen out of everything, all your travels around the world?

MW: Well, of course, you've got special memories from everywhere, especially when you don't travel any more than I do, but I guess...well, like with Marylou for example, if we go on a trip somewhere, it's not that she doesn't like Jimmie or Jimmie's fans, but she wants to be separated from it. She doesn't want to go somewhere and visit people because of Jimmie. Now with me, it doesn't bother me.

I enjoyed going to Los Angeles and seeing the studio where Jimmie worked and going to Barney's Beanery where he used to hang out some and that big hotel, the Chateau

Marmont, where *Rebel* was worked on. I enjoyed seeing that, just going into the lobby and just knowing that Jimmie had been there.

I really hated to see the old Competition Motors building get torn down, not that it was a good building, just because it has so many memories. Jimmie bought his Speedster there and then he got the Spyder there. He was very happy around cars and he was able to have a nice new car. His Speedster was new and the Spyder was new and he was being successful at racing them and that was something he really enjoyed, so I enjoyed seeing the building and seeing old pictures of him and seeing how it used to be, but I've been to the crash site two or three times.

It's not a place you enjoy going to, but still it's kind of good to go there for some reason. Of course, I've been to Cholame, just down the road less than a mile. Jimmie never really reached Cholame, so in a way, it really doesn't have a lot to do with him, but in a way it does. That's the name of the town closest to the intersection there.

LA: When was the first time you went up to Cholame to see where Jimmie was killed?

MW: It was in '96 when I was in California for the museum opening. We spent a few days there before they had the opening. Charlie, Coy, Brian Hatton, and I rented a car and we drove up there.

LA: And the memorial that Mr. Ohnishi...?

MW: Yeah, I think it was there at Cholame. We got turned around somehow. Don't ask me why because I don't know. I wasn't driving, but we ended up coming in from the opposite way. We got around behind the wreck site somehow and came through Paso Robles and we went by the funeral home, beautiful brick funeral home.

We stopped and got out. We weren't going to go in, but this guy saw us out there taking pictures and he came out. He figured we were James Dean fans and he said, "Well, come in if you want to." There wasn't anybody in there then, so we went in and looked around, a nice old place. I think it was added onto since Jimmie's body was there, but it was a very nice old funeral home, Keuhl's Funeral Home.

Then we went on through to Cholame. I'm sure that memorial was there. Then we went on to where the wreck happened and then on back towards Los Angeles. Of course, Jimmie came from the opposite way. In 2006 I was there again when the highway department put up the James Dean Memorial Junction sign, plus it seems to me there was another time I was there. I don't know, maybe it was only the two times.

There's nothing really to see at the wreck site. There is and there isn't. The intersection has been changed some. It's kind of a sad place to be. A lot of people apparently stop and get their pictures taken with the sign. I don't think you can tell where the original road was anymore, but you can tell about where it was. Apparently, a lot of accidents happened there over the years.

LA: Were you at Cholame around dusk? To see what happened?

MW: No, but I can imagine how it could be. It's a long hill Jimmie would've been coming down and then there's kind of a low spot and you come out of that low spot and you get to the intersection. I can see how it could be a very dangerous intersection.

Vivian Sherwood leans on Marcus Winslow after the emotional unveiling of the marker designating the James Dean Memorial Junction where Jimmie was killed. Vivian was a publicist working in New York City when she met and was charmed by him and she lobbied the State of California for years to honor him at this site. This event took place on September 27, 2005, so the fans visiting on September 30th, the 50th anniversary of Jimmie's death, could see the tribute that California had given.

James Dean, the photographer, experiments with the angles of New York City.

LA: You mentioned New York City when you talked about Coy Bronson. Have you spent a lot of time there?

MW: I enjoyed New York years and years ago. A lot has changed since then, but when I first went, things were still around from Jimmie's time. I've been up to the outside door of where he lived last and I've seen the Ed Sullivan Theater and a lot of places that were there when Jimmie was in New York.

I enjoyed seeing those places. Even though I wasn't there when Jimmie was, it kind of made me feel he was along beside me. Los Angeles and New York were both very interesting. Of course, going to foreign countries was interesting, but I enjoyed going to places where Jimmie had been more than anything.

LA: Was the Iroquois hotel there?

MW: Yeah, it was there. Iroquois, I don't remember whether I went in it or not. I don't know. It was close by where he lived last, I think.

David Loehr used to do that James Dean Walking Tour when he lived in New York. It was handy for him to do when he lived there. I wish he was still doing it. I'd enjoy doing it again, but physically to walk that much... (pause) ...David investigated and found all the sights, restaurants Jimmie used to loaf in, different places where the TV shows were shot. He had a nice walk for the fans. I always appreciated the fact he did that for them.

LA: Would David go back to New York after he moved to Fairmount?

MW: Not much. He used to go back and forth for a while, but then it got so he just didn't go back at all. David and Lenny had an apartment in a two or three story building. They had a big sewing machine set up and a couple of rooms where they sewed. It wasn't in downtown Manhattan, but it was a decent district as I remember it.

One time I was in New York when Dave and Lenny were living there and I stayed at their apartment for a couple nights and it was quite an experience for me. Of course, New York is much different from Fairmount, and it really amazed me to think about Jimmie coming from little old Fairmount and all these buildings and all these people. And he really didn't have anything when he came and didn't have anywhere to go, especially to do what he did. It was just an accomplishment that I think is amazing.

It was interesting to be on Broadway, to walk down the street and see where so much stuff happened, and I guess is still happening today. New York's a busy place and a lot of productions come out of New York and a lot of TV shows still today. It's a neat city. I wish I had the time to go and have someone really show me around, but that'll probably never happen now.

When I was visiting David, we went out to the Statue of Liberty and we got inside the statue and went clear up into the crown. For a while they wouldn't let people go in the crown, but I think maybe they are again now. It was neat to get to do that. You felt like you were observing a lot of history there. We went to the Empire State Building. I've been up in it two or three times, up to the observation tower. I enjoy getting up there. You can just see forever.

Jimmie and Martin Landau discussing their craft in New York.

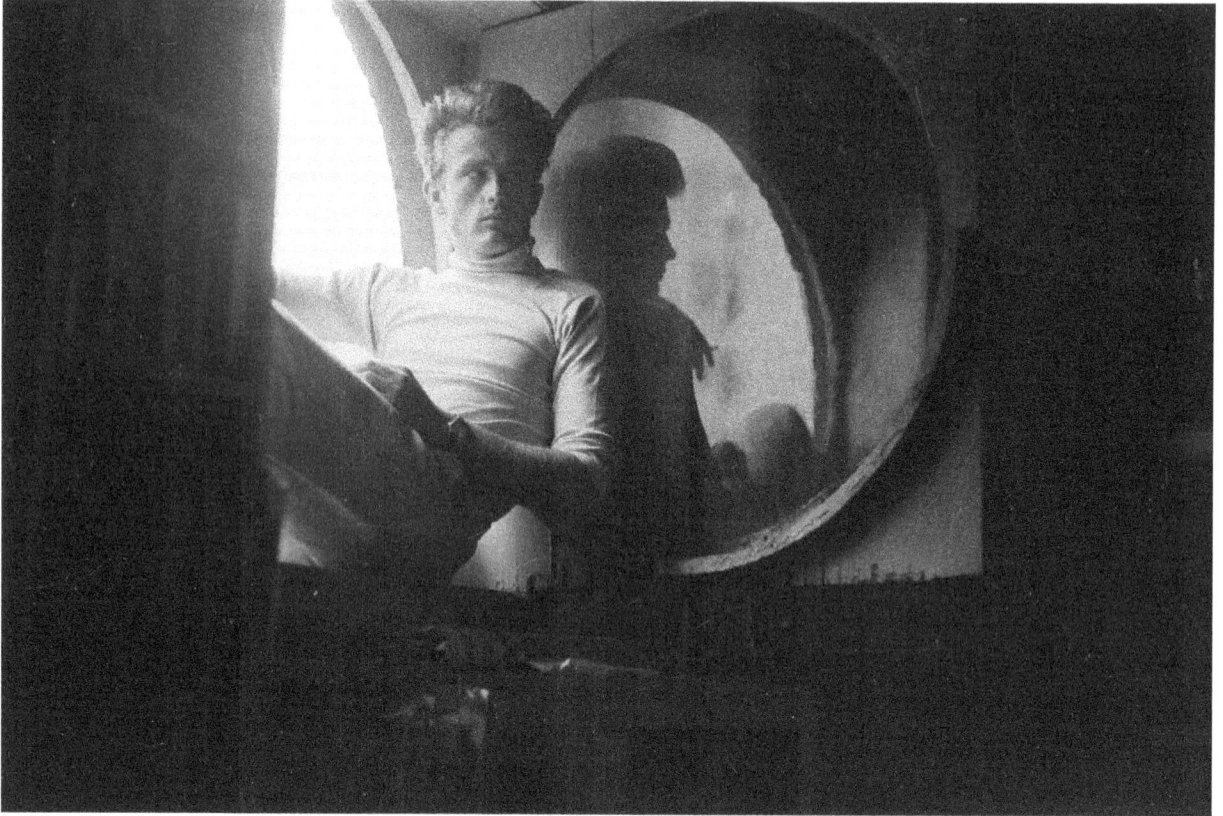

Dean's small New York apartment offered him comfortable nooks and crannies to read and contemplate.

We also went up in the World Trade Center, one of the buildings. There were two of them. We just went up in one, but we went to the observation floor and I'll never forget they had windows that went from the ceiling down to the floor and kind of a wooden bar going around for you to come up against, but, my gosh, you just walked up and looked out the window and you felt like you were going to fall out the window because there wasn't much there. They designed it that way on purpose, and it was very neat. I couldn't believe it when those terrorist attacks took them both down. They were really nice pieces of architecture, but apparently, they weren't designed to be flown into by 747 airplanes. They should've been, but they weren't.

Greenwich Village, we walked around it, and that was interesting. We saw a lot of movie memorabilia shops and many of them were in basements. You'd look down and right there would be a shop. I was very impressed with New York. I enjoyed it. Wouldn't want to live there, but I enjoyed visiting there.

LA: Did Lenny or David point out the Broadway theaters Jimmie's plays were in?

MW: Some, yeah. I don't remember which ones they were now, but I remember David showing us at the time. I don't know if Jimmie did anything at the Ed Sullivan Theater or not. I'm not even sure it's called the Ed Sullivan now. That's where David Letterman had a

It was New York itself, always alive, that stirred Jimmie's thoughts and drove his creativity.

MUrray Hill 2-7464

BETWEEN FIFTH AND SIXTH AVENUES

HOTEL IROQUOIS
49 WEST 44th STREET
NEW YORK 18, N. Y.

Dear Mom and Mark,

I hope the weather there, is much more pleasant than it is here. It couldn't be warmer if it tried; 98° to 114° degrees with 70 to 80% humidity. no breeze. The hard part is the maintaining of a respectable social standing. Meaning clothes. You must be fashionable even in the heat. Shirt & tie and suit. Wow! You know how I love to dress up.

I apologize with all my heart for not writing. As you may or may not detect. this is the first letter I have written in many months. Completely out of practice. My only concern is that you

over

In the summer of 1952, Jimmie announces to Ortense and Marcus Sr. that he is now a member of the Actors Studio.

can read this and will forgive me.

You wanted to know what I was doing, also if you could help me in any way. Yes, you could help me very much but first I must tell you what has happened. I have made great strides in my craft. After months of auditioning I am very proud to announce that I am a member of the Actors Studio. The greatest school of the theater. It houses great people like Marlon Brando, Julie Harris, Arthur Kennedy, Elia Kazan, Mildred Dunnock, Kevan MacKelly, Monty Clift, June Havoc, and on + on and on. Very few get into it and it is absolutely free. It is the best thing that can happen to an actor. I am one of the youngest to belong.

It is fine but an actor must also live. The summer presents a problem. T.V. shows go off the air + summer replacement shows go on, making your chances even slimmer. There just isn't enough work. I have many good prospects for Broadway Shows but that won't happen until the fall. T.V. will also come back. I work now, but the jobs are few and far between.

MUrray Hill 2-7464   BETWEEN FIFTH AND SIXTH AVENUES

HOTEL IROQUOIS
49 WEST 44th STREET
NEW YORK 18, N. Y.

I was taking dancing and fencing lessons but they will have to wait for a while. I would more than appreciate it if you could spare 10 dollars or so. I need it rather desperately. I'm sorry that when I write I always need something. Sometimes I feel that I have lost the right to ask; but because I don't write isn't an indication that I have forgotten I shall never forget what you and mom have done for me. I want to repay you by being a success; It takes time and many disappointments; I'll try very hard not to take too long. If I have asked for help at the wrong time please forgive me and I will understand.

Love to all

Jim

MUrray Hill 2-7464

BETWEEN FIFTH AND SIXTH AVENUES

HOTEL IROQUOIS

49 WEST 44th STREET

NEW YORK 36, N. Y.

Dear Mom + Mark + Marby

Please forgive me for not sending Christmas this year. I had hoped to; but man can do nothing against the designs of Providence. The show ran one week in N.Y. (a flop) However it was a personal success say the critics and others. It *was* true and now I'm out of work again. I wish you could have seen me make the debut in N.Y. or Philadelphia. You would have been proud. Maybe next time. I would like very much to share with you the talents you and mom engendered and nurtured. An action that may soon be at my convenience. With all due respects to the

Jimmie writes the Winslows in December '52 about his personal success in *See the Jaguar,* a play that bombed on Broadway.

85

significance that a present bears during Christmas. I would be at this time, much happier with the money.

My best to all and to you, my love

Jim

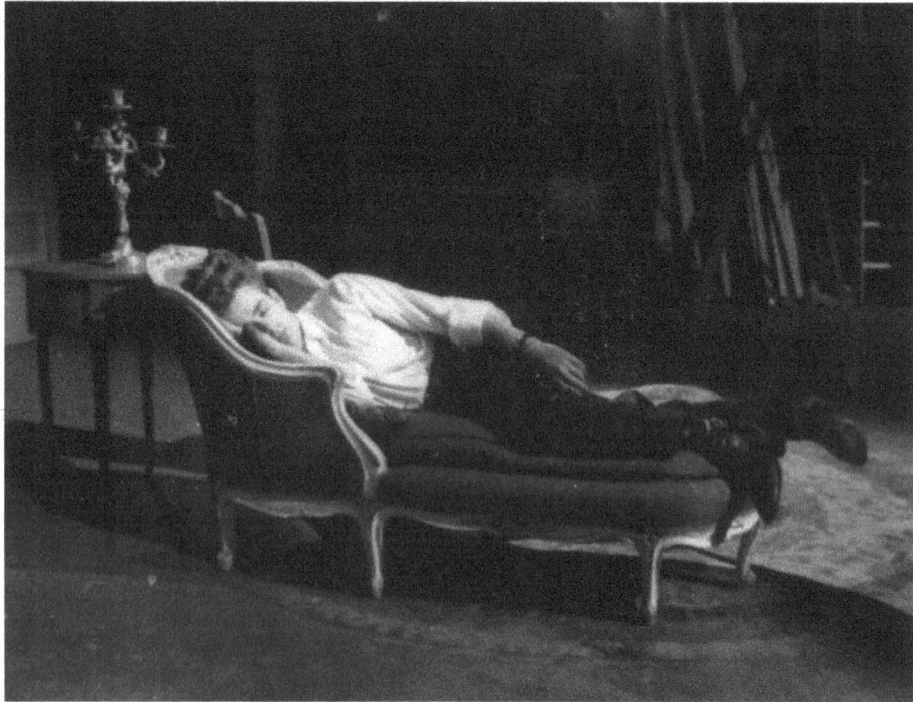

Jimmie takes a quick nap on set in New York while rehearsing
"*The Thief*" for live television, January 1955.

MUrray Hill 2-7464   BETWEEN FIFTH AND SIXTH AVENUES

HOTEL IROQUOIS
49 WEST 44th STREET
NEW YORK 36, N. Y.

Dear Mom, and Dad,

I sincerely hope you have a pleasant Christmas.

I'm happy to know Daddy misses me. He is the only real genuine love in my life. The "Friends" I brought to dad. met Dad and fell madly in love with him and his kind. They can now more readily accept me for what I am. Understanding my remorse having to tolerate people much unlike him.

I was a personal success in my B'way debut. The show flopped but the critics were more than kind to me. Anyway I am out of a job. I would appreciate to greater degree the money itself, rather than present, with all due respects.

Jimmie's letter to his father and stepmother in December '52 tells of the closing of his play and asks for Christmas money rather than a present.

to its significance at Christmas time.

I hope this year I could send you some Christmas but fate would have it otherwise. the show only ran 1 wk. in N.Y. Sorry! next time.

all my love

Jim

James Dean...always thinking...in his dressing room for "*The Thief*."

late night show, so whether they changed it to his name or not, I don't know.

LA: Let's go back to the Cannes Film Festival and after the screening of *Forever Young*... was the reaction really, really good?

MW: Yeah, everybody applauded for it. I don't know if it won any awards. Brian wanted it shown in a theater so many times to make it eligible for an award. As far as I know he did get it shown that many times, five or six, but I don't think it ever won anything.

I think *Forever Young* is one of the best documentaries on Jimmie, and it is narrated by Martin Sheen and Martin Sheen did an excellent job. He's got one of those voices that you can just go along with, but as far as I know, they didn't win anything with it. It is really a good documentary, the very best, I think in my opinion.

LA: In Japan, it only showed in one theater?

MW: We were only there for one showing. It may have been shown more than that, but it was only shown once when we were there. I don't remember too much about the Japan deal. Of course, Mark Roesler and I went to see Ohnishi when we were there. I guess that's what I remember the most.

Jimmie with his tripod and 16mm camera outside Marfa, Texas on *Giant*.

5

Curtis Management & Jimmie's Father

Leith Adams: When did the Curtis Management Group come to you?

Marcus Winslow: It was in February of 1984. Mom had moved to town in 1980. She was always afraid out here in the country and when Dad died, Mom was really afraid. She wanted to move into Fairmount and a house became available. Matter of fact, Uncle Winton and Aunt Ethel lived in that house when they moved back here from California. They thought they wanted to live in Fairmount and they did live here for at least four years, but they didn't like the winters.

Ethel had lived in California all her life and Winton had been there since moving out with Mildred and Jimmie, and they didn't like the cold. They decided to get to a warmer climate, so they went to Florida and bought a house. That left this house in Fairmount available. Mom's cousin, Margaret Thomas, owned it and lived next door and was happy that Mom would move in. It worked out real well. It was a nice little house. I'd love to have it. I wouldn't mind living in it.

Anyway, Mom moved in and one Sunday afternoon she called and said, "Can you come in here? There is somebody you need to talk to." I said, "Yeah, I can." So, I went up to her house and Mark Roesler and another guy were there. Both of them had gone to Indiana University together, and Mark had started up this licensing business called Curtis Licensing Company. His father-in-law owned Curtis Publishing and that's how he came up with the name Curtis Licensing. At that time, Mark was representing Elvis Presley's image and Norman Rockwell's art. He only had a couple licensors.

He was talking to Mom and me about Jimmie. I told him Jimmie has a dad, and he's the one to be involved because he owned the rights. We knew Winton didn't want to talk to anybody, so we told that to Mark.

Mark asked if we would contact him, and I wrote Uncle Winton a letter about Mark Roesler and Curtis Licensing and how he and Ethel could check them out if they were interested. I even told them, "If you don't want me involved, that's okay. You go ahead and do what you want with them."

Winton Dean Retired Aug. 3 After 32 Years Service

Winton Dean, Dental Laboratory Technician Central Dental Laboratory retired Aug. 3 after 32 years service.

Born at Fairmount, Ind., Mr. Dean began federal employment with VA Hospital, Marion, Ind. on Jan. 7, 1929 after completing a course with McCarrie School of Mechanical Dentistry Chicago. He transferred to VA Center on Sept. 16, 1936. During World War II, Mr. Dean entered military service on Feb. 18, 1943 and was discharged Sept. 13, 1945, returning to V A Center. On April 30, 1957. Mr. Dean resigned to go into business for himself as Motel Operator. After a year's absence, Winton Dean was reappointed to his old job on April 14, 1958.

A quiet, affable gentleman, Winton Dtan is the father of Motion Picture star, J a m e s Dean who met his untimely

WINTON DEAN

death in an automobile accident several years ago.

To Winton Dean, VA Center extends its best wishes for much happiness to a career employee who served VA for 32 years.

A Veterans' Administration newspaper article announces Winton Dean's retirement circa 1964.

Well, Winton said they didn't want to do it on their own, but if I wanted to, I could go ahead. I felt kind of skeptical about it at first, but it worked out well.

This was around the time when someone was causing us a slew of trouble. A guy in California caused us a lot of grief for a while. He was really a scumbag no-account. Matter of fact, after we got together with Uncle Winton and Curtis Management Group for licensing, this guy was calling himself the James Dean Memorial Foundation and taking donations from people, but there was never any accounting for it. Who knew where the money was going?

He was supposed to build this statue in some cemetery in Los Angeles. He said if Jimmie couldn't be there, well the least he could do was put a statue up for him. Who knows whether the cemetery even knew about it? He was just a no-account troublemaker. He knew Uncle Winton didn't want anything to do with anybody and somehow found out where Ethel and Winton were living.

If you want to know where someone lives bad enough, you can find out. He got their address and wrote them a big letter about Curtis Management Group and how we were exploiting James Dean's name and he wanted to do this and we wouldn't let him and blah blah blah. Winton and Ethel were smart enough they just saw right through it. Pretty much they turned him over to us.

Stuff like that has happened over the years. It's not the only time we've had some trouble. You think you're trying to do the right thing, and there's always someone else who really doesn't have anything in it other than their own selfish desires to do something, but we haven't heard from this guy in years.

I think he kind of fell out of the picture. He was in Fairmount a couple years ago, but he naturally didn't bother to look me up. I didn't want to see him anyway, but he was in the Museum in Fairmount and he'd written a book.

A guy I know bought the book just because he wanted to see what he'd written, and he mentioned us in there. I don't remember what all he said. I never read it. Never worried a second about it because I know anybody that knows him wouldn't take any stock in anything he said. You always have somebody like that. Even though they're not bothering you right now, it's in the back of your mind and you're wondering if they're going to reappear.

Mark Roesler and Joan and Marylou went down to Florida to Winton and Ethel's. I was sick. I had some kind of a stomach virus, but they flew down and Mark talked to Winton and Ethel, and they really liked him. They were willing to sign right up and have Curtis represent Jimmie's image.

Over the years, a lot of people had tried to get Winton and Ethel involved in things using Jimmie's name. I think they got involved in some, but never made a dime. Mark guaranteed them so much a month for the rest of their lives and Ethel said, "What if something happens to Winton?" He told her, "It won't make any difference as far as your part is concerned. We'll still pay you the same amount every month as long as one of you is living." They were really pleased. It was after that meeting when this guy sent them the letter and they just turned it right over to Mark. It didn't even seem to worry them, and I was tickled with that.

Another time we got into a lawsuit with the photographer, Roy Schatt, in New York City over some photos. They even sent a lawyer here to Fairmount while I was in New York because they knew I wasn't here. It was after Uncle Winton moved back up here from Florida. They snuck into the nursing home in Marion where he was and tried to interview him. It was a dirty deal, just a bunch of no-account thieves. They were the same people that talked Warner Bros., I think, into suing us. It was an outside law firm.

LA: Did Roy Schatt find these lawyers or did they find him?

MW: I don't know. I don't know. I always heard that Roy Schatt's wife was a lot younger and she wanted to make all the money they could, but I really don't know. I wish I had talked to Schatt after it was all over, because I think he was basically a good person. He sat there during the trial and went to sleep half the time. The lawyers were doing all the talking and all the thinking.

Later, Roy Schatt was at the stamp ceremony at Warner Bros., and I shook hands with him. I probably should have been nicer. I was never not nice to him, but I didn't go out of my way. I should have. He was just an old guy trying to make a living. I feel he was being used by his legal team, but he's the one who initiated the lawsuit. We didn't.

I think we found out Warner Bros. even helped pay part of Roy Schatt's lawyers' fees.

They were sort of setting us up, or that one law firm was. I don't know if Warner Bros. was behind it, but the law firm set us up against Warner Bros. What an experience. What an experience. I wouldn't go through that again for anything. We had a guy come here four times serving me with a summons to appear in court…I was ready to kill that guy.

LA: He came to the house?

MW: Oh, yeah. He came here four times in about a two month period. Seemed like he was even beginning to get ashamed, but he had come to serve me this summons. He lied to me the first time. I was over at Coy's house, working on his house, when Coy called and said, "Dad, there's some guy here who wants to see you. I think he may have some kind of court papers." I said, "Well, let me talk to him."

Oh, he talked real nice, you know. I felt the same as Coy. I could tell from the way he was talking, he was up to something, but I knew I was going to have to face him sooner or later. I could have avoided it. I didn't have to agree to meet him, but I thought I might as well face the music.

He came up to Coy's house, and I said, "Are you going serve me with a subpoena?" "No, no, no." Well, he did, you know. I said, "You lied to me. You told me you weren't." "No," he said. "You said 'subpoena.' This is not a subpoena. This is a summons." "You lying bastard!" It's all the same, but whatever. There's a reason for everything, I believe.

When we settled the suit with Warner Bros., we never had anybody dispute our rights to Jimmie's image after that. It got to be where we knew who Warner Bros. was, and they were good to us, all they've done and all you've done. I know you didn't have anything to do with the lawsuit, but to start with, it was hard to even agree to work with them.

Man, I hated Warner Bros., but I've gotten to where I don't have any bitterness at all towards them. It feels like that's just life. That's the way things are. It turned out to be probably the best thing for us. I'm very thankful for the people I've met over the years and the help and assistance I've gotten. I like to think I helped them, too.

LA: You did. You made the Warner Bros. Museum look great. Jimmie's Triumph motorcycle right in front as you walked in the door. That was just a knockout.

MW: I'm glad you were able to make use of it. I'm thankful we are even able to have it. We've been so fortunate about a lot of things over the years. Everything has worked out. We've had our share of problems and disappointments, but overall, we've been pretty fortunate.

From what I was told, and that's all I know, the big lawsuit with Roy Schatt in New York came about because a watch company wanted to use some of Schatt's photos of Jimmie to promote a watch in Japan. Winton and Ethel had told me, when I first talked about Curtis Licensing with them, that they had some kind of an agreement in Japan. At the time, we didn't know what their contract said, so I told Mark we couldn't do any licensing in Japan.

We did finally get a copy of the Japanese agreement and it didn't amount to anything. It was just for some photos, but Curtis was very, very cautious. When the watch company came to Mark and wanted to use Roy Schatt's photos of Jimmie, Mark said we couldn't license anything in Japan, that it wasn't part of our agreement. Of course, he didn't want to tell them everything, so he just said he couldn't do the deal.

The watch company had told Roy Schatt they'd pay him so much money for the photos.

I'm not sure how much, but the company told Schatt that Curtis Management had turned them down and that made him mad, so he sued us. It really got nasty. His wife may have been okay. I don't know, but at the time I didn't like her because we got sued. She was the one who was wanting to do all this stuff, make all this money. I think she was probably behind the lawsuit or had a lot to do with it.

About that time is when a piece of steel went through my eye. It was only about a week after that happened when they wanted me to go to New York. I didn't feel like going. I didn't want to go anyway, but I really didn't feel like going. I was real depressed from my eye injury, but I agreed that I would go if that's what I needed to do. I got there and spent three or four days listening to a bunch of lawyers argue back and forth. I thought I was going to have to testify, but I never did have to.

The lawyers even brought some guy up from Florida, down where Uncle Winton had lived. He supposedly was a friend of Uncle Winton. He didn't testify to anything that hurt us. I guess he was trying to testify that Winton and Ethel weren't in their right minds, something about how he had sent a meal over to them and that Winton wouldn't come out of the bedroom; it kind of made him sound like Howard Hughes, a hermit.

The lawyers paid his way to come to New York, made him feel like a big shot. That's really what it amounted to. It didn't mean anything. The next week the trial was supposed to resume again. I thought, *Boy, this is a bunch of b.s.* Nothing was happening and we didn't know what the outcome was going to be.

We had to go back to New York the next week. We had only been there a day. I think it was on a Monday, and Mark said,

"They're wanting to settle and they want to settle outside of court and they want to sell us the pictures." I didn't figure we could buy them, but he wanted to sell the photos and we thought, *This has turned out to be a pretty good deal.* We ended up buying the photos off of Schatt and the lawsuit was dropped. It was a good move for us. We've used those pictures and used them and used them and as far as I know, Roy Schatt was happy.

On the other hand, I don't know what he thought the future was going to bring. I think he thought we'd pay him for those pictures and he already knew Warner Bros. was going to sue us because the same lawyers he was using were some of the same ones involved in the Warner Bros. suit.

It was only about a month later, Warner Bros. sued us. That's when we found out Warner Bros. had been paying his lawyers. They were trying to say we didn't have any rights to the name of James Dean, so the studio could have them. Maybe when they found out they weren't getting anywhere with this lawsuit in New York with Roy Schatt, they told him they would sue us and get his pictures all back eventually. Well, that didn't work.

Anyway, after we had Roy Schatt settled, Warner Bros. sued us, and that was really a devastating experience. While that was going on, every morning I'd wake up and it was like a death in the family was hanging over us. I knew we hadn't done anything wrong, but you never know. We really didn't know, to start with, what kind of a contract Jimmie had with Warner Bros., because we didn't have a copy of it and they didn't want to give us a copy of it. They eventually had to. That was really something. I tell you; I never, never want to go through anything like that again.

At the trial, Warner Bros. would bring up stuff and this judge—I felt the judge might want to vote in their favor because Warner Bros. is in Los Angeles. They do business there, and we're here in Indiana, you know. The lawyers would bring something up in the trial. They'd want to present something and the judge would say, "All right, go ahead." They'd want to do this or do that. I'd think, *This hasn't anything to do with what we're doing here,* and the judge would just let him go ahead and do it.

As it turned out, he didn't want them to have any grounds for an appeal. That's what it turned out to be. A lawyer from Warner Bros. was there, and these other two lawyers from this outside firm convinced the studio if they hired their firm, they would get them the rights to James Dean. This old guy from Warner Bros., he sat there and went to sleep every day. I don't think the judge was too impressed with that (*laughs*), but anyway he did.

We hired a law firm from Los Angeles and it apparently was a pretty good law firm. Our lawyer was real clean cut. He told us before the trial…of course we didn't have a jury, but anyway, he said, "Now don't wear any fancy jewelry or any rings or any fancy stuff." We had suits and Marylou had on a dress suit and we didn't have on any fancy jewelry.

Everyone got a haircut before the trial and this guy, their lawyer…I didn't think I would ever forget his name, but I have… three or four times he came to Indianapolis to get me to come down for a deposition. He's the lawyer who sent that guy up here with the summons. Every time he tried to get me down there, nothing ever happened. The last time, I did have to go down and he started asking me some questions and our lawyer said, "Don't answer that. It doesn't have anything to do with this."

That made him mad right off the bat. He said, "We'll just get the judge to order you to have him answer these questions." "Go

ahead." Well, we sat around for two or three hours and finally they told me, "You might as well go home. We'll let you know in the morning if you have to come back." That was the end of it. (*laughs*) I never did have to give him any deposition.

The Screen Actors Guild signs up every actor and they have different categories for the actors. If they're just starting out, more or less an unknown, they're in a certain category. I've forgotten what it's called, but if they get to be famous, then that puts them in another one. Jimmie was in such a low category, because he was so unknown when he signed with Warner Bros., that his contract wouldn't allow the studio to have any rights other than for those three movies. I mean they had all the rights in the world to those three movies forever, but they didn't have any rights to his name or likeness. Warner Bros. claimed they did, something about one sentence in Jimmie's contract gave them that right.

I'll never forget the judge saying, "Now wait a minute. I want to get this right. You're saying if I'm in a restaurant and James Dean came in and I took his picture with my camera, Warner Bros. owns the rights to that picture?" This guy said, "Yep." And the judge said, "Ohh-kay." (*laughs*)

The trial lasted for a week and then the next week, on a Friday, the judge said, "I'll mull over this for a few days and I'll give you the answer in a week." He had a certain date and a time. It was one week later.

I said, "Do I have to come back for that?" And our lawyer said, "Not if you don't want to." "I will do whatever I need to," but they said it wasn't going to make any difference. The judge would have his decision made. They felt we were going to win. They felt real good about it, and sure enough, the judge gave us the rights to the name and likeness and he even gave us the rights to his voice. We didn't ask for it, but we got it.

Right away, Warner Bros. was going to file an appeal. All I know is what Mark and our lawyer told me. They said they heard that a law firm that did a lot of appeal work told Warner Bros. there wasn't anything to file an appeal on. That old judge let them bring in anything they wanted.

Finally, they wanted to settle and they had to pay our lawyer fees. They'd also sued Curtis Publishing Company separately for something and Mark told me before our trial, he was going to sue Warner Bros. for damages for suing Curtis Publishing Company because they didn't have a reason for doing that.

I told him, "I don't want anything to do with it. All I want to do is get the thing settled and for us to have the rights like we're supposed to have." I said, "If you want to sue them, you go right ahead, but I don't want to be involved in it."

They did sue them and part of that settlement was Warner Bros. paid them something. It wasn't a great amount, a few thousand dollars. It made them feel better, I guess, but I just wanted to get the damn thing settled and move on.

We had gone for a whole year taking everything we made on licensing to pay the attorneys' fees. That was back when licensing was doing really good. Thank God we were able to pay the attorneys. We paid them over one and three-quarter million dollars and we got that back.

There was about $100,000 we didn't get back because the judge said there were overlaps. In other words, the attorneys in Indianapolis had charged for doing this or that and the attorneys in California charged for the same thing. They probably both did the same research, but he felt like one of them...

LA: He looked at the billing statements and he made that decision?

MW: Yeah, but it took him about six or eight months. He gave us all the rights, but just as soon as he gave us the rights, our attorney in California said we were sued under some 990 act or something where whoever is the prevailing person in the lawsuit, their fees have to be paid by the losing party. He said, "We want our attorney's fees."

Warner Bros. didn't think we would win, but they ended up having to pay our fees amounting to, like I said, $1.6 million or something. That was okay with me. I was tickled to death when it was all over with.

I've heard people say this...and sometimes I think it counts and sometimes it doesn't... but I've heard people say there is always a reason for everything. I believe that's probably true because we went through hell for about a year there with the Schatt deal and then the Warner Bros. deal and when it was all settled, we were in better shape than we had ever been. No one ever sued us again after that because they knew if Warner Bros. couldn't beat us, then no one could. *(laughs)* And really, we never gave anybody any cause to sue us that I know of.

We got our money back from the lawyers' fees and the lawsuit put us in a better position than we'd ever been in. You have to wonder why things happen the way they do, but there is usually a reason for it. Things turned out so good. Probably, we would always be wondering what our position was with Warner Bros., and it turned out we were in better shape than we ever thought we were because we didn't know what the contracts said.

I hate to say it, but I just hated Warner Bros. after that for quite a while. I thought, *Yeah, there's no way I'll ever have anything*

97

to do with them. They're a bunch of crooks. Then you came along. We got involved with you. Then, when the Post Office made the James Dean stamp, why, they had the stamp ceremony there at Warner Bros. and they had us there for the opening of the museum and, as far as I'm concerned, they've treated us like kings ever since. I don't know. We won't give them any reason not to, but I'm sure we'll never get along with them like we have because you're not there anymore and they change their presidents and stuff like that about how we change our underwear.

LA: Let's go back to when Mark Roesler came to Fairmount and met with your mom and you said you needed to talk to Winton. What had been done with James Dean's image before that?

MW: Nothing. There hadn't been a thing done.

LA: So, if there were posters being sold…and there were a lot of posters in the Sixties….

MW: Mm-hmm, yeah.

LA: Then Winton didn't make any money?

MW: Yeah.

LA: But he probably didn't even know about it?

MW: I don't think he pursued it. He and Ethel just didn't pay any attention. Didn't care. Didn't want to be bothered.

LA: Were you aware that college kids had James Dean posters on their walls?

MW: Yeah. We'd see a lot of people coming here to visit that had on James Dean shirts. I

don't know for sure, but it seems to me it was around 1980 when a lot of licensing started happening on personalities. There may have been some before then, but not to the scale there is now.

About that time, they started putting celebrity pictures on everything, not just tee shirts, but all kinds of products. We didn't get involved until 1984 and until that time, there hadn't been any money made for the family on Jimmie. That was tough, too, because once you set a precedent of no one paying royalties and then you start telling people they have to start paying, they don't like that. They'd rather not have to pay anything.

LA: Right.

MW: Well, most of them would prefer not to pay. There are people who know how business is and they didn't mind, but there were some who didn't think they'd have to, but we don't have much trouble anymore with anybody.

LA: So, Winton never wanted to get involved?

MW: No, he didn't want it on his mind. But he did get involved in it. They let us license, and we gave them so much a month for the use of it.

LA: For the Foundation?

MW: Yeah.

LA: And the Fairmount Museum?

MW: Well, not the Museum. The Museum didn't have anything to do with it. It's just when Curtis first started out, they had to have some kind of an entity and they suggested we call it the James Dean Foundation, so that's what we did.

It wasn't too long until we had to change it to James Dean Incorporated, because a lot of foreign countries wouldn't recognize a foundation. They would recognize a corporation, so we had to go from the James Dean Foundation to James Dean Incorporated.

LA: Was there a lot of marketing being done overseas that you found out about?

MW: Yeah, quite a bit. That's one thing about Jimmie. He has a worldwide presence, whereas a lot of people might be famous in the United States, but they're not famous overseas. He happened to be very well known overseas.

LA: So, when you started the foundation and the corporation, Winton was promised a certain amount of money a month?

MW: Regardless of whether anything sold or not. He didn't want a percentage. He just wanted "*x*" amount of dollars period, and it was very reasonable, so we went along with it. He got that as long as he lived.

LA: As business picked up, how involved were you in everything? Did you get to see what the product was going to be?

MW: I used to always see what it looked like before it came out. That sort of changed a little bit. I don't know why I don't see things like I used to. I'm supposed to see the design of everything they're going to do, and it has always worked out pretty well. There hasn't been very much over the years that I've had to turn down or that I did turn down. It was probably something that was said on a tee shirt or something that I didn't think was in good taste. So much stuff anymore, they use the name in advertising somehow instead of

on a product to sell, so there hasn't been as much for me to see as there used to be.

LA: Like using Steve McQueen in a car commercial, but his image is not on the car.

MW: Yeah, right.

LA: Would you see the commercials?

MW: I used to see some of them. Recently I saw that a shaving company is using Jimmie as a spokesman or whatever. I mean he's not really saying anything. It's just a picture of him with the shaving products, but they look fine to me. A lot of that stuff goes on. Posters and other things, at least of Jimmie, have died down.

They used to put Jimmie's pictures on all kinds of stuff, but you just don't see that like you used to. I don't know why. It's just the changing times, I guess.

LA: The James Dean tee shirts in the Fairmount Museum, are those created by the Museum?

MW: Most of them are bought from companies.

LA: That have the license?

MW: Yeah. The Museum used to have a lot of their own tee shirts made up. They always had to find a picture and do this and do that and a lot of these tee shirt companies are already making them and they're nice tee shirts. They're professionally designed, so the Museum is better off just buying and reselling them than trying to create the shirts themselves.

LA: You get the statements from CMG, right? From Curtis Management Group?

MW: Yeah, it lists the companies that are licensing and what they are supposed to be making.

LA: So mostly it is Jimmie in commercials or in advertising campaigns?

MW: A lot of it is anymore. The market is flooded with calendars and posters and tee shirts and stuff so that companies are afraid they can't sell them because everything has already been seen. I can only speak about Jimmie. Licensing things on James Dean went way down, but I think it has on all celebrities.

LA: So, Curtis Management's business has kind of fallen off a little bit?

MW: With Jimmie anyway, but I'm not complaining. I'm tickled to death for what we get. It's just not near what it used to be. I don't know about the other people CMG handles. They represent a couple hundred different people, but I would guess there are probably only half a dozen that are really big.

LA: Yeah, you just don't see much of anybody anymore. You're right.

MW: Mm-hmm, used to be Norman Rockwell was a big thing. You saw Norman Rockwell everywhere. Now you don't ever see Norman Rockwell stuff.

LA: So, Winton Dean and your mom, they were brother and sister?

MW: Right, right. Uncle Winton and Mom and Uncle Nolan grew up southeast of Fairmount in the Grant Church area. Winton was seven years younger than my mom and Uncle Nolan was about seven years younger than Uncle Winton.

I think that's right because when Uncle Winton was sick and was in the V. A. Hospital, that's when they said he was born, 1907. People have told me he lied about his age, that he was a year younger, but I don't know if it's true or not. As far as I know, he was born in 1907.

LA: Did he go into the military before he started working in Veterans Administration?

MW: No, he worked for the V.A. here in Marion. Then he got the opportunity to go to California to work at a V.A. hospital there. It was a lot better job than the one he had here, and he felt he had gone as high as he could go here so that's the reason he went to California. Then while he was there, he got drafted into the service. He made false teeth, dentures. I don't think he ever had to go overseas, but he was in the service during World War II.

LA: Jimmie's mother, Mildred, where was her family from?

MW: They were from Jonesboro, just north of here. That's what our address is—Jonesboro, Indiana. How Mildred and Uncle Winton met, I don't know. But it would've been around 1925 or so, probably, when they got together, met, and so forth. Her name was Wilson originally, and I really don't know too much about her family.

I used to know her brother. He would come in at the implement store in Fairmount and get parts for an old Ferguson tractor he had. Howard Wilson was his name. Mildred also had a sister that lived in Texas. I can't think of her name right now, but I'm pretty sure she had a couple of other sisters, too.

Then after she passed away, why, Mom and Dad took Jimmie back here. I'm not

Jimmie and his mother, Mildred Dean

sure how much interaction Jimmie had with the Wilson family. I never heard too much about them, but I don't know if there was any reason he didn't see them. I think it just happened that Uncle Winton's family was a little closer to him.

LA: Did you ever talk about Jimmie with her brother?

MW: No, never did. He was an older guy. I guess to be honest about it, when he was coming in the shop, it would have been in the early Seventies and I just didn't have any reason to ask him anything about Jimmie. Jimmie had been very popular, let's see, in the late Fifties and then maybe the early Sixties. There were always some people who

were fans, but a lot of people kind of moved on to something else. I just didn't have any reason to ask him anything.

Really, it was around 1980 when Jimmie's popularity started getting big again. Seemed like there was kind of a Fifties craze that came along about that time. People got to be interested in Jimmie and others. Jimmie usually gets compared with Marilyn Monroe and Elvis Presley. Elvis Presley and Marilyn Monroe made gobs more movies than Jimmie ever did, but his popularity, his acting legend, is still very strong. For someone who only made three movies, it's pretty unreal. That's a really good sign he had something special or people wouldn't still be interested in him.

LA: You were pretty young at Jimmie's funeral, but do you remember her family at the funeral?

MW: I'm sure they were there, but I don't remember seeing them. At that time, I was eleven years old, almost twelve. I don't think I even knew who his mother's family was. That was something I never ever gave a thought about because he had lived with us so long, it was like this was where he'd always been.

It wasn't until two years after he died that people would ask me about his mother and I'd say, "Well, I don't know. I'll find out." His mother had been buried in Marion in Grant Memorial Park. Matter of fact, I was by there about a month ago. I hate to say it, but it was the first time I'd been over there for a long time. I was surprised by how many flowers were on her grave. Fans had put flowers on her grave.

LA: Did Winton ever talk about her?

MW: No. When I was around, he never mentioned her. Even when I was old enough to start knowing much, I never heard him mention her. Of course, he remarried in 1946, married Ethel, and I suppose that might've made a difference. Maybe he didn't want to say too much around her. Jimmie's mother just wasn't mentioned much.

Now Mom and Dad, I heard them say a lot about her. They really thought a lot of her and said she was a good "mimic." That's what Mom called her. Joan, my sister, said they'd just sit around and laugh because she could just do imitations of anybody. Maybe that's where Jimmie got some of his talent. Maybe he inherited some from her. I guess she was really, really good at that. And there's the story about her making up this little playhouse with puppets that she and Jimmie would play with. I don't remember seeing anything like that, though. It could have been when they were in California.

LA: When his dad got the job out there, how old was Jimmie?

MW: I would guess it was around 1935 and that would've made Jimmie about five years old. He came back here in 1940, so they were out there about four years. He was nine when he came back.

Jimmie in California circa 1936, age 5.

Winton and Mildred had bought a house in Marion. I just went by it yesterday. Most of the places where they lived, they just rented around here. They lived in a couple of houses in Fairmount and at least one in Jonesboro and one out here on the farm. Winton really did like to move around quite a bit, but then they finally bought this house in Marion. It's only about a half mile from the V.A. Hospital, maybe three-quarters of a mile.

When Winton took the job in California, he rented a house out there, and his Aunt Flossie looked after the house in Marion for him. Flossie was Grandma Dean's sister. I don't think Winton and Mildred were gone too long before they had Flossie sell the house. Not many people know they lived in that house. I've never heard anyone say anything about it, other than my sister, but it's over there in Marion on Adams Street.

LA: Since Jimmie came back on the train with his mother's casket, did Uncle Winton come back for the funeral?

MW: No, he didn't come back. I was told he had taken off so much work to be with her when she was sick that by the time she passed away, he just couldn't come back. He'd have lost his job if he had. I'm sure he wanted to come back, but he just wasn't able to.

LA: When you think about it, it always sounded like the plan was, once Winton got his feet back on the ground, Jimmie would go back to California.

MW: Yeah, that's possible.

LA: But then he was drafted.

MW: Yeah, that's right. I've always imagined they didn't know how long Jimmie would be here. I think Mom and Dad were happy he stayed, but I imagine when he came, they didn't really know. He fit in here really well. He got acquainted with a lot of the boys that were his age.

Then his dad got drafted and by the time he got out of the service in 1946, Jimmie had already been here five or six years. I'm sure Winton getting married again, that was another problem or event, whatever you want to call it. Jimmie was just...I think he was satisfied here, so there wasn't any point in pulling him out of school and sending him back to California. I imagine Uncle Winton probably felt the same way.

LA: Jimmie never went back to California for a visit?

MW: Not to my knowledge. I don't think so.

LA: And then Uncle Winton...how often do you think he came here?

MW: Oh, I don't know for sure. I'm going to say three or four times.

LA: Over the whole time Jimmie stayed with your mom and dad?

MW: Yeah. Of course, part of the time he was in the service. And there are some pictures of him here in his army uniform, so he was here at least once during the war, maybe a couple times. I think he and Ethel came back a couple times after they got married. And he communicated with Jimmie some because he told Jimmie he'd help him in college if he came back to California after high school. It's not like they weren't communicating or anything.

LA: Jimmie knew he was going to go out and stay with his dad?

Jimmie's uncle, Nolan Dean, and son, Joe, Winton, Jimmie and Jimmie's grandfather, Charlie Dean

MW: Yeah.

LA: Did Jimmie go out right after graduation or did he stay around here for the summer?

MW: He went right to California. He was only here a couple weeks after graduation, maybe three weeks.

LA: Do you have the letters that he wrote your mom and dad?

MW: I have some of them, yeah.

LA: Did he write about UCLA?

MW: I don't know. I don't remember. We can get them out and look at them sometime.

They're in a lockbox up in Fairmount, but I don't remember him mentioning UCLA. He may have made a statement like "school's going well" or this or that, but I think that's probably about the extent of it.

LA: You mentioned that Ethel and Jimmie didn't really get along?

MW: I don't know for sure if they didn't get along, but I don't think he ever felt very close to Ethel. You know, she was his stepmother, and sometimes kids do and sometimes they don't. Ethel never had any children. I'm sure she loved Jimmie because he was Winton's son, but I don't imagine she was too experienced with kids either, so things were probably just a little awkward between them.

But I don't think Jimmie disliked her or anything. I don't know if she disliked him. There was a little conflict there. It could have been Jimmie. I'm not saying it was her. It might have been more him than her. I don't know.

LA: Do you know if they saw *East of Eden* in California?

MW: His folks? Yeah, I'm sure they did.

LA: Did Winton ever talk about him as an actor?

MW: No, Winton didn't want him to be an actor, from what I understand. There are so many actors in California and, of course, there are a lot more now than back then, but Uncle Winton had lived in California since 1936, you might say.

When Jimmie came back out there in 1949, Winton had seen so many people wanting to be actors and just kind of drifting around from here to there, never able to get

a solid job. I think he felt acting was a dead-end profession.

He wanted Jimmie to be an attorney and from what I understand, Jimmie did study and took some basic classes, but Jimmie wasn't really interested in being a lawyer. He wanted to act. Even after Jimmie quit UCLA and told his dad he was going back east to New York, I don't think Winton was too crazy about it.

But Jimmie was old enough to make his own decisions, and Uncle Winton had to let him do what he wanted to do. I think before Jimmie died, his dad saw the talent he had, especially from *East of Eden*. I don't know if he got to see a preview showing of *Rebel* or not, but he realized how talented he was when he died.

They were getting back together. I don't think Jimmie wanted to live with his dad and stepmother, but he'd come over and visit them fairly often. And his dad was with him the day he was killed. He was with him that morning. I think they were beginning to get close again.

The fact that he had lost Jimmie for nine years probably weighed on Uncle Winton's conscience, plus the fact that he didn't support him, didn't support his idea of being an actor, and then Jimmie turned out to be such a tremendous actor. I don't know for sure, but I feel it weighed on his mind after Jimmie was killed.

LA: Did your mom and Winton communicate?

MW: Yeah, they wrote letters back and forth. I haven't seen it for years and years, but there's a letter up at the house where Winton wrote to Mom and said he didn't think Mildred was going to survive. Other families have had the same experience, but it was a sad ending for everybody involved.

Jimmie in the mountains of California after returning to live with his father and stepmother in 1949.

LA: Do you know where Winton and Ethel were living in California when they moved back here?

MW: They moved so much. They probably moved twenty-five times or thirty. They moved so many times they knew just what to do. I imagine a lot of their stuff was never even unpacked. I heard Ethel make a comment once that they could go from nothing packed to being ready to move in twenty-four hours. They just did it so much they knew what they had to pack, what they had to take with them and what they could ship. They moved an awful lot.

They both apparently didn't mind moving. I'd say it was Ethel. She'd say it was Uncle Winton too, but I'd say it was more her. She

never wanted to be bothered about Jimmie. Uncle Winton got kind of a raw deal with the writers and magazines right after Jimmie died. The fact that he let Jimmie come back to Indiana and live and be raised here fit in with Jimmie's character of Cal Trask in *East of Eden*.

I believe a lot of people thought Jimmie's dad really didn't want him. That was written in books and magazines, and it was very unfair to him. He and Ethel got so they just wouldn't give interviews. They wouldn't ever talk to someone who was writing something. Wherever they lived, their next door neighbor never knew who they were, unless somehow, they found out by accident, and then they'd move. They'd just leave. They're gone. It's just the way it was.

They were here in Fairmount from about 1975 or '76, somewhere in there, until around 1979. I don't think Ethel ever felt very much at ease here, because word got around who they were and she just liked her privacy. I'm not knocking her for that. She was nice. She was good to her family, I mean, if you wanted to come visit them, they were always welcome to have you.

She just didn't want strangers bothering them. When they came back here, they moved into the house in Fairmount I told you about and when they left here, they went to Florida, which is the last place they lived together.

LA: So, when they came back, they were only in one house in Fairmount?

MW: Yeah.

LA: And everybody knew where they lived?

MW: Yeah.

LA: Knocked on their door?

MW: Some did. The local people respected their privacy, but people doing interviews, they bothered them some. Ethel told the people who asked that they didn't want to be bothered. I can't say they were bothered a lot, but occasionally. It was always on their mind, I think.

LA: So, they really left here because of the weather?

MW: Yeah. They were used to warm weather. We had some harsh winters then, back through that period, late Seventies. The thought of an earthquake didn't scare them at all, but thunder and lightning did, and

they wanted to move to a warmer climate, so they went to Florida.

They moved into a new home. I don't know how they ended up there, but they were the first people to live in it. It wasn't fancy or anything, just a little house in a housing addition. They were in it from around 1980 till 1988. Ethel died in 1987, I believe. It was probably less than six months later when Uncle Winton moved up here.

He moved into our little house here on our property where Phil Zeigler lives. It's the same house where Marylou and I lived, but it's been remodeled. When Winton came a girl was living in it, and I had her move out. We remodeled the kitchen. We painted every room in the house and re-wallpapered one room and put all new carpet down. We made a nice home out of it for him. He lived by himself for a year, year and a half. Then he went to the nursing home and got along there pretty well, I think.

LA: Would you see him a lot?

MW: In the nursing home? Yeah, we'd try to get over there a couple times a week?

LA: When he was in the house here, would he come over and have lunch or anything?

MW: Yeah, occasionally he would. I never pried into his affairs, but I tried to keep an eye on him, see if he was all right. I did see him about every day.

LA: And Jimmie rarely came up in conversation with him?

MW: Occasionally. Now when Ethel was living, Jimmie was never mentioned, but when Ethel passed away, he started talking about Jimmie. I think she probably thought she was doing the best thing by protecting him and not letting him talk about Jimmie, but really, he might have been better off if he had. He had a lot of things on his mind and he didn't get to talk about them when she was there.

Marylou and I went to visit him. It may have been when Ethel was in the hospital. She was in the hospital for quite a while. We were down there quite a bit, for a month and a half or two months. I remember one evening he said, "I've got some stuff I want to show you." He got this box out that had all this stuff of Jimmie's in it.

Ethel had even made the comment once that…Well, she had a coffeemaker in the kitchen, and Marylou was looking at it because it was an old one. Ethel said, "Yeah, one of the last things Jimmie bought was that coffeemaker. Do you want that?"

Marylou said, "Yeah, we'd probably like to have it." And Ethel said, "Let me talk to your Uncle Winton." And he didn't care one way or the other. She said, "You just take it with you. We don't use it anymore." She said, "I think that's the last thing we've got around here of Jimmie's." I don't know if she thought it was or whether she just said it was, but Uncle Winton showed us a lot of stuff while she was still in the hospital.

The next time we came down to Florida, we went to Daytona Beach because Marylou and I liked to go over there. We always stayed at the same hotel and always tried to get a room that looked out over the ocean. We were there for a couple days at Daytona and we thought we'd call Winton and Ethel and tell them where we were and tell them we'd come over and visit for a few hours.

Ethel was real panicky. She said, "Can you come over here right now?" And I said,

"Yeah, why?" Well, she had fallen down and she was in bed, and Winton didn't know how to do anything and she needed some help. We told her we'd be right over, so we went from Daytona Beach to where they lived. Brooksville was the name of the town, although the house was outside of Brooksville.

We drove over and Ethel had fallen somehow and, boy, her hip had the worst bruise I've ever seen in my life. I mean it was black, so Marylou started fixing their meals, and we stayed at a hotel real close to their house. Ethel said, "Why don't you just stay here?" They had a spare bedroom, but we said, "No, we'll just stay over at the hotel and we'll come back over here and check on you," so that's what we did.

We were around for two or three days. I took Uncle Winton over to Brooksville. It seems like we went to a grocery store and got some stuff. It was obvious they were kind of in a bad way because she was bedfast for the time being. She just did about everything for Uncle Winton. That's just the way it was. She really babied him. She got his clothes out for him and all this stuff.

I needed to get back because I was Trustee Assessor here in Fairmount Township and the girls in the office could run the office okay, but if there were any bills or anything that needed to be paid, I had to sign the checks. Marylou said, "Why don't we drive home." I had the car there because we had driven down. She said she'd come back and stay till Ethel got up on her feet. We told Ethel and she said it would be fine. That just made her real happy so that's what we planned to do.

We got home a couple days later and called down to be sure they were okay, and Uncle Winton said, "Ethel's in the hospital." I said, "In the hospital?" He said, "Yeah." And I said, "Did her hip get worse?" And he said,

"No, her head." I said, "Her head?" And he said, "Yeah, she had a stroke or something."

We told him we'd be right back down, so we made arrangements to get on a plane right away and fly to Tampa and rent a car and we drove on to their place.

She was in the hospital in Gainesville, a real nice hospital. They had one complete floor where all they dealt with were head injuries. That's the reason they sent her up there, I guess. She had gone to the hospital locally, and they transferred her up to Gainesville, so the next day I said, "Do you want to go up to Gainesville?"

At first Uncle Winton said he didn't think he did. I felt he was afraid of what he might find, but he did go. He went with Marylou and me. Ethel was unconscious or in a coma, whatever you want to call it. The nurse said the best thing to do was talk to her. She said she might understand you. She said you don't know whether they do or whether they don't.

We talked for a little bit, but Ethel didn't act like she understood anything, and so after a while we came back to their house. It was an hour, hour and a half drive up there, so the next day I said, "Do you want to go back up?" He said, "No," he didn't want to go. He'd been up there the one day and she was unconscious and he didn't think he wanted to go back. I said, "I think somebody ought to go up, so I'm going to go." Marylou would stay with Uncle Winton, and I would go by myself.

That day she was conscious and she seemed to know what was happening and she and I talked for quite a bit. I was real happy. I thought, *Well, I think she's going to be all right*, so I said to her, "I'll get Uncle Winton and I'll bring him back tomorrow." She said, "Okay," and that's what I did.

I got Uncle Winton and Marylou and we all went back up the next day and, you know, she was in a coma again, never came

out of it. I asked this nurse a few days after, "What's the deal with her?" She said she didn't know. She'd worked there for years and said that's just the way people are. She thought what happened was that Ethel had a blood clot come out of her hip because it was terribly bruised.

The nurse said, "We've had people come in here and we could never find out what was wrong with them. The brain is a very delicate organ." She said even though Ethel was on a floor that took care of brain injuries, there was a lot they didn't know. She said, "I've seen that before. I've seen people come in and wake up and be conscious and go back to sleep and some of them wake up again and some of them don't. We don't have any answers for it."

I went up about every day for the next couple of weeks. Part of the time Uncle Winton went with me and part of the time he didn't. Part of the time Marylou would go and part of the time she didn't. I finally decided, "She's not going to wake up." And I needed to get back home. Like I say, I could be away from the office for a while, but I needed to get back to do things I felt I had to do.

Uncle Winton said he'd be all right, although I don't think he had any intention of driving back up there. We came home and it wasn't but three or four days that I talked to him and he said they had taken Ethel to a nursing home there in Gainesville. He was hoping she'd come out of it. A couple days later he called and said she had died.

One evening Marylou fixed supper and afterwards Winton said, "I've got some stuff I want to show you." He opened up the closet and he had three boxes in there and they were all full. I don't even remember now what all was in there, but there was a gob of stuff. I couldn't believe he had all these things.

LA: What do you remember seeing first, is there anything that hit you?

MW: That belt that says "James Dean" was one of the first things I saw. I about passed out when I saw that. I forget what all was in there now, clothing and letters, but, like I say, that belt was in there and these little figurines.

When Jimmie was home that last time, he had some little figurines that I thought were presidents, but they weren't. They were musicians. They were about this tall. What is that...three inches? He had them all wrapped up and I remember he had this drum with him. Bongo drum. He packed a lot of stuff in the bottom of this bongo drum to take back with him.

I assume he bought those figurines either here or in Marion or else he got them in New York. I'd always wondered whatever happened to them. I just supposed they were gone, but they were in one of those boxes. Uncle Winton had kept them rolled up in paper.

There were a couple of little toys. I guess I should be able to remember more than I do. There were at least two, maybe three boxes full of stuff, but one in particular had a lot of stuff in it.

Most of it I put into the Historical Museum. I don't know of anything that I've kept out especially, maybe some checks that he'd written. If I was at the Museum, I could point things out and say what came out of that box, but it's been so long ago, I just forget what all was in there. A bunch of stuff.

LA: Where did Jimmie's school papers come from?

MW: We had most of those here at home. Some school papers have shown up for sale

that we didn't have, and I don't think he had them either. I suppose one of his teachers maybe kept some papers, his and other students' papers too. I don't know.

David Loehr has several pages from school and he didn't buy them from us, so I don't know where he got them. Like I say, maybe something his old teachers had, but there was some school stuff in those boxes Winton had. All his sports ribbons were in there.

LA: The baby clothes?

MW: No, we had those at home. One time when I was in the attic, I found this box and Mom had written on it: "Jimmie's Baby Clothes." That's where that stuff came from.

LA: I wonder how she got that.

MW: I don't know. Maybe Mildred just left them here.

LA: Did any of Mildred's puppets survive?

MW: No. I've never seen anything of Mildred's other than Uncle Winton still had her driver's license, and that's in the Museum. I think it is the only personal effect of Mildred's I can think of that anybody has.

LA: Did Winton have the photos of Jimmie and Mildred in California?

MW: Yeah, he had those.

LA: Were they in the boxes he showed you?

MW: They probably were, now that you mention it. There were a couple of acting plaques Jimmie had received. In the spare bedroom where we were staying, I went to hang a coat in the closet and looked down on the floor and there was some kind of a plaque there. I picked it up and looked at it and it was another of Jimmie's awards. What it was doing in there, I don't know, but I do know Winton had that rifle of Jimmie's. It still was in the case, not a leather case, but it was in a cloth case.

I could go in the Museum and point out a lot of the stuff. Some of it was the New York things that I have. The bullhorns and the bullfighter's cape were already here in Fairmount since Winton loaned them to the James Dean Memorial Foundation. He just left all that stuff here with Mom.

All those awards were in the closet in Florida. The three boxes were from a grocery, banana boxes. You lifted the top off of them and they were filled with stuff. Those estate papers were in there and he had letters Jimmie had written to him.

LA: Pier Angeli letters?

MW: No. Those are what Lew Bracker had taken off of Jimmie's desk in California. Whether they were Pier Angeli letters or not, I don't know.

LA: They don't look phony.

MW: No, they're not phony. I'm just not sure the person who wrote them was Pier Angeli. I thought they were at the time or I wouldn't have paid such a price for them, but since then people have said that's not her writing. I don't know whether it is or not. I think it was one of his girlfriends from New York, Barbara Glenn maybe. The letters are not signed, but I think she wrote Jimmie those letters.

Lew Bracker, it was an honest mistake. He thought all those letters from Jimmie's desk were Pier Angeli letters. I didn't know for sure, but I just had a hard time believing

they were. Someone wrote a book in the past three or four years mentioning I have letters in the Museum and say they're from Pier Angeli, but the writer didn't think they were.

I don't remember if she says who she thought they were from, but the postmark is from Pennsylvania, Erie, Pennsylvania, I think. I'd have to look at them again, but none are signed. They all have this kind of handwriting just like Jimmie's. If you didn't know better, you'd almost think he wrote them, but he didn't. Just recently a lady told me she thought they were from Barbara Glenn, and they could very well be.

Lew wrote a book a few years ago about Jimmie (*Jimmy and Me*, Fulcorte Press, 2013) and a fan from France wrote him a letter. Lew answered it, and they were so thrilled that he answered their letter that they sent him back a letter with a photo they'd gotten of Cisco, Jimmie's horse. They bought it in an auction with some papers like this letter that Jimmie had written to Barbara Glenn, so then Lew said he thought those letters must be from her. I don't know. I've never pursued it any further, but I always thought it was strange that none of them were signed.

Another reason I doubted they were from Pier is they were from Pennsylvania. Someone said she may have sent them to a friend in Pennsylvania who then re-sent them to Jimmie. If you let it, I guess your imagination can run wild.

LA: Oh! ...and they weren't signed because she was still in love with Jimmie. The thought was Pier Angeli was still in love with Jimmie and didn't want her husband to know?

MW: Yeah, she was married to Vic Damone when the letters were written.

LA: That is pretty complicated. Huh?

Dad,

Gone to New York. Will be on "Danger" week from tues. Be back wed. Am leaving motorcycle with you, Keep an eye on her for me. Traded my MG in on a new Porche will get it around Dec. 1st. Was terribly hurt for a while about Pier, but I'm ok now.

Love.

Jim

P.S. Don't worry about picking me up when I return. I think it's all arranged. If need be I will call.

In November 1954, Jimmie wrote his father about his break-up with Pier Angeli.

MW: Anyway, I was really surprised all that stuff was with Uncle Winton. When he moved back here, I made it a point to put everything where nobody could find it. After he went to the nursing home, I thought it was surely okay to take some of it out to display, but I didn't. I waited till he died before I put any of it in the Museum.

We had things here at the house we hadn't put in yet, so I bought one or two showcases and took them to the Museum and brought some of that stuff to display. Uncle Winton's will said everything that was Jimmie's was to go to me, so after he passed away, I went ahead and put about all of it in the Museum. I guess it's not a hundred per cent there, but a big share is. I didn't want Winton to die, but I didn't want to put his things in there and have something happen to them. I didn't think I should do it as long as he was living.

LA: So, you had all the Agriculture class papers Jimmie wrote?

MW: They were here at the house. Those track ribbons, Winton had all those. Apparently, Jimmie had taken them with him, and the Bible the Back Creek Church had given him when he graduated from high school. Winton had that.

Most of the childhood things, we had here. I know I was surprised to see those track ribbons. They must've meant a lot to him, since Jimmie still had them, same with the Bible from the church. I always thought that meant something.

Back to Ethel, she was very, very protective of Uncle Winton. I'm sure whatever she did, she thought she was doing the best for him. Who knows what kind of problems he may have had from Jimmie's death that we don't know anything about?

But she did go overboard in protecting him. Anytime they'd come here to visit, if it was a little cool outside, she'd run out with a sweater. He was the only thing she had, really. She did have some family of her own, a sister or two.

One sister I know of was disabled and in a home. I think Ethel and Uncle Winton sent her money all the time, but Uncle Winton was her life. She really looked after him. I have to give her credit for that.

It did make it difficult for everybody else, though. We didn't dare mention Jimmie if they were around. I never saw her get mad, but she always made it pretty clear she didn't want anybody talking about Jimmie in front of Winton. I think he had a lot of stuff bottled up inside him because of that. Ethel was awfully nice to me. I hate to say anything unkind about her, but she was the one who made all the decisions. Uncle Winton, for some reason, just kind of went along with whatever she wanted.

I don't think Jimmie and Ethel got along real well. They tolerated each other, but I don't think there was a lot of love between them. Ethel, like I say, was always very nice to me. I don't feel I can say too much bad about her, but she was not easy to get along with.

As I've gotten older, I look back and I have a lot more sympathy for her than I used to have. Sometimes I can see where she was coming from. She was just very, very protective of Uncle Winton. She's the one who always talked on the phone. Whenever the phone would ring, she's the one who answered it.

Now she would let Uncle Winton talk to me whenever I'd call down to Florida to see how they were, but, as a rule, she's the one who talked on the phone. If anybody did get in touch with them, asking something about

Jimmie, I don't think she was very cooperative. She didn't want to be bothered. Who knows why for sure?

I speculate she and Jimmie didn't see eye to eye, but I don't one hundred per cent know that to be a fact. I guess you would have to say she was a very selfish person. She looked out for herself and Uncle Winton and nobody else. That's just the way it was. I always tried to be careful and not give her any reason to be upset with me.

LA: Did she get along with your mom and dad?

MW: Yep. When Winton and Ethel would come to Fairmount for a week or two, well, they'd stay here, and whenever Mom and Dad would go to California, they'd stay with Winton and Ethel. The only time I ever remember they didn't stay here was when they came back for Jimmie's funeral. They probably stayed at Grandma and Grandpa Dean's because of all the turmoil here.

LA: Because your house was the center of all the activity, and they would have been in that?

MW: Yeah, but after Jimmie's death, here's where they'd stay whenever they came back, so yeah, Mom and Dad and Ethel and Winton got along pretty well. I don't think they always agreed on everything, but it was another case where they tolerated each other to some degree.

LA: Ethel had to know that Winton had all of Jimmie's things?

MW: She knew it or she just had mentally forgotten it. I think she knew he had it, knew they had it. After Ethel died, Winton talked quite a bit about Jimmie.

LA: Was it all good?

MW: Oh, yeah. He never said anything bad.

LA: Did he talk about how impressed he was with him?

MW: Not too much. He talked more about when Jimmie was a little kid, when he was still living with Mildred and him. He talked quite a bit about that. I guess there was a lot I would like to have asked him, but I didn't think I should because Ethel had instilled in us all how much it would upset Uncle Winton and I didn't want to upset him. I just listened to what he had to say.

LA: Do you remember some of the things he talked about?

MW: I can't remember everything. They were just casual conversations about when Jimmie was a little kid, some of the stuff he did. As for Mildred passing away, I never discussed that with Winton. I guess I'd like to have known more about what happened the day Jimmie died, but I didn't ask any of that. From what I've read, Dick Clayton, Jimmie's agent, came and told Uncle Winton that Jimmie had been killed.

LA: He came to the house?

MW: Yeah, he came to their house. I told you Mom and Dad had been there visiting just a couple of days before, but they'd started back to Indiana. My Uncle Nolan had gone out to California at the same time as Mom and Dad. Nolan had a Chevy pickup truck with a canvas top over the back of it. That was before you could buy all these "toppers" to put on trucks to make it like a motor home.

Nolan and his wife, Mildred, her name was Mildred too, they would sleep in the truck on their trips sometime. Nolan was still there when Jimmie died. Matter of fact, he's in one of the pictures Sanford Roth took at Competition Motors that morning when Winton met Jimmie and they had breakfast.

Nolan and his wife left for Indiana right away. They knew Jimmie's funeral would be back here and they'd have to get back to Indiana for it. I think Winton and Ethel went to Paso Robles and identified the body. Of course, they had to go through Cholame where the accident occurred, but whether they stopped there and saw the car, I don't know. I found a picture of the car in Jimmie's stuff that was all wrapped up. It looked like it was taken with a Polaroid camera because it was in color. That's the only color picture I've ever seen of the Spyder from the accident.

Uncle Winton talked a little bit about Bill Hickman who was driving behind Jimmie that day. Bill Hickman helped him clean out Jimmie's house and Jimmie had just bought some real expensive speakers, the ones I told you about. They were expensive for the time.

Uncle Winton talked about how they were cone-shaped, but I'm not sure what he meant. There were four of them. Jimmie had put them up in each corner of the room. I seem to remember Winton saying Bill Hickman had those speakers.

Bill Hickman also wanted Jimmie's billfold as a keepsake. I didn't know it, but Winton did give it to him and the billfold came up for sale around 1990. Bill Hickman had given it to someone else and this person was the one selling it.

I had a chance to buy it, but I didn't feel it could be true that Winton and Ethel would have given away Jimmie's billfold because they were so protective of everything. I would have thought it would have been a pretty

special memento of Jimmie's. He probably was carrying it when he was killed, and so I didn't believe it was the real thing.

It wasn't too long after that, maybe a month or six weeks, when I went into one of Uncle Winton's boxes and in there was a writing tablet with notes Ethel had made and one of her notes said Bill Hickman had asked for Jimmie's billfold. He said he hadn't known Jimmie too long, but he'd liked to have it for a keepsake, so apparently, they gave it to him. By that time, the guy had sold the billfold, and that was a mistake on my part.

Ethel was a stickler for notes. She had notes about the funeral home in Paso Robles and how much the funeral was going to cost here in Fairmount and what the shipping would be to send the body back. She had down the serial number of Jimmie's tape recorder that she thought had been stolen.

I think the whole inventory of the estate is in courthouse records in Los Angeles. Apparently, all estates are public record, so people have gone there and made copies of it and everything was listed, his motorcycle and his Porsche Spyder and the station wagon and all his racing trophies and everything, even dirty clothes that were in his apartment in New York. Apparently, they just put them all in a bag and sent them back, books too.

LA: Jimmie's tape recorder? They thought it was stolen because things were stolen?

MW: Apparently someone did break into Jimmie's house the night he was killed, like Jack Simmons saying he took Jimmie's movie camera. That's always been something I've heard. Someone also broke into his New York apartment before Winton got everything out of it.

When we had that Roy Schatt lawsuit, there was this fellow, Bobby Heller, who testified he broke into Jimmie's apartment and took some photos of Jimmie that were by Roy Schatt. Heller was an acquaintance of Jimmie, I think, and he was a friend of Roy Schatt. It was all something to try to justify the lawsuit, but it didn't work.

He said he took all of Schatt's photos out of Jimmie's apartment. I remember the judge said, "Now, wait. Wait. You're telling me that you broke into James Dean's apartment?" And he said, "Yeah." And the judge said, "Well, I suppose the statute of limitations has run out by now, but," he said, "you have a lot of nerve… (*laughs*) …telling this to us in court."

I was told Heller was unhappy because I had never talked to him. I didn't even want to talk to him. I was told he was pretty unhappy he had to testify. I suppose Schatt's attorney said he was going to have to testify that he went in Jimmie's apartment and took these photos that Schatt had taken of Jimmie.

It had something to do with the copyright, that if Jimmie didn't have any Roy Schatt photos, then he didn't own his image in them. Bobby said, "Oh, it was easy to get in there." He said the latch on the door was one where you could just fiddle with it a little and open the door.

Knowing Jimmie, it probably didn't worry him. He never worried about stuff much. Anyway, someone else might have gone up there and taken things no one knows about. I doubt Jimmie had anything of any value in there. I mean, it is valuable to us, just not of any monetary value.

But there was this tape recorder Ethel and Winton thought had been stolen. They found the receipt in Jimmie's things. It turned out Bob Hinkle had it. Bob worked on *Giant* and taught Jimmie how to talk and act like a Texan. One time he was here for the James Dean Festival and made mention he had it.

He said, "I can tell you the serial number," and he rattled it off. After the festival was over, I got that notebook out and it was the right number.

Ethel even had the serial number down for Jimmie's 16mm Bolex movie camera. She had all these serial numbers and the amounts he paid for everything because of the insurance money. As far as I know, the insurance paid off for them.

Back to Uncle Winton, he got to be kind of a problem. His mind got to wandering. He lived by himself, and I think that makes a difference when you don't have anybody with you. I about worried myself to death over him.

One morning, it was in the winter, I came out of the house and happened to glance around to the right of me and he was standing there. This was about 7:30 in the morning and it was cold, and I said, "What are you doing here?" Well, he didn't really know. He'd just walked over, so I took him home and I got his breakfast for him and got him warmed up because he was really cold. I told him, "Don't ever do that again." I said, "You might've fallen and froze to death." "Oh, I won't. Oh, I won't."

It wasn't a week later, around nine o'clock at night, someone knocked on our door at home. I went to the door and it was Uncle Winton. He'd walked over here from the other house. I finally took him home. I think I might have even spent the night over there.

It got so I had to go and get him up in the morning and get him in the shower and help him shave and get his breakfast for him…and then I'd go back and take some lunch to him and go back and take his supper, because it got to where you couldn't depend on him to do anything. It really got to be a burden.

I'll say one thing. He made the decision to go to the nursing home. I had talked to the nursing home before, and a lot of times you can't just get right in. They're full, you know. They called me and said they had a private room coming up available and would I be interested in it for Uncle Winton, so I talked to him about it and he agreed he would try it. And he did real well. He adapted as well as anybody possibly could. We took his TV over there and some of his furniture and tried to make it as "homey" as we could. At the same time, we were stressed because we didn't want people over there bothering him, asking him about Jimmie.

LA: Let's go back to the scrapbooks your Mom would show to fans. Who put those together?

MW: She did, I think. People would give Mom and Dad photos. I don't remember where they all came from, but people would get them somewhere and they'd get an extra one and give it to Mom and Dad and they'd

put it in a scrapbook. I think that's where all that stuff came from.

LA: You never saw your mom put the scrapbooks together?

MW: I don't remember, but I don't know how else they would've gotten together.

LA: Before George W. George came here and made *The James Dean Story,* had reporters started coming to town to interview people?

MW: Oh, yeah. Yeah, there were a lot of people requesting interviews from Mom and Dad. They tried to accommodate most of them. A lot of times they got tired of it and didn't really want to be bothered, but I think mostly they made arrangements to talk to them. There were people wanting interviews right after Jimmie's death. Since Uncle Winton and Aunt Ethel would hardly talk to anybody, Mom and Dad did.

6

A Quaker Town

The Fairmount Museum sign...2020...Intersection of State Route 9 and State Route 26.

Leith Adams: They say Fairmount is a Quaker town. What does that mean?

Marcus Winslow: Fairmount, when it was originally established, had a lot of Quaker churches. They were called "Friends Churches" and they used to be real strong in this area. As time went on, Methodist, Wesleyan, Baptist and so forth came in. Fairmount now has one Baptist Church, one Methodist Church, one Wesleyan Church, one called the Church of

God, and a couple of smaller churches. I don't know all of their denominations.

The Friends Back Creek Church just down the road is one of the oldest churches around, established way back in the 1800s. There used to be two churches, two buildings, one for the women and one for the men. Later on, they built a bigger facility and the women sat on one side and the men on the other. The church that's there now was built around 1890 on the same spot. Of course, the traditions the Quakers used to have aren't really followed anymore

This little Back Creek Church, probably ninety or a hundred people would fill it up, would be my guess. Jimmie went to it with Mom when he lived here. She was in an organization called the Women's Christian Temperance Union, a group of women that got together to study the Bible and have a lot of programs, plays, and things.

Jimmie got a lot of experience being in front of people there because Mom would have him in programs, mainly at Christmas and Easter. Jimmie liked to act and play his parts out. A neighbor lady who is deceased now, I'd hear her talk sometimes about Jimmie playing a certain part. She said he really, really did a good job because he was starting to figure out how that character might be in real life. And this was all at a very young age. I'm not sure if he ever went back to the church when he came to visit or not. I can't answer that.

The Quaker Church is very much like a Methodist Church these days, except Friends Churches don't baptize like a lot of churches do. The larger Friends Church in Fairmount, where Jimmie's funeral was, holds a lot of people.

Quakers are not what they used to be. At one time they were more like the Amish than they are now. There's not a whole lot of difference between the Friends Church and the Wesleyan Church and the Methodist. Some people might feel real strong one way or the other, but basically they're all pretty much the same.

In around 1996 or '97, they put an addition on the church, and now it has a good place for groups to gather, whereas before they had to go down into the basement. They didn't think much about it, but the basement was pretty crude. Jimmie's plays and the WCTU

meetings wouldn't have been down there, though, but up in the sanctuary.

When Marylou and I go to church, we still go to Back Creek. It struggles to make ends meet, just like a lot of churches. Some of the old churches have to work to get people to come, while the newer churches are just overflowing with people. I don't understand it all, but that's the way it is.

The older people I remember from when I was younger, they are all gone. Even the farmers around here that I grew up with and kind of looked up to, they are all gone. They've all died. It's hard for me to realize, as much as I hate to admit it, but I'm getting to be one of the older ones in the neighborhood. (*laughs*)

Mom was always regular about going to church. She was really a good person and, like I say, was in the WCTU. In the movie *East of Eden*, I couldn't help but notice the World War I parade. One of the old cars had some women in it, and there was a sign on the side that said, "WCTU." I always got a kick out of seeing that sign. I don't know whether it was originally planned that way or whether it was something Jimmie suggested, but I couldn't help thinking of Jimmie when I saw that.

The ladies would meet maybe once a month and they'd go around to different members' houses for coffee and to do whatever they did. Up until Jimmie was killed, Mom was very active in the church. Then I think she was so hurt over what happened to Jimmie that she kind of backed off from going for quite a while, but she did get to going back loyally again, like she should.

Dad didn't go to church very regular until the last six or seven years of his life. Then he started going about every Sunday. He always got a kick out of taking our sons, Coy and Chuck. Mom and Dad would pick the boys up from our house and take them with them. He enjoyed having them down at Back Creek sitting with him in church.

After Marylou and I got married, we used to go to the Friends Church in town, the reason being Xen Harvey married us and he was a very special person. We did go to his church just trying to decide which one to attend.

Xen Harvey married about all the young kids in Fairmount. It didn't matter what church they went to, if they wanted Xen to marry them. He didn't insist they go to the Friends Church, but he did insist they be married in his church. If he was going to be the minister, he didn't think it was right to go into other churches and be the minister.

I think Marylou and I were the last people Xen married before he moved out of Fairmount on to Richmond, Indiana. He was involved in the publication of a Quaker magazine there, but finally he came back to Fairmount and was pastor again at the Friends Church.

Back Creek had a minister who did a really good job. He was a young guy and was getting a lot of young people so that's where we went. We even had to have church over in the parsonage because there wasn't room enough in the old church structure.

LA: When Jimmie's mother died and Jimmie moved here, where did he go to school?

MW: That was in Fairmount in the West Ward where Dad went to school, the Old Academy Building. I went there too. It was built by the Quakers as a school for Quaker kids, but as time went on, it became part of the main school district in Fairmount. Grades 1 through 6 went to West Ward.

There was another school in Fairmount called the North Ward. It was about a block

from the old high school in Fairmount, and they also had one through sixth grades. That school was about all town kids and the West Ward, where I went, had some town kids who lived near it, but the country kids went there, too.

Of course, I wasn't born when Jimmie came here, but I imagine Dad took him to school at first, and then he'd ride the school bus like me. Riding the bus was quite an experience. It'd take close to an hour every day, especially since I was one of the first onto the bus, probably Jimmie too. You'd just ride and ride and ride until finally everybody was picked up and you got to school.

Then in the evening I'd be one of the last ones off of the bus. Dad would come get me quite a bit in high school. He'd get me, and I'd plow in the evenings with the tractor, help him get the crops in. As I look back on it, it was a good time in my life, but I didn't think it was all that great at the time. (*laughs*)

LA: Having to work after school?

MW: Yeah.

LA: You were so close to town; I'd have thought you'd be the last person to be picked up. Did the bus go north after you got on?

MW: It went every direction. One reason I was picked up first was my bus driver lived around here. There were three or four other families with kids he'd pick up before he got to me, but he'd go west of here and he'd go south of there. They had pretty good-sized routes, especially the bus I rode on.

Some of the newer ones had good heaters in them, but my bus had one little heater up front and if you sat more than two seats back from the driver, you might as well have been sitting outdoors. By the time I got on, even though I was one of the first ones, all the kids were huddled up front around the heater and, boy, that was a cold ride. Same way coming home.

I'd always be one of the last ones off, and sometimes it would be getting dark out, late in the day. In the morning I'd go to school in the dark sometimes, too. The town kids got to sleep a little longer because they didn't have to ride the bus. They'd walk to school. Now kids won't even walk a block to school without the school bus picking them up. It's all changed compared to what it was when I went to school.

I went to West Ward for six years and then to the Fairmount High building for seventh and eighth grade because, like I said, junior high was in the same building. In junior high, we participated in all of the activities, just like the high school kids. We'd go to the programs they'd have there in the gym or in the "auditorium," they called it. That's where they had the class plays.

In grade school, sometimes there'd be something special, maybe a play put on by the high school kids and we'd walk to it from West Ward. That was always a big deal. You got to walk all the way from West Ward to the high school for some kind of a program and then walk back to West Ward again. It was a pretty good walk.

The best program I remember was a guy from Eaton, Indiana. "The "Marshal of Eaton," he called himself, and he really was the marshal there. He had a gun display. He actually shot a gun in the high school gym and did some pretty fancy tricks. I don't think they would let him do that today with all the kids in there because he was shooting live ammunition.

He'd shoot at a file that he had mounted somehow. It was a three-cornered file and,

on each side, on up a little ways, he had two balloons attached and he would shoot and split the bullet in two with that file. One half of the bullet would go to the left and pop that balloon, and the other half would go to the right and it would pop that balloon. I remember that show real well.

The West Ward was a big old building, but when I went there for first, second, third, and fourth grades, we only used the downstairs. When I came back from summer for fifth grade, the upstairs had opened up after some remodeling and fifth and sixth grades were upstairs.

It was really a pretty good old building. They quit using it because Fairmount built a new building, and they shut down two or three schools to send the kids to the new school.

Then they tore down West Ward and that was a far better building than the old Fairmount High building. Even though Dad went to grade school there, Mom was born and raised kind of east and south of Fairmount, so I think she went to one of the township schools for grade school.

Fairmount High was a good school in its time. I remember the new gym was built in 1955 because when I was in the sixth grade at West Ward, all the high school had was the old gym, but when I went into seventh grade at the high school, the brand-new gym was there, so apparently they built that gym in the summer of '55. Jimmie was killed in September of '55. And I remember the high school then, and it had one of the nicest gyms in Grant County.

LA: When you were in grade school, where would you shoot baskets?

MW: It would be in this gym that's still there.

LA: But you didn't go to the high school building until seventh grade. Didn't you play basketball before seventh grade?

MW: No, I didn't. When I was in grade school or even in high school, I was kind of short. Matter of fact, I was real short. I really wasn't tall enough to be playing basketball or anything. Today, I could go to the Youth League in Fairmount and get some experience, but when I was a kid, they didn't have anything like that.

We started playing basketball in junior high in the new high school gym, but you didn't do much until you became a freshman or sophomore. Then you might get on the varsity team. Today it's changed compared to the way it used to be. There are more opportunities to do things now.

LA: When you started school, were you buddies with other farm kids or town kids?

MW: Mostly town kids, now that I think about it, or farm kids who lived on the edge of town. On a Friday night, I might go home with one of the kids or they would come home with me and we'd do whatever we did. If I stayed in town, a lot of times we would go to the show in Fairmount. It was a big deal to me because I wasn't used to going to shows often.

Country kids usually had to work when they got home, because their dad was farming. The town kids, most of them, didn't have a job, so it was always a treat for me to stay with a city kid and spend the night and go to the show on Friday or Saturday night or maybe both, plus playing around town doing something.

In town, you always had kids to play with, but out in the country, you didn't have that. The farms were far enough apart that unless you got on your bicycle and rode somewhere, you were pretty much at home by yourself unless you had some brothers or sisters, and I was sort of an only child. I mean, I had a sister, but she got married when I was just a year or two old, so I really didn't have anybody to play with when I was a kid.

LA: Did you ever detect animosity between the town kids and the farm kids?

MW: Not that I remember. I don't remember any. There were always kids that hung around with each other and, I suppose like today, there were always two or three bullies in every class who wanted to cause some trouble, but most of the kids were all pretty nice kids and came from pretty decent families. I don't remember there being any major problems between the town kids and the country kids. They were all raised different, of course.

Country kids had more responsibilities and more of a work ethic to them, I'd say, but that wasn't the town kids' fault. It's just the way it was. Most of the town kids' parents worked somewhere or at least their fathers did. That was back when a lot of women didn't work outside the home. It's just been in the last forty or fifty years that women started working outside of the home. Back when I was a kid in high school, most of the mothers were still at home.

In 1955 over in Marion, I remember the big Fisher Body plant opened and they started hiring a few women. Everybody thought that was pretty unusual, a woman working in a factory. RCA used to employ a lot of women in Marion. You don't think anything about it today, but back then you did. The man, the father, did most of the support for the family and the mother stayed home and took care of the kids, but it's not that way so much anymore.

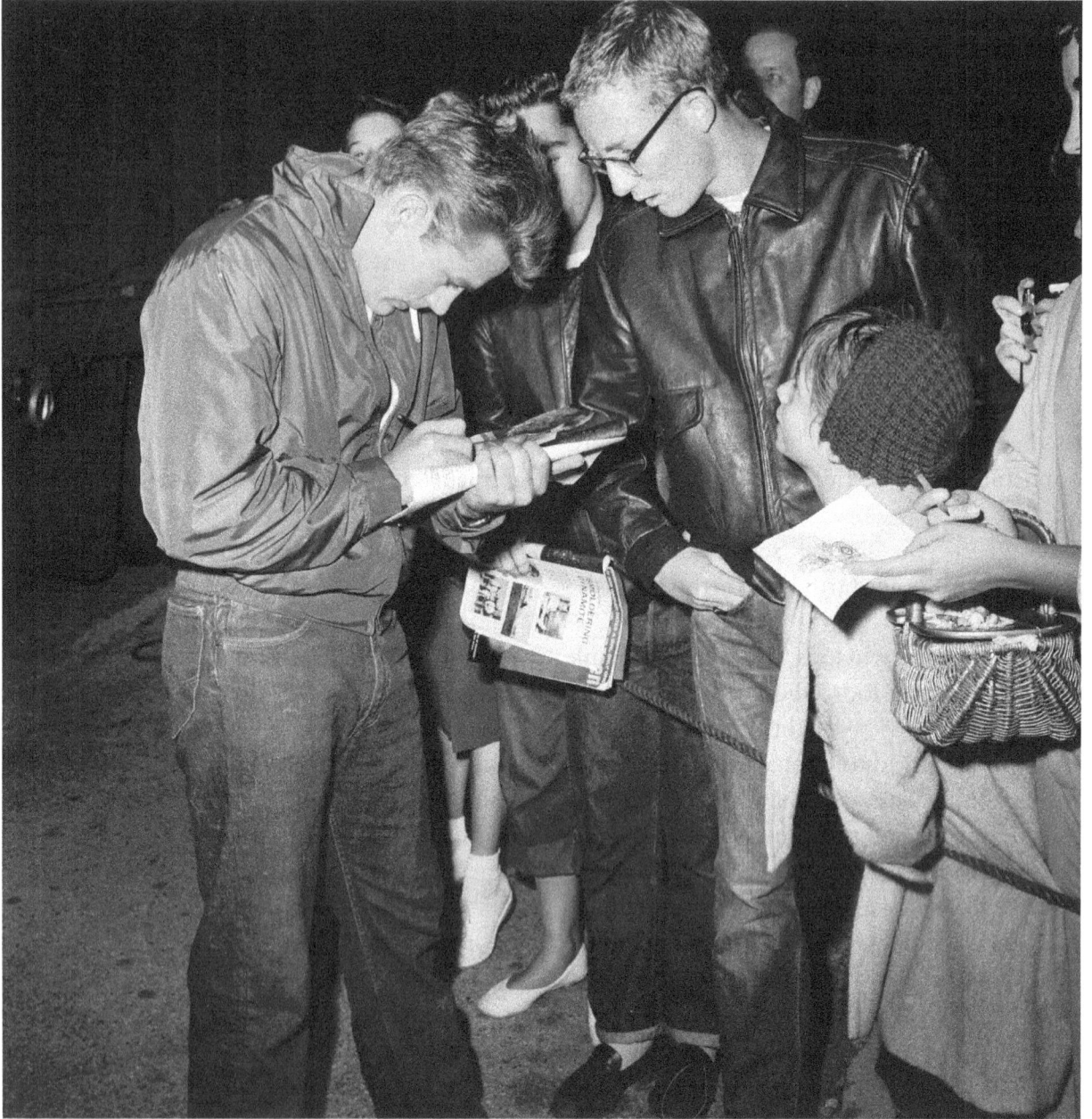

A young fan is in awe as she watches Jimmie sign an autograph.

7

Jimmie's Fans—Part One

Leith Adams: When fans came to visit your parents, your mom and dad never took pictures of those people?

Marcus Winslow: No, they didn't. Why? I don't know. Maybe they felt that would be invading their privacy. There were a lot of people who used to come to visit, I'll tell you. As a little kid, I really didn't have a normal life because somebody was always coming to visit Mom and Dad, and it always had something to do with Jimmie.

Mom and Dad were very nice to them. They never turned anybody away that I know of. They didn't let just anybody stay here. It had to be somebody who knew Jimmie or had some good reason, but they were awful good to the fans. It's a wonder someone didn't break into the house and steal some stuff, but we never had any problems.

LA: When Nick Adams came back, did he stay in the house?

MW: Nick Adams came back in '57 for the premiere of *The James Dean Story*. It had something to do with the Foundation. I think he stayed with Bob Middleton and his wife, the people who kept him when he was here

for the funeral. Bob was raised over here a half mile away, but he moved to Marion and got a home after he got married.

When Jimmie was killed, the Middletons and other friends of Jimmie kept some of the people who came here. Whitey Rust lived on Washington Street in Marion in a big old house and he kept Jack Simmons. Henry Ginsberg, the producer of *Giant*, probably stayed at the hotel in Marion. I don't remember if Dad arranged it or what, but people that knew Jimmie and came for the funeral stayed with people who knew Jimmie here.

LA: So, Nick Adams only came a couple of times?

MW: Mm-hmm. He came for the funeral and he was here for the premiere to help the James Dean Memorial Foundation, because its purpose was to give scholarships for young actors and actresses in Jimmie's name. Money from the movie was to go to the Foundation, so Nick came back. There are pictures of him here. It was August 1957.

By that time Nick had done a little bit more work. He'd finished *No Time for Sergeants* (1958), a movie with Andy Griffith

Marcus and Nick Adams when *The James Dean Story* premiered in Marion in 1957.

where they jumped out of an airplane. If he was here after that, I don't remember. He may have been. Sometimes things just kind of run together from years ago, but I really don't think he was here more than those two times.

Jack Simmons was back once or twice after the funeral just for visits. We heard that a lot of Jimmie's friends seemed to think Jack Simmons was the one who got into his house. Apparently, Jack had a shady reputation. I was always kind of afraid of him. He was a strange little guy. I was afraid he was into drugs or something. I don't know why... whether someone told me that or what.

I wasn't very old then. This was only two or three years after Jimmie's death. At least once when he came back here, he stayed with Mom and Dad. They had another bedroom upstairs he could sleep in. I was always kind of edgy around him. But like a lot of things, I've thought about it over the past three or four years and I kind of wish I had gotten to know him a little better.

Joe Hyams wrote that *Redbook* article and much later wrote a book. I've never read it, but I've had people tell me he interviewed Jack Simmons and Jack Simmons said he took Jimmie's movie camera, the one he used down in Marfa during *Giant*. Jack had

124

Jimmie, Perry Lopez and Jack Simmons joke around on location for *Rebel*.

it stored in a room somewhere and the roof leaked and ruined it. Now whether that was true or not, I don't know.

Michael Sheridan, in researching Jimmie's TV shows, discovered him out there in Los Angeles. He looked him up thinking he might have some films or something. Michael was at his place and said where Jack was staying wasn't fit for a human being. He also said something to the fact that Jack mentioned he wished he'd never met Jimmie. Jimmie's death had ruined his life. Evidently, he felt real close to Jimmie and said he never really got over Jimmie's death.

When Jack Simmons died, there was a guy who had kind of been looking after him.

I have his name up at the house. I think he had been a cop there in Los Angeles and got acquainted with Jack and when Jack passed away, he got all of Jack's stuff. Jack lived in an old Masonic Lodge building from what I understand. This guy even sent me some pictures of it, real ornate looking building on the outside, but apparently it had been empty for years.

Jack had taken over one of the rooms. That's where he lived. He'd shown this guy a bunch of napkins Jimmie had drawn on: "doodles" are what they're called. They were from Googie's, the restaurant where everyone hung out. Apparently when they'd leave Googie's, Jack would pick up Jimmie's drawings and take them, so when Jack died, he had all these little doodles on napkins. And he had one or two paintings that were sold.

This guy called me about a year ago and said he had a great big painting Jimmie had done and wanted to know if I was interested in buying it. I'd never heard anything about this painting, so I said I wasn't interested. The way he talked, it was like five feet tall or something, a great big huge painting. He said it was at Warner Bros. when Jimmie died, like Jimmie was doing it there at the studio.

Somehow Jack got it, so the story goes. It's not signed or anything by Jimmie. He sent me a picture of it. I don't even remember what it was of now, kind of an abstract painting, an oil painting, I think, but who knows whether it was Jimmie's or not? He seemed to think it was and evidently Jack had told him it was. It was boxed up when Jack had it.

This guy said he had an awful job getting it out of there since it was so heavy all boxed up. He was going to put it in an auction and he wanted me to verify it. I said, "I can't verify it. I've never seen it and I never heard anyone else say anything about it."

"Well," he said, "I'll be willing to give you some of the money when we auction it, if you authenticate it." And I said, "I can't authenticate it. I don't want that on my conscience. I don't know if Jimmie did it or not." And so, he was going have it in an auction a month or six weeks after that. I don't know whether he got it sold or what he got out of it. I never did hear.

LA: Nick Adams claimed he and Jimmie were going to do a nightclub act. Do you know anything about that?

MW: No. I always got the impression Nick Adams looked up to Jimmie a lot, but I'm not sure how much Jimmie looked at him. They were sort of friends at one time, but no, we didn't see Nick Adams after that premiere.

Just to tell you how people are, there was a guy who came here when they started the James Dean Foundation. They had plays for two summers up there on the stage in Fairmount. I suppose they rented the auditorium.

Anyway, this guy got to coming here from Chicago. His name was Robert Conrad. He ended up having a couple shows on TV, *Hawaiian Eye* (1959–1963) and *The Wild Wild West* (1965–1969). He came here several times and got acquainted with a guy, an older guy, probably wasn't as old as I thought, but at the time he seemed like an older guy, Hudson Pope. He was a banker in Toronto, a pretty well-to-do guy. Matter of fact, I think he's the one who footed the bill for that monument down at the cemetery and putting the bust on it. He paid for all that.

This guy got to be close friends with Bob Conrad. Nobody knew it, but Conrad was married and had a couple of daughters, but as far as anybody knew, he was just single. This fellow paid his way to California, paid his rent and everything in Los Angeles. Conrad wanted to be an actor, and this guy more or less supported him for quite a while until he got on his feet and started getting some acting jobs. He got *Hawaiian Eye* first, then *Wild Wild West* and it seems to me he might of had one or two other series over the years.

I can remember playing badminton with him. We had a badminton net set up south of the house in the yard and we'd play badminton out there, but after he went to Hollywood, I never heard from him again. There for a couple of years, he was here every three or four months for something.

LA: Really? Every three or four months?

MW: Yeah.

LA: And he always stopped in and saw your mom and dad?

MW: That's the reason he came down, to see them. He might have thought something else was going on, too, but that's when the James Dean Memorial Foundation was still in existence. He might have come here for the opening. It seems like I have a picture of him standing in front of that building.

Anyway, I always thought it kind of strange, not that I cared a lot, but he really got his start here in Fairmount. If he hadn't

met this fellow from Canada, he never would have gotten the breaks he did because this guy paid for housing for Conrad and his family. He put them all up and apparently had a lot of faith in him, you know.

LA: Nick Adams always said that he brought Robert Conrad out to California, but maybe that's not true?

MW: If he did, I'm not aware of it. Not that I can remember everything, but I just remember Robert Conrad being here. I was thinking he was from Chicago.

LA: Yeah, he was.

MW: Maybe he'd even done some nightclub work or something.

LA: I heard he was a singer, a nightclub singer.

MW: Could be. Now that you mention it, I believe he was.

LA: Are there letters between your mom and dad and Robert Conrad?

MW: Not to my knowledge, no.

LA: Maybe he was seeking encouragement from them. If your mom and dad nurtured

Robert Conrad getting discovered in Fairmount, Indiana.

somebody like James Dean, maybe they could nurture him. So...this Hudson Pope, would he come down every year?

MW: He came down a couple times a year for a while. Matter of fact, a couple years after he was here, he asked Mom and Dad and me to come up there. We took a train and traveled around some, but we ended up getting on a boat going to Quebec. Most of the people there were French, didn't speak English. I remember a beautiful hotel right on the river and walking around the old part of town, looking in a lot of windows.

I think he paid for our vacation. Nice old guy, I keep saying "old." He probably wasn't as old as I thought. About ten years ago, the phone rang and I answered it and it was Hudson Pope. I figured he'd died, but he said he was retired and apparently had a farm. His nephew farmed it. He called two or three times over a period of five or six years. I'm pretty sure he's died by now because I haven't heard anything from him for quite a while now. He was a nice guy.

LA: He never came back again?

MW: Not after, I'd say, 1960 or '61. He was a successful banker, single, wasn't married. Now whether he ever got married or not, I don't know, but he wasn't married when I met him.

I always liked Bob Conrad. He seemed like a nice guy. I always thought it was kind of strange; he came down several times and really got his break here to get to go to California and he never did come back. Never called. Never wrote or anything that I know of. Kind of makes you feel like you got used, but on the other hand he probably got busy, and...well, I never thought a lot about it.

LA: How'd you first meet Kenneth Kendall?

MW: When Mom and Dad took me out to California for the showing of *The James Dean Story,* somehow, we visited Kendall's. He was in a commercial type building where you walk in off the sidewalk. I remember he had a bunch of those little busts of Jimmie, like the one sitting on that shelf over by the door. It had a little square base on it, looked like it had seashell indentations on it. He gave me one of them. He just took it out and gave it to me. I've always had it.

After that, the next time I met him he was in his house. It was years and years later. I think Mom and Dad were probably acquainted with him because of some magazine articles written about him, with pictures of him. He had made that big bust of Jimmie. I don't think at that time anything had ever been done with one of those busts. There probably wasn't even a bronze.

Then he had one cast in bronze and sent it here and they took it down to the cemetery. Later, he sent one for the little park downtown in Fairmount and he also did the one at the Griffith Observatory in Los Angeles.

Kenneth was a pretty devoted fan. He did a lot of paintings and sculptures of Jimmie. He always paid tribute to him. Kenneth had a style. His style wasn't an exact...I don't know how to say it...it's kind of a caricature of the person, seems to me. Jimmie's hair is extreme and the chin and the nose are extreme. His work has a lot of thought in it. I like it.

He did that big bust and later on he did a smaller sculpture of Jimmie as the boy in *The Immoralist.* He made one for somebody, and the other one, David Loehr got. David had to sell it in that Heritage Auction. I had a notion to buy it, but I thought, *What am I going to do with it?* Jimmie has a pair of scissors in his hands. It didn't bring a whole lot of money, probably not near what it was worth.

I really didn't have any business buying it financially at the time. There were other things in the auction I would have rather had. I thought, *What the heck would I do with that?* It seems like it brought $1,800. It was pretty cheap. Somewhere I have that catalog and I have the prices written down in it for everything that sold, but I don't have it out here in the Car Barn.

I did buy some things out of that sale. I bought the fence that went around the roof of that *Giant* house and I ended up buying that big Kenneth Kendall bust, the one on top of the plinth they carried around the Observatory to decide where to put that permanent statue. I always liked that. I always did want it, but it brought over $8,000 in the original sale. I didn't think I wanted it that bad. When it ended up being broken in the shipping, I bought it for $5,000 and Heritage Auctions shipped it to me at no cost. I thought it was worth that.

I don't know if Kenneth realized it or not when he made it, but some places on that neck were only one or two inches thick. Other places it was thicker. Kenneth probably figured since it was sitting on that round pipe, it would carry all the weight. He didn't think about anybody hitting it or something. I don't know what happened to it, but it was all busted up.

LA: Did Kenneth come back here once or twice?

MW: He was here twice, maybe three times. The first time was probably in '85. The fan club had some kind of a deal over at Marion and they wanted him to come. I think he was a little bit backward about leaving Los Angeles to come here, but he did. Then David brought him back two or three times after that. I'd say he's been here at least three times.

LA: That was when he was older, not back in the Fifties?

MW: He was older then. I have to laugh. He had his black hat, wore all black and some kid came up to him in town when I was talking to him and said, "Can I have your autograph?" Kenneth said, "Yeah." And the kid said, "I don't know who you are, but I know you've gotta be somebody." (*laughs*) Had the moustache and the pointed beard.

LA: Did you ever talk to Maila Nurmi who was Vampira?

MW: Yeah, she came here one time, not too long after Jimmie was killed. She came and visited Mom and Dad. I don't remember if she spent the night or not, but she was here in the evening, I know. I don't remember a whole lot about her. She seemed like a nice person at the time. Of course, the movie magazines made her out as being real weird, strange and everything, but I don't think we thought she was.

I've been told she came to some of the birthday parties Kenneth had later in his life, but she never would tell anybody where she lived. This one guy said to me, when they got ready to leave, she said she had quite a ways to walk and this guy told her, "I'll take you home." So, she said, "All right." But when she went home, she made this guy let her off uptown somewhere, not where she lived, and she walked on home from there. He said, "I don't know where she lived."

There's a picture in one of the movie magazines of her sitting in front of an open grave, supposedly talking to Jimmie or something. I remember Mom and Dad used to get so upset with those movie magazines and the stuff they'd write.

Today you wouldn't think much about it. You'd think, *"Well, that's just more garbage those magazines put out,"* but Mom and Dad took it all pretty serious. I know Maila Nurmi told them there wasn't anything to a lot of that stuff. Whether that's the reason she came or not, I don't know. She seemed like a pretty decent person.

I don't remember whether she flew or came on the train or what, but she was here for at least one full day. Like I say, I don't think she stayed with us. A lot of people who came here stayed at the motel that used to be at the crossroads of State Road 9 and State Road 22. I'm guessing that's where she stayed. It seems to me Dad may have gotten her and brought her here and then took her back. I don't remember her driving. That's the reason why I think she stayed over there. Probably the bus stopped there and picked people up.

LA: The statue of Kenneth Kendall's that is in the Fairmount Historical Museum, is it the same head as the one in the Fairmount Park?

MW: Well, Kenneth took one like he used at the cemetery and constructed a neck for it, so now when it sets down onto something, it's not just a shaft going up to the head, it's a whole big square neck. About the only way you could get it off would be to hook a chain around it to jerk it off and you'd probably tear it up doing that, but the head is the same. It is the only large sculpture of Jimmie.

Kenneth Kendall's monument to Jimmie in Fairmount Park.

Kenneth did some little sculptures, but that was the only big one he ever did.

LA: The statue in Fairmount Park, when was it dedicated?

MW: The stamp ceremony was there in 1996, so I'd say the statue in the park was probably in '94 or '95. When they had the stamp ceremony, there wasn't any wall around the statue. Now it has a little wall around it. I think they ran out of time and built the wall the next year. It still wasn't built when they had the stamp ceremony, but it looks pretty good up there now. It always did look okay, but now with the trees and bushes growing up around it, the statue looks more like it's supposed to be there.

LA: Kenneth's painting of Jimmie that's in the Museum, did you buy it from Kenneth?

MW: No, he gave it to the Museum before he died. I have a painting in the office here, a big painting I bought in David's auction, but Kenneth was very generous. He'd send things to the Museum and not charge them anything for it or charge them very little, so they could resell what he sent to make money. He was a good fan.

He was different. It seems like artists, their mindset is: don't try to tell them how to do anything. That's kind of the way he was, so I never tried to tell him anything because I knew how he was. I liked Kenneth. He and I were good friends, as far as I know.

LA: He seemed really appreciative of people.

MW: Yeah, he did. There were a lot of fans who came to visit Kenneth and became good friends with him. He was eccentric. I don't know if that's the right word or not. That house he lived in; I think it really could have been nice. It had a round ceiling for the living room, but he was just an old bachelor. I don't think he ever cleaned anything. It needed a lot of "TLC," but I enjoyed it. I enjoyed being there.

I was at his house three or four times. When that Warner Bros. trial was in Los Angeles, I saw him. He had Marylou and me come over for supper one Saturday evening. I was also there once or twice before. His studio was right next to his house or maybe it was hooked on. I think he made a bust of Marlon Brando first and then he did the one of Jimmie.

I get a kick out of his story about Leonardo DiCaprio. Kenneth made a sculpture of him and Leonardo wouldn't come and get it and that made Kenneth mad. I don't know what it looked like, how good it was or anything, but Kenneth wanted him to come over and get it. His agent said they'd send someone over to pick it up and Kenneth said, "No, Leonardo's going to have to come and get it."

LA: Never got it?

MW: Never got it, no. I can understand where Kenneth was coming from. He had a lot of time in it. I understand his thought.

The Winslow Farmhouse where Jimmie was raised...2020. (Photograph by Matt Scott)

8

Marylou, Mom, Dad & Joan

Leith Adams: So...you went to the surprise going-away party for Jimmie in 1949 and Marylou was there because it was held at her house?

Marcus Winslow: Yeah, but I didn't know her at the time. I'm pretty sure she was one of those little girls I went down to the store with that evening. She always probably knew who I was, but junior high was when we met.

North Ward and West Ward School kids both went to the high school building in the seventh grade, and she and I got acquainted then. I don't think we dated until I was sixteen. I know the first time I picked her up I was driving Dad's car. It was before I had that '56 Ford. Her family always knew Jimmie.

LA: When you picked her up, were you going to a movie?

MW: Seems like we were going over to the park. The Shelter House used to have dances there. We did go to a lot of movies. If it was summer it was usually a drive-in and then in the winter we'd usually go to the Indiana or Paramount in Marion. I really miss those old theaters with the fancy curtains along the sides.

Marylou and I got married in 1964. The old house on our farm where our helper, Bill Burwick, had lived was in bad shape and wasn't worth remodeling, so Dad and I pushed it down with the tractor and set it on fire and burned it. We took the road grader over there that we had and graded the ground and made a place to put a mobile home.

I bought a mobile home off of Marion Howell who lived about a mile and a half from here. The Howell's daughter had gotten married and had bought it and had the mobile home in their backyard when she decided she wanted a house. They only lived in it a year, then they moved into this house in Jonesboro. Marion, he wanted them to get it sold and get it out of the yard.

After I looked at the mobile home, I was interested in it. We brought it here and put it over around the corner where that old house had been and landscaped it with evergreens. We lived there from 1964 to 1970, until Marylou was wanting to get into a house because she felt the walls were coming in on her. Coy and Chuck were both born, so there were four of us in that ten-by-fifty mobile home.

MARCUS DEAN WINSLOW
A fast lad with a super-charged Ford
Class Plays 2,3,4; Thespians 2,3,4;
Art Club 2,3; Breeze Staff 4; Whirl-
wind Staff 4.

MARYLOU THOMPSON
Be glad, and your friends are many
FHA 2; Booster Club 1,4; Cheerleader
1.

Marcus Winslow and Marylou Thompson's senior photos from the 1961 Fairmount High yearbook.

Ralph Riley, a friend of mine who sold cars up at the Ford dealer, also had a filling station, and I pulled in there one evening to get some gas and Ralph and I started talking. He said, "Hey, I've got a house you ought to have."

I asked where it was, and he said it was down on Elm Street and that he was going to move it. The Marathon Oil Company had a storage place across the road and one of the tanks had sprung a leak and gasoline had gone under the road and it came up underneath this house.

Matter of fact, Marathon had moved the people out of the house and paid for their hotel for a while. Finally, Marathon bought the house from them. And Ralph Riley bought it off of Marathon and was going to

move it down the street to another lot. He told me to go look at it. He said they had it on blocks up in the air, ready to move.

The next day Marylou and I arranged to get into it and we went in and looked around and really liked it, so I think I gave $4,800 for the house. It was only about five-years old, and the guy who moved it was a professional house mover.

Before we even had the house ready to live in, this guy came along and wanted to buy the mobile home and take it up to the lakes. That tickled us to death. We actually didn't want to get out of it that soon, but we felt if you have a buyer on the hook, you had better take advantage of it.

We completely repainted the house inside and out. We were just so happy with that little house. We lived there from 1970 until 1980. Dad passed away in 1976 and Mom was really afraid, so she moved to that home on First Street in 1980, and Marylou and I have lived here in the big Winslow house since then.

Mom and Dad already owned the burial spots at Park Cemetery. Apparently, they had three, three or four. Jimmie was buried on one of them and Mom and Dad eventually were buried right beside him.

A year or so after Jimmie died, some people came to Dad. They owned the plot right north of Jimmie's and wanted to know if Jimmie's dad would be interested in it. Uncle Winton and Aunt Ethel ended up buying it, so when they passed away, that put them right north of Jimmie's grave and Mom and Dad are south of Jimmie's grave. There's kind of an empty spot on each side and we never will put anybody in them because of people walking around the grave. I bought two or three burial spots south of where Mom and Dad are. I reckon that's where Marylou and I will be.

LA: How do you think your dad would feel, sitting here in the Car Barn with all the vehicles in here?

MW: He'd be shocked to death.

LA: He'd love it though, wouldn't he?

MW: Oh, yeah. Dad loved this farm. Dad's father bought this ground in, I think, 1893, and Dad was born in 1900. The house and big barn were built in 1904 and the smaller barn in 1910. This farm was Dad's life. Mom and Dad got married in 1924 and it was only a year or two later when they moved into the house here. I don't know how well Dad liked to farm, but he did farm.

I think he felt he had to because his dad was here. I think if Dad had a choice, he would have been a photographer. He was very interested in photos and photo equipment. It seems to me he even took a class one time, but as much as I hate to say it, he never was a real good photographer.

He bought a used camera. I think it was a Leica, a real expensive camera, because he wanted to take good pictures. Even then, a lot of times, his pictures didn't turn out. That was back when you had to adjust the light yourself and the speed, whereas now you just pick up a camera and push the button. It does it all itself, but back then you had to do it manually. Dad tried, but I don't think he was ever a real good photographer.

Dad was kind of stuck here on the farm after his father got to where he couldn't farm and then passed away. Dad did pretty good from the late Forties up to the mid-Fifties. He bought a truck in '54 and new car in '54 and also this tractor back here, the yellow one, in '54. I don't know how he was able to buy them all at once, but he did.

Then Jimmie was killed and that kind of took the push out of him. There were so many people coming here after that. It took a lot of Dad's time talking to people. Then the James Dean Memorial Foundation was started. Dad had never intended to make any money off of it, but he never intended to lose any. He didn't intend to do anything, but he ended up having to put money in it from his own pocket. I don't know how much, but we were all surprised when Dad died and we found out how much money he owed. We didn't know he had all the notes he had at the bank. I worked here then and let Mom have all the money from the cattle I was taking care of.

My sister Joan's husband farmed the ground and for a couple of years, he was giving Mom all the money they made off the farm.

We paid off all the notes. I always felt bad we couldn't have done that when Dad was living and helped him out, because I know it was a burden on his mind. Mom didn't even know Dad owed any money. Mom didn't even know where to pay the light bill and the gas bill at the time. Dad paid all the bills. He did all that stuff and then when Dad passed away sort of suddenly, Mom didn't know anything.

My sister and I were used to paying bills, so we showed her where she had to go or what she had to do. This happened back when you didn't mail your bills in, but you took them to town and paid them. I was proud of Mom. She had a load on her shoulders there for four or five years.

Mom had fifty-seven acres that had been Grandpa Dean's southeast of Fairmount, and Dad had taken some mortgages on it. Joan bought that farm. We agreed to let her buy it, and she and Myron paid off the notes. Things turned out okay, but I always felt bad for Dad because he struggled, struggled for years and years. A lot of it was because of what happened with Jimmie.

I've always felt bad that he and Mom weren't able to enjoy the licensing. Now, Mom did for a little while because she was still living for several years, but she was so old, she didn't realize what was going on.

Dad was wonderful. If there was anyone I could talk to who has died, it would be my dad because I always felt he was just the most wonderful person there ever was, but I'm sure there are other people who feel the same way about their parents.

LA: You went to him for advice?

MW: Oh, some. Probably more than I realize.

When we bought the house and moved it from Fairmount out here, it was the luckiest thing that ever happened to me. That was really a good deal, but when I went to borrow money for the house, the bank said I had to have more collateral because the land was Dad's land. It wasn't mine.

Dad gave me two and a quarter acres over there. It didn't really cost him anything, but he gave it to us. I paid to get it surveyed and paid to get the house moved and all the utilities hooked up. If Dad had been able to, I'm sure he would have been glad to help pay for everything, but he wasn't able to and I knew it. I never asked him to. If I needed money or I wanted to buy something, I went to the bank and I borrowed money and did it on my own.

I always tried to help Dad here on the farm, working on the buildings and doing this and doing that because I always knew he didn't have the money to hire someone to do a lot of the stuff that needed to be done.

Naturally, you miss your parents when they're gone, but I've never, never felt guilty that I didn't do everything I could for my Dad. Actually, I let my own family go, Marylou and the boys. I would come over here and do things, but I should have been there with them, helping them do things and taking them places. Instead, I was over here helping my dad. I can honestly say I've never had any guilt feelings that I should have done more because I did all I could.

LA: You wouldn't take vacations with the family?

MW: I would, yeah. I was working somewhere and I'd get a week off. After a while, maybe I'd get two weeks off and we'd go to Disney World. Marylou had a brother in Florida, and we'd go visit him. We've never done a lot of traveling, but we have done some. I don't want to leave the impression I didn't spend any time with them because I did.

I know there were times when Marylou or the kids wanted to do something and I couldn't go because I was over here helping Dad and therefore, they didn't get to go. I don't know if my life's been different than anyone else's. I'm sure other people have done the same thing.

I've always been proud of this farm. I knew it meant a lot to Dad, so I've tried to fix it up and I have fixed it up. The barns were in bad shape, so I started working over here. I'd spend weekends and every evening over here working, doing repairs, because I knew Mom didn't have the money to pay someone to do it, so I did it. Put a lot of new siding on the barn. Put new windows in the barn.

We did hire somebody to paint the barns. I didn't have the bucket truck then, probably a lucky thing. Did a lot of repair work on the house, tore old gutters off and put new ones on and painted the house myself. I remember that.

LA: Did the boys help?

MW: A little, but they were pretty small. There really wasn't much they could do. I painted the roof on the house two or three times. Painted the roof on the small barn over here. I don't think I was able to paint the roof on the big barn. It was too high and too big. I don't mean to be bragging. I don't mean it that way, but I'd find used boards and use them to fix stuff with. I tried to save Mom every penny I could. Mom did really well. She had all the bills paid off, and I was able to buy stuff to fix things with after a while.

LA: Did she find out about the notes?

MW: Yeah, she found out about them. She was pretty shocked too. You look at them today and they weren't very big by today's standards, but back in 1975 they were more than what you'd like to have. They weren't un-payable or anything. It's just that no one knew about them. Both banks in Fairmount were very, very good and very cooperative. Neither one of them threatened anything. Dad didn't have any notes on this farm. The notes were all on that other farm, the one Joan bought.

We paid off most of the notes before she bought that farm, so Mom ended up having money to do things she wanted to do. The sad thing was, by that time, she was eighty. When you get to be eighty years old, you don't have much ambition to travel and do the things you once wanted to do. She enjoyed living in town. It was a nice little house and she could see people coming and going and the fire station-police station was right across the street.

I think she really enjoyed it, then something happened with her feet and legs. The circulation went out of them. One Sunday Joan called me and said, "You'd better come in here." I went into Mom's house and Mom was sitting in a chair and she couldn't get up. Her feet, they just wouldn't hold her up. I didn't know what was wrong with them, so we called an ambulance and took her to the hospital and finally she had to go to a nursing home in Marion. I sure hated that, but there wasn't any other alternative.

And it was a nice nursing home. She got good care. Matter of fact, that's the same place Uncle Winton went when he came here and lived for a while, then had to go to a nursing home. I was always thankful we had enough money from the licensing to pay for Mom's nursing home, pay for her upkeep and so forth. At least she got to enjoy a little bit of it, not that being in a nursing home is enjoyable, but there are worse things.

She was in a wheelchair from then on. Maybe she had neuropathy like I have. I don't know what was wrong with her. A lot of it was circulation because they ended up having to take her foot off. That's what she died of. She was ninety then and didn't have any circulation in this one foot. It was turning black, you know, just dying. Finally, the doctors said they were going to have to take her foot off. We knew when that happened, she might or she might not make it, and she didn't. It was too much stress on her body.

Mom was a really good person. She'd do anything for anybody. I was very fortunate. I had two of the nicest parents anyone could ever have and, talking about Jimmie, they treated Jimmie just like they treated Joan and me. They tried to give Jimmie anything he wanted and probably did more for Jimmie than they did for my sister and me, because of the circumstances.

I can remember, up till Jimmie was killed, Mom and Dad talking about Jimmie this and Jimmie that. They just thought he was the greatest thing there ever was. Then when he died, that just killed them. I don't think they ever got over it. I don't think Uncle Winton ever got over it. I suppose there are other families that have had the same experience, you know?

My sister, Joan, and I never argued over anything. I was more like her child than her brother because there was so much age difference, but when we had to divide up Mom's stuff, neither one of us argued about a thing. We just took whatever each of us wanted. Mom had a table that was a real nice table and Joan wanted her daughter to have it. That was Mom's and I said, "Okay." I got the rocker, but those personal possessions don't seem to mean as much to you when your parents are gone.

After Mom died, then we had to do something about the farm. We didn't say anything about it for a while and finally… well, Grandma and Grandpa Dean had fifty-seven acres and when Grandma and Grandpa died, Mom and Dad bought it from the estate because Dad was farming then and really needed the ground to farm.

After Dad died, a couple years later, Joan asked me, what I thought about her and Myron Reece buying the ground over there. She told me what they'd pay for it, which was quite a bit below market value, but it was okay with me. I said, "Well, just so I'm treated okay when the time comes." She said, "Okay," so they bought that ground over there.

When Mom died, there were a hundred eighty acres here and, of course, I inherited half of it, ninety, and Joan inherited ninety. She said, "Well, what do you want to do about the ground?" She said, "You want the ground here, don't you?" And I said, "Well, I'd like to have it." And she said, "Okay. What do you think it's worth?" I thought it was worth about what she paid for the ground a few years before, probably worth less because ground here isn't as good as it is over there. I told her, and she said, "Okay, it's all right with me." I don't think her husband was too happy about it. He thought I ought to pay more for it, but she said it was none of his business. (*laughs*)

She and I have always gotten along just as good as a brother and sister could. I hear so many people feuding around with their siblings, especially when their mom and dad die. They argue about who is going to get this? …and who is going to get that? …and it can get kind of nasty. Joan and I never had the least bit of argument about it. If one of us had something we wanted real bad, the other one said, "Okay" and vice versa. Boy, some families, it's a mess. Some of them never get over it. You know they are mad the rest of their lives at each other over some dumb little thing. It shouldn't amount to anything, but sometimes it does. Life is really short when you stop and think about it.

LA: For me, thinking about your dad being a Quaker, how did he learn to play tennis?

MW: I don't know. He was very athletic, and I know he played basketball. I'm not sure if they had football back then when he was in school, but he was pretty active in sports. Whether Quakers were against sports or not, I don't know about that. If they were, I never heard anything about it, but they did have some funny ways.

LA: What were some of the "funny ways" you saw?

MW: They were pretty strict as I remember it, but this was all before my time. What I'm saying is what I've heard. They definitely didn't approve of smoking or liquor or going to shows. When I was a kid I wasn't allowed to go to a show on a Sunday. I could go during the week or of an evening, but Mom and Dad were a little uneasy about it. I did end up going on Sundays when I got to be fifteen or sixteen. They said, "If you want to, go ahead," but up until then, they were against going to a show on a Sunday.

I suppose they felt Sundays were supposed to be a day of rest. Today, of course, people work on Sundays here in this part of the country. A lot of farmers, come spring and fall when they have to plant their crops and harvest them, they'll work on Sundays but not all of them. There are a few of them that when it comes to be midnight Saturday night, they shut the tractors down and don't go back until early Monday morning, but the majority, if they're getting behind, they'll work on Sundays. And a lot of people around here work in factories or in stores or smaller businesses and they're required to be there on Sundays. That's the way it is.

The young fan watches Jimmie sign her sister's purse.

9

Jimmie's Fans—Part Two

Leith Adams: David Loehr recently wrote a story that Bob Dylan stopped here at the house one night and talked to you.

Marcus Winslow: Yeah, it was late at night. It was probably one or two o'clock in the morning. Apparently, they'd been down in Indianapolis and did a concert. At that time Coy and Chuck were both living in town. Chuck was living with Coy in that big house, and Chuck called me and said Bob Dylan was on his way out.

Well, you know, he woke us up. I was sound asleep. And I said, "What?" "Bob Dylan is on his way out to your house. Get up and get ready for him." I said, "Well, how is he getting here?" He was walking. Apparently, he and his entourage walked all the way from Fairmount out here.

I'd heard of Bob Dylan, but I really didn't know him. Didn't know much about him. I knew he was a singer. He had Lainie Kazan with him...this woman singer. Marylou recognized her right off the bat and asked her if that's who she was, and she said yeah and they kind of struck up a conversation.

I talked to Dylan a little bit, not too much. Honestly, I didn't know who he was, really. He kind of had this coat on or a sweater or

something kind of pulled up around his neck. He didn't look like a movie star, but that's all that happened with him.

LA: Do you remember what he asked you about?

MW: No, I don't. I just remember him being here. He was in the living room and there were probably half a dozen other people with him, counting Lainie Kazan. There was so much going on I didn't have much time to talk to him. And I don't even remember what he saw while he was here. I just don't remember that much about it. He woke us up out of a sound sleep.

Anyway, he walked out here from Fairmount or from the cemetery, at least. They had a big tour bus and I don't know if they left it at the cemetery or what they did. The walk wouldn't have been as far if they had walked from the cemetery, but anyway... that's the Bob Dylan story.

LA: Coy and Chuck probably talked to him.

MW: They may have talked to him some, yeah. I don't remember them saying. Probably Chuck, if anybody talked to him, because Chuck is more outspoken than Coy. He probably went right up to him and started asking him questions.

LA: According to David Loehr, Dylan walked all over the farm just to get a sense of it.

MW: Yeah, the barnyard and stuff up here, I don't think they went out back.

LA: Not to the pond?

MW: Not that I know of. Not that I remember anyway.

LA: You didn't come outside with them?

MW: No. I guess I really wasn't that impressed with him. Kind of a scruffy-looking guy, but since then I've seen pictures of him and pictures of him performing and I wish I'd have known who he was when he was here, but when he was here, I just knew he was a singer and that's about all I knew. Chuck follows all that music stuff and he knew exactly who he was. I think Coy did, too.

LA: I guess Lainie Kazan wrote in her autobiography that Dylan sang "Blowin' in the Wind," one of his most famous songs, at Jimmie's grave.

Do you remember Martin Sheen coming here?

MW: Yeah. He was here in 1980, I believe it was. I think Mrs. Nall had something to do with getting him here. That may have been the 25th Anniversary. Marylou and I got married in '64. I kind of had a life of my own for a while.

I think Martin Sheen visited Mrs. Nall's home. She might even have brought him up here to meet Mom, since Dad was gone then. I remember meeting Martin Sheen, but

I wasn't really acquainted with him. I never got to be close to him.

I also I met him at a dinner in California in 2005. It was when Warner Home Video had a private showing of *James Dean: Forever Young*. Martin Sheen narrated it. I thought he did a good job. Anyway, I talked to him in California that one time at the dinner and that's about the only conversation I've ever had with him. I guess he's a big fan of Jimmie's and really respected him for his talent.

LA: After Nick Adams and Jack Simmons, was Bob Hinkle one of the earliest of Jimmie's co-stars or co-workers to come to Fairmount?

MW: He was most probably one of the first to make himself known. I don't think anyone like Elizabeth Taylor ever came to Fairmount. Bob Hinkle worked on *Giant* too and taught Jimmie about Texas, how to talk like a Texan. Jimmie would go over to Bob's and bring his tape recorder and they would practice dialog and his Texas accent on it.

Bob said Jimmie sometimes left things and when Jimmie died, he had that tape recorder at his house. Bob said he didn't even know who Jimmie's dad was. Hard to believe he wouldn't have known his dad was in California, but he told me, "I didn't even know anything about his dad," so when Jimmie died, he just kept the tape recorder. It's in the Historical Museum now.

LA: Bob Hinkle writes about going rabbit hunting with Jimmie in Texas. Did he ever talk to you about that?

MW: He said they used to hunt for jackrabbits, pretty big rabbits. Jimmie enjoyed hunting rabbits and apparently in Marfa in the evenings when they didn't have

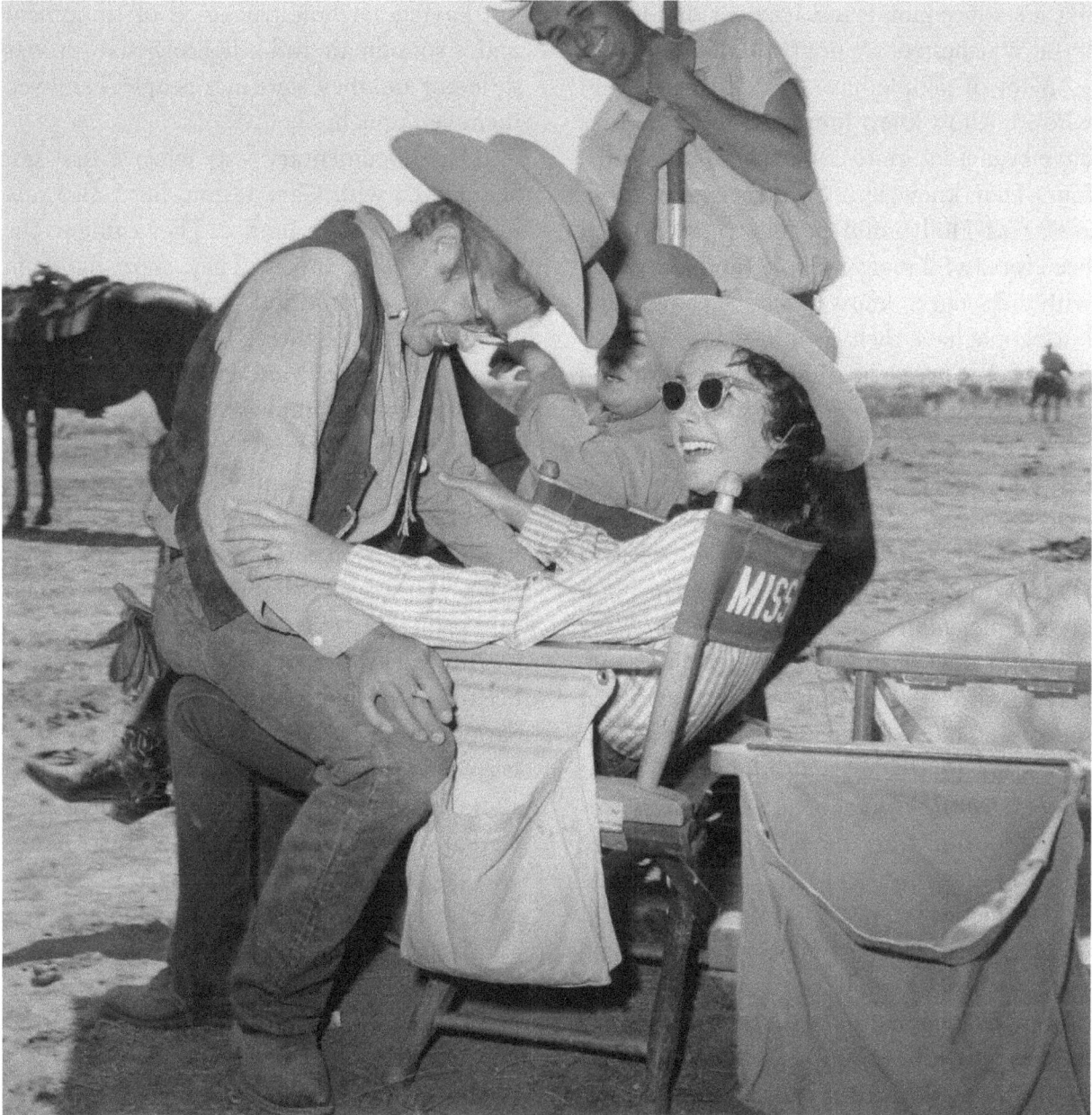

Jimmie finds a comfortable place in the sun with Elizabeth Taylor
as Bob Hinkle shares their laughter on location for *Giant*.

anything to do, he and Bob Hinkle would go out rabbit hunting. Jimmie bought a brand-new Winchester rifle.

The first time I saw it, Uncle Winton was showing me some of his guns and this Winchester was still in the gun case. I took it out and looked at it. He said, "That was Jimmie's gun." And I said, "It was?" "Yeah, I've never shot it." Apparently, it never has been shot since Jimmie used it in Texas shooting rabbits, which couldn't have been very much. I put it in the Museum for fans to see. It's a single action. You have to cock a handle underneath the wooden handle every time you want to shoot, but it's a nice gun. It just happens that today, those Winchesters are pretty desirable.

A lot of people have come to Fairmount who somehow knew Jimmie. Of course, there have been a lot more come who didn't know him. They knew him from the movies, but as far as Hollywood people, there haven't been too awful many. People Jimmie worked with did seem to know where he came from, but people have their own lives to live. They didn't come here when Jimmie was living and as time went on, people did their own thing.

LA: How did you meet Gary Legon?

MW: Gary Legon is a brother-in-law of David Dalton, the guy who wrote an early book on Jimmie, *James Dean—The Mutant King* (Chicago Review Press, 1974). Sarah Legon, David Dalton's sister, and Gary Legon worked together. They were married, of course, but they were producing a documentary called *James Dean—A Portrait* (1988). Sarah was the editor and Gary directed and they came here to film it.

To me what was so different about them was that some of these people doing documentaries would come in and they'd have to change this and change that and they have to have the lighting just so and they have to put the shades down and they have to put this screen up to reflect light and all this stuff and Gary and Sarah Legon didn't do any of that. All they had was a camera and they just came in and filmed whoever they wanted to film, interviewed them and left.

I've forgotten who taught them to do that type of work, but he convinced them they didn't need all that stuff. I have to say that when you watch their show and watch some of the other shows, you can't see much difference as far as lighting and so forth. I felt they were really on top of it, as far as

not having a whole truckload of equipment and a soundman and a lighting man. It was different and they were nice people. I enjoyed them very much.

That documentary was when I first got acquainted with Gary Legon, but I also saw Gary and Sarah in France. They came to the Cannes Film Festival. They were living in France at that time and somehow, they knew I was going to be there. There was a big tent where Dennis Stock and Phil Stern and I were taking questions from the audience.

I talked to Sarah and Gary before it started. I think they used to know Dennis pretty well, maybe years ago, but Dennis, as I remember it, hurt Sarah's feelings pretty bad somehow. I don't remember what the deal was. He had said something that offended her.

Anyway, this program started and people began asking questions. I noticed Gary and Sarah get up and start to leave and they waved at me. I don't know if they had something else they had to get to or if they were disgusted with some of the stuff Dennis was saying. I don't know. I haven't talked to them since, but they were nice people.

Matter of fact, for the 50th Anniversary I was interested in doing a book with them, so I had Mark Roesler get in touch, but they said they were tied up. I've forgotten what project they were working on, but they didn't have the time to do the book, so we got involved with George Perry from England. He wrote that book called *James Dean* and he did an excellent job.

LA: Did David Dalton come here?

MW: Yeah, David Dalton's been here. He was here back in the Seventies when he wrote *The Mutant King.* He interviewed Dad and some other people, but I don't honestly remember him being here then. At that time, I had a job and had other obligations. I didn't have time to chitchat with him, but he came back a few years ago. Time flies by so fast, it might have been fifteen or twenty years ago now.

It was probably when he did *James Dean: An American Icon* (1986). And David Loehr furnished a lot of the pictures for that book. I think David Loehr got him here to help promote book sales. He came out to the park where I was at the car show and he and I talked for a while and he seemed like a nice guy. I really don't know him other than meeting and talking to him for a few minutes. He did a pretty good job on the books he did on Jimmie. I don't know what he's done since. I'm not that familiar with him.

LA: Now, this gift here of the framed Sectional basketball ticket and program brings up a good point: that the fans, the people who like James Dean, seem to be the kind of folks who want to share.

MW: This guy was really nice who did that. I have several things people gave me that had something to do with one of Jimmie's movies. Up at the Gallery, David used to have things people had given him. Of course, a lot of people did want to be paid for what they have, but some folks, if they know you'll make good use of it, why they'll just give it to you.

LA: Just like this ticket and program right here?

MW: Yeah, that's true.

LA: It seems the fans respect him so much that they respect everything about him.

MW: Yeah, it does seem to be that way. Of all the years since people have been coming here, sixty years now, we've never had any-thing bad happen. The house has never been broken into or no one's ever gotten into the barn or stolen anything.

The tombstone has been stolen a couple times, but I never felt the fans did that. It was just some kids who wanted to be mischievous. We've had real good luck with the fans over the years. They've all been very courteous and generous and they seem to realize that the farm is private property. They seem to appreciate and respect the idea that we let them stop and take pictures and walk around or whatever for nothing. It's not like we charge them and most of the fans appreciate it.

LA: Your mom and dad started that?

MW: They were much more generous than me. I've never turned anybody away, but they would invite people into the house and get scrapbooks out and show them to the fans. Mom and Dad took an interest in everybody.

I can't tell you how many times when I was a kid, we'd be getting ready to go somewhere to eat and here would come somebody and Mom and Dad would stay and talk to them. They thought so much of Jimmie that I think they felt if they weren't nice to the fans, then the fans wouldn't think of Jimmie in a positive way. They were really good to all the fans.

Matter of fact, my parents became acquainted with several of them. One girl was here from Spain and she came back several times over the years. Mom and Dad always let her stay here at the house, and they got to be good friends. They would even pick her up at the airport. They made friends with a lot of Jimmie's fans.

I guess some of my best friends too are people I've met who were fans of Jimmie. I've gotten acquainted with them, and after a while you don't think of them as fans and they don't think of coming here for Jimmie so much. They are still interested, but that's not the reason they're here. We've met a lot of nice people over the years; a lot of strange people too, but never have had any trouble with any of them.

LA: I remember you said you didn't think the projector was Jimmie's, the one I bought for Warner Bros. at David's auction in Dallas, that it wasn't on the inventory of everything Uncle Winton got when Jimmie died.

MW: No, all you got there is...

LA: ...a projector...

MW: ...somebody's word for it, you know. I don't know if it was ever Jimmie's or not. I guess I've learned to be very skeptical of a lot of things and unless I know whose it is and I have some kind of proof or a pretty good idea that it was Jimmie's, I don't swallow some of that stuff.

I know David Loehr had things that were never Jimmie's, but he honestly and truly believed they were because he wanted to believe it. I'm not knocking David because of it, but I'm sure that was the case.

LA: What about the fence from *Rebel*?

MW: Yeah, that was probably legit. He was lucky there. When he was in Los Angeles one time, David drove by the place and they were tearing the fence down. It was piled up behind the house.

LA: That's the backyard fence from Jimmie's house? The one when he's jumping up and down, talking to Natalie Wood on the other side of it?

MW: Yeah, David drove down that alley, and they'd torn that fence down and had it piled up there, so he just grabbed a bunch of it.

LA: Do you have that fence?

MW: No, he still has it.

LA: It didn't go up for auction?

MW: It was in the Heritage Auction and it didn't sell for some reason. This guy, Doug, who worked there told me it didn't sell. I asked what they wanted for it, and he said David was trying to get it back, so I thought if he wants it back, I'll just let it go.

LA: On another subject, were you always aware of the Indy 500?

MW: Oh, yeah. The first one I can remember was when Dad took Lew Bracker and me down. That was in 1956. We went down with a guy from Fairmount by the name of Hod Gaddis who used to build race cars. He was real familiar with a lot of the guys down at the track, so we sat right on Curve One. I think there were five or six wrecks in that race and they all happened in front of us. No one was killed or anything, but several of them lost it and hit the wall right there.

One of them was Paul Russo. I've always remembered that. He was driving a Novi and those Novis had a totally different sound than the rest of the cars. Whenever one of those Novis came around, you always knew it by the whine of their turbocharger. They were neat cars, but the crews couldn't seem to keep them together for some reason. I don't think one ever won the race. Some Novis were up close to the front when the finish happened, but a lot of them would drop out. Over the years, they just seemed to have mechanical problems.

LA: So, Lew came back specifically for the race?

MW: No, he came back to visit us. See, Lew was here for Jimmie's funeral, which was in the first part of October 1955. I think Dad and Lew communicated back and forth some. Lew said he was coming back that next summer, and Dad told Lew, if he could work it out, to come for Memorial Day and he would try to get us tickets to the race.

They worked it out and we had a real good time. I think Lew enjoyed it, because he was used to road racing and it was totally different down at the 500.

LA: Did he talk to you about racing?

MW: Not that I remember. A year or two after he was here, I was buying a lot of car magazines and I picked one up and was reading through it and there were pictures of some road races and one of them was a Porsche with Lew Bracker's name on it. I

didn't know it at the time, but it was Jimmie's old car.

Lew had bought Jimmie's old 1500 Super Speedster. Originally, he had a newer one, but Lew's was just a 1500 and he said he wanted one like Jimmie. When Jimmie traded for the Spyder, Lew went right down to Competition Motors and made a deal and traded his in for Jimmie's.

After Jimmie's death, Lew started racing more. He became a driver for Porsche. The Porsche factory sponsored him, and Lew had the first black speedster they built. Porsche always painted their cars white or silver or red or something. They'd never had any black ones and when he requested they build him a black one, he had to take it to the head of the company. After that they built a few more and now I hear that's their most popular

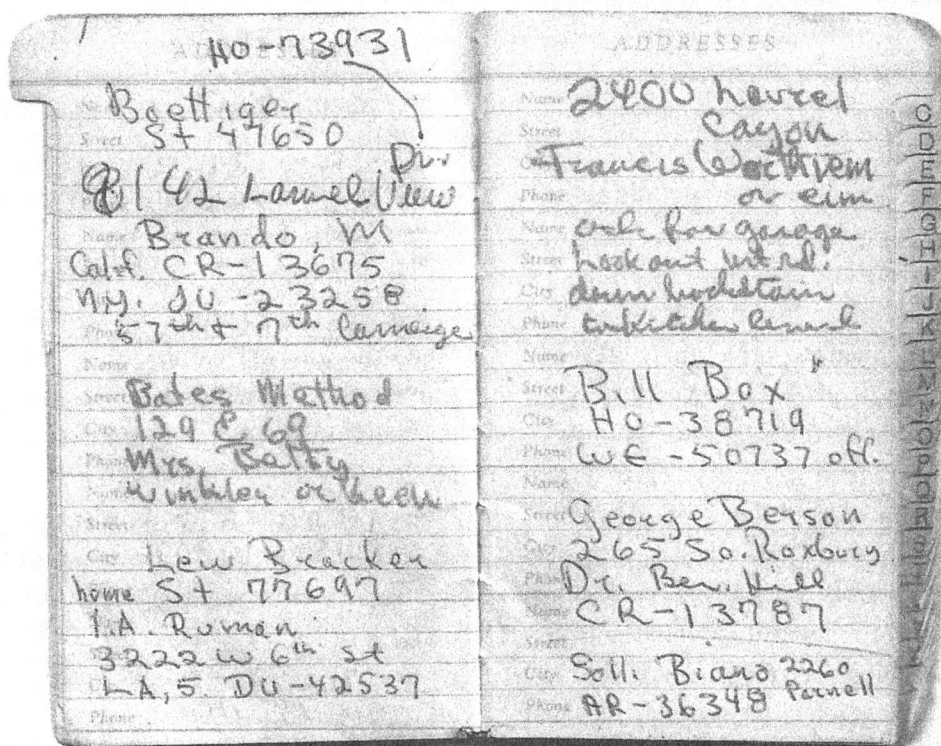

Jimmie's address book is open to Marlon Brando, Lew Bracker, "Boettiger" (American director and bullfighter Budd Boetticher) and "Solli" (Solly) Biano, head of Warner Bros. Casting Department.

color. Lew raced for two or three years, but after he got married and had a couple of kids, he kind of backed off of his racing career. Apparently, he was pretty successful.

LA: Did your dad and Lew stay in contact the whole time?

MW: Dad and Lew wrote to each other for at least three or four years and then, I don't know, we kind of lost track of Lew for a long time. Lew seemed to be a good friend of Jimmie's and that meant a lot to Dad, so he kept in contact with him the best he could.

LA: Lew is a really good writer.

MW: Yeah, he is. He did a good job with that book, *Jimmy and Me*. I think his daughter Lesley helped him quite a bit on it.

LA: His daughters are great. They're really taking care of their dad. And the cool thing is their dad is still teaching them…which is even more cool. Marlin Wilson is a longtime fan. I met him when he came to USC to look at stills. He came down here as a little boy, didn't he?

MW: Marlin Wilson was only thirteen or fourteen maybe when his folks brought him down from Michigan. At that time, it was a long drive to here from where they lived. They didn't have interstate roads like we do now.

Marlin got to be a big collector of James Dean photos. He almost has a photographic mind when it comes to pictures of Jimmie. He can see a photo and if Jimmie has his arm at a little bit different angle or something, he'll know it. Most people are like me. If I see a photo and then see another one that looks just about like it, I'll think it's the same photo and Marlin will say, "No, it isn't the same. Look at this and look at that," and he's

usually right. He notices all that stuff. He probably has more photographs of Jimmie than anybody I know.

Some of them are photographs from magazines and things like that. They're not all nice, glossy 8 x 10s, but he has the most pictures of Jimmie I've ever seen. He has a knack for getting them.

I guess I'm kind of backwards. I won't call people and ask them about their photos, but he will. If he sees a photo and he can find out whose it is, he'll call and ask them if they'll sell it or if they'll send him a copy of it. That's how he's gotten what he has. Marlin is a really nice guy. He's a good friend. He and I both have some photos his folks took of him here and some with both of us together. He's been coming here a long time. About every September, he'll be here.

It used to be, some of the fans would come in September and they'd exchange photos and stuff. He really got a kick out of that. It's not that way so much anymore. He comes down still, but the old fans he used to see have either died or quit coming. None of the new fans have more photos than him anyway, so (*laughs*) there are hardly any photos for him to get anymore.

Now and then, he'll call and want to know if I've seen a certain photo on the internet. Since the internet came out, photos are a lot more available than they used to be. Marlin has learned how to copy a photo from the internet, so that is where he's gotten a lot more, plus he bids on eBay and at auctions for photos.

If there's one on eBay he doesn't have, he'll bid on it and he usually gets it. Occasionally he'll be outbid. He has learned that there are no guarantees he's going to get it, so he'll copy it regardless. Then if he gets it, well, he has a better copy. If he doesn't get it, at least he has something. I've never learned how to do that, but he has.

LA: When you were in high school, was Adeline Nall still teaching?

MW: Yeah, she had come back from New York and went back to teaching again. Yeah, she was still there.

LA: Was her son born when she went to New York?

MW: David was about Jimmie's age, maybe a year or two younger. He was probably married when she went to New York.

LA: Was she divorced or...?

MW: I think so. Her named used to be Brookshire. She used to go by the name of Mrs. Brookshire, and I suppose Nall was her first husband because her son's name is David Nall. I guess she got a divorce or he died and she married some guy by the name of Brookshire. Mrs. Nall lived over in Marion.

LA: She didn't live in Fairmount?

MW: No, but I didn't know that much about her personal life. I never made any effort to find out. As we talk about it, her first husband would have been named Nall and her second husband was apparently Brookshire and then for some reason she took the Nall name back.

She lived west of Marion in an old family homestead, I think. Her mother lived with her for years. I'm not sure if her mother lived with her or she lived with her mother, but she lived in the same old brick house west of Marion for years and years.

LA: Did she teach English or just Theater?

MW: I didn't have her for Theater, but I did have her for a couple of years. We all had to take Speech in sophomore year and I think I took English from her, too.

This is changing the subject, but there was a guy brought a woman and a boy to the door Saturday. This guy recognized them as being tourists walking down the street in town and he brought her and the boy out here. I believe she was from Germany, and this boy had to be at least sixteen or so.

The woman had been here thirty-five years ago and the boy was her son. I said, "How long ago were you here?" And she said, "Thirty-five years." And I said, "You don't look old enough to have been here thirty-five years ago." And she said, "Well, I was." *(laughs)* Can you imagine that? I said, "How long are you going to be around?" And she said, "Two weeks." "Two weeks?" "Yeah," she said, "I wanted to see what the Midwest was really like." I don't know what she's going to do here for two weeks.

LA: So, she's going to drive around Indiana?

MW: I don't know if she drives or not. I told her, "Well, come back sometime next week and I'll show you some cars and stuff." She remembered me from thirty-five years ago, but I didn't remember her.

LA: Now, Bob Pulley was Jimmie's classmate, and we met him when we came back for the 50th Anniversary. Are his daughter and her husband still working in that business making shirts and stuff?

MW: Yeah, Christy makes a lot of vintage type clothing, not of Jimmie especially, but just vintage style clothes, Fifties-type bowling shirts and that kind of thing. Evidently, she and her husband hit at just the right time and were smart enough to know what to do because they have one heck of a business.

And it's all mail order; they don't have a store.

Their business is almost all from the internet. They have made some clothing like Jimmie used to wear, which they sell through the Fairmount Museum to try and help it out, but they have a heck of a business. They are both very, very talented in that way. They seem to know what to stock and what to make.

LA: They live in town?

MW: They live in Marion. They bought an old bank building a block off the square a few years ago and that's what they work out of.

LA: So, they're probably selling directly to stores then.

MW: Yeah, they are. They sell to stores. They sell to individuals. I don't know how they have it all set up. But they're so busy they're not even open on Fridays anymore, just Monday through Thursday. They are constantly shipping stuff out.

LA: That's kind of neat...the daughter of Jimmie's old classmate.

MW: Yeah, it is. They really hit on something good. You have to give them credit. The business is called "Daddy-O's."

LA: Is Bob's widow still alive?

MW: Yeah, she lives in Fairmount in that little house Mom used to live in. Bob and his wife sold their house out in the country and bought that house in town. They did a lot to it. It's a nice little home.

LA: At the 50th, when Frank and Catherine Mazzola came here, they stayed with the Pulleys out in the country. Catherine was amazed when Mrs. Pulley asked if she and Frank wanted some breakfast and she said "Yes," and Mrs. Pulley went out to the yard and pulled some apples off the tree, brought them in, cut them up, put them inside a crust and said, "You'll have it in however long it takes to bake an apple pie." She just thought that was unbelievable. You go to your backyard and you pull the apples and you bake the pie. Are you still in contact with Liz Sheridan, Dizzy?

MW: I haven't talked to Liz for a while. She used to call me occasionally. Of course, she's getting up there, too. She's eighty-five to ninety, somewhere in there. I've forgotten whether she lives with her daughter or what the deal is. The last time we talked, it seemed to me the daughter was getting involved somehow, but I don't contact her. I don't want to interrupt her schedule or anything.

LA: Do any of the fans stick out as being, you know, more special than some of the others?

MW: I suppose the very first ones from the first five or six years that we're still hearing from, you kind of think they're special. I have three or four people I've gotten very well acquainted with in the last twenty years that I wouldn't have known if it hadn't been for Jimmie. Like I say, they first started coming here because of Jimmie and after a while they became friends of ours.

I don't think the Jimmie aspect was quite as important once they got to know us. We've really met some nice people over the years. We've had some problems, but not with the local fans.

10

Work—Part One

Leith Adams: You said you worked in a factory. What factory did you work in?

Marcus Winslow: I was helping Dad here on the farm. To be honest about it, the farm wasn't big enough for both of us as far as income. I was hardly making anything and I think he was probably giving me more than he could afford. So, I decided to get a job at a factory, for a while at least.

I worked at Pierce Governor in Upland, Indiana. They make governors for gasoline engines, mostly industrial engines, combines and things like that. Governors maintain the speed and control the fuel going into the engine. The factory had been in Anderson, Indiana, for years and years and years and they got into some kind of a conflict down there and they just pulled out—sort of like the Irsay Family did in Baltimore with the Colts, moving them here to Indianapolis. Pierce Governor pulled out of Anderson and came to Upland; built a brand-new factory over there.

I was Number 37 on the Pierce Governor time clock—one of the first workers they hired. Until they got the factory going, they set up these little shops around Upland where we worked. I was drilling little holes in bolts. You

had to use these little teeny drill bits, about like a needle. And, boy, you had to be so careful with them, or you'd be breaking a bit.

Once or twice, they sent us to where they were building the factory. They began construction in one corner and as that corner was built, they started setting up these automatic screw machines.

I don't remember if I was running a drill press down at the shop or what I was doing, but I thought, *My God, I'll quit before I run those automatic screw machines.* Those things would index around and index around, rotating, and they were noisy and they had oil shooting in them all the time onto the tools. And I just thought, *Man, if they ever send me down here, I'm quitting.*

One day, this guy said to me, "When you come back tomorrow, you report down to the factory." I said, "What am I going to do down there?" "You're going to run the screw machines." I thought, *Oh, my God,* but that's what I did.

The parts they'd make, some were pretty small, maybe no bigger around than your little finger. Others were pretty good-sized, almost like a 2-inch piece of steel. It could kick a part out every fifteen or twenty seconds or it could go for a minute and a half or so.

The quicker you'd have it kick out a part, the better the factory liked it.

When I first started, I was bound and determined I was going to get out of there somehow, but I ended up staying with it and ended up liking the work. It was an oily job. All that tooling was cooled with oil. So, when you opened the door on the side of the machine to look at something, oil was spraying inside and it could get onto you, get on your shoes more than anything. I used to buy a new pair of shoes about every six months, just because the old ones were so saturated with oil that I couldn't stand it.

It became a pretty decent job. You'd get your machines set up, and if you had enough parts to run, you could just let it run all day. As long as it was putting out good parts, you'd let it go. I always checked it pretty close because I didn't want to run a bunch of junk.

LA: So, you did the quality control on the pieces?

MW: Yeah. They had an inspector who came around every day. He was supposed to come around every hour or two and check a part, but after you ran good parts time after time after time, they got kind of lax on checking you. I always ran pretty good stuff.

The next thing I knew, they had me on these big machines, five spindle machines. Warner and Swasey was the name on them. Some of the stock we fed into the machine was heavy, 2¼ inches was the biggest and some of those bars were 12 feet long. Hell, it would take two of you to pick one of them up and put it into the machine and you had to load five of them.

At first, we didn't know anything about these machines. And this foreman, he didn't know anything either. He was mean, I'll tell you. I hated that guy. He was always chewing me and everybody else out about something, but he didn't know how to run those machines either. He had come up from Anderson. He'd been a foreman down there, but he wasn't a foreman because he knew anything. I've always thought a foreman worked his way up and knew everything about the department. Well, this guy didn't.

We had to figure out those machines ourselves. After a couple of years, I got pretty good on them. They had me running two machines, one of them was a six-spindle Bradley, that was the name on it. Then I ran these Warner Swasey machines, five-spindles. They were older, but they were nice machines.

When I started, I thought being a foreman was a step up. But after I'd been there a year, I could see it was just a step closer to the door because every time something went wrong, they blamed it on the foreman. He wasn't watching what the operators were doing or this or that and they'd fire them.

I saw some good people fired, but I also found out, no matter how good they were, there was always someone who came along and took their place and things just kept running. I used to think, *Boy, if something happens to that guy, this place will be a mess.* Well, usually this guy would get let go and the place just kept on running. So, I guess I changed my outlook on that.

I went there in 1965 and in 1970 I quit. For years, I had been working part time evenings and weekends at Union Implement in Fairmount, just down the road. They sold Massey Ferguson and Minneapolis-Moline farm equipment and I would set up equipment for them. New combines would come in for sale, and you had to put a lot of stuff on them: corn heads and grain tables and other pieces. You had to put them together. I did a lot of that.

I'd come home from the factory and work at Union Implement for four or five hours. Sometimes I'd work until pretty late in the night. They even had me back in the shop tearing a motor down or fixing something. Forrest Smith and his brother owned the dealership and Forrest finally bought out the brother. The one leaving ran the Parts Department. Anyhow, Forrest wanted me to come be the Parts man, especially because I had worked part time for three or four years.

Dad would go there a lot and loaf. He'd get a Coke or something out of the Coke machine or a cup of coffee if they were making coffee. He encouraged me to think seriously about working there full-time. I thought about it a while. And since it was only a quarter of a mile away and Upland was about a half hour drive, I decided to do it. And I enjoyed it.

I guess I enjoyed working with farmers. And I'm not bragging, but we had a good Parts Department. I liked being the Parts man. I liked meeting people, different people coming in. I got kind of disgusted with the way the place was being run, but it wasn't up to me to run it.

After setting up equipment for several years and working in the shop some, I was familiar with everything. Many places hired someone to be a Parts man who didn't know anything about anything and I knew all that stuff.

I had a chance to take over the shop if I wanted to be the shop foreman, but I didn't want to do that. I was pretty satisfied up there in Parts. I had worked enough that I knew where all the bearings and all the sprockets and all that stuff went on a combine and if people came in and said they needed a bearing for this or that, I didn't have to look in a parts book.

I had a micrometer I'd used to check parts over at Pierce Governor, so if someone brought in a bearing that wasn't a Massey Ferguson product, I'd take out the micrometer and check it and I could go to our stock and bring back a bearing that would get them running again.

Finally, Massey Ferguson came out with a book that gave a crossover for our bearings, but for at least two or three years, I just had a sheet I'd made up myself of bearings.

If somebody came in with a combine and it had broken down and they needed something really bad and I was out of the part, I'd go out to a new combine and take it off and let them have it and then order a new part and put it back on the new combine. Sometimes I'd order two parts, one to stock and one to put on the combine. We did that a lot, stripped parts off a combine. I'm not saying it's a good practice. You want to definitely be on top of it, if you do, because if they sell the combine and want to use it and there's a part gone, the Parts man is in hot water because he took it off. We always tried to get it back on.

Like I say, I really enjoyed that job. Forrest was a heck of a nice guy, but he just sold too much, too cheap. And Massey Ferguson started getting into financial trouble and their quality control got kind of bad. And it hurt all the Massey Ferguson dealers; some of them went out of business over it.

It hurt our dealership some. But as much as anything, he was just selling too much, too cheap. Guys were driving right by other Massey Ferguson dealers and coming to us and I wondered why for quite a while. *There has to be some reason for this,* I was thinking.

It was because he was selling stuff cheaper to them than what the other dealer was, and that is a good way to get a customer. But you have to make money to stay in business. I worked there from 1970 until 1979 and when the bottom fell out of farming, it really hurt all the implement dealers and he finally went out of business—closed it down.

Out west of Fairmount, there was a big farm, a father and two sons, Norman and Dave Love. The father had been elected State Representative and so he turned the farm over to his boys and they did really well. Since they had quite a bit of Massey Ferguson equipment, they thought it would be a good idea to get into the farm implement business. Their father didn't think so, but one of the sons, Norman, was a real go-getter and he convinced their dad they'd make a success of it.

Norm and Dave talked to me saying they were interested in starting another Massey Ferguson dealership, but they wouldn't do it unless I agreed to work with them. I thought it was a good idea at the time. I felt kind of bad for the people who bought so much equipment here in Fairmount because they didn't have anywhere to buy parts. So, I agreed to go in with Norm and Dave and be the Parts man. There turned out to be about a half a dozen investors—one other guy and I voted to keep the business here in Fairmount—but the rest of them wanted to build a new building.

I even borrowed some money and invested in the dealership. It was a bad move. When we started in 1980—and we were open, I think, until 1987—the interest rate was 8% or 9%, which is a lot today, but at that time it wasn't because within a year the rate went clear up to 20%. We were operating on a fair amount of borrowed money, and it just killed us. The farmers were in just as bad shape as us. They weren't buying equipment, plus we really didn't have a good salesman.

It was in the summer and Marylou and I had gone to Michigan. Charlie and Bill Bridenfield were brothers who came down here as fans and became good friends. They had rented a cottage up there and wanted us to come up and stay for a week. We debated about whether to go or not. It was something new for us, but we ended up going. A year later we went to another cottage. Really it was just a house that this fellow owned and rented out on Lake Michigan, right on the lake, a beautiful setting.

On a Sunday night, I got a phone call and it was my sister. And she said Norm had been killed in a tractor accident. I knew at that instant we would be going out of business because Dave was a nice guy, but we were already struggling and when Joan said Norman had been killed, I knew we wouldn't be in business long, and we weren't.

Norm was on a tractor mowing a ditch bank and he had a rotary mower attached behind. As I was told, the front wheel fell into a washed-out place and the tractor just flipped right over and threw him into the creek. And as luck would have it, the rotary mower came down on top of him.

After Norm was killed, his dad came right in and took charge. And he wanted to close up and sell all of the equipment, sell the building, and that's what we did. We were open for another six months to a year, kind of cleaning up on stuff. Then we closed her up. There wasn't any choice, and I really didn't care. I loved selling parts and dealing with people, but after seventeen years, it got to where it was just a nightmare. It was okay with me if they closed it. I thought, *I won't have to deal with this anymore.*

It was a bad experience for me, very bad. That was in early '87 when we went out of business and I had just been elected Fairmount Township Trustee. Dave and I had talked it over. Dave said, "If you get elected and you want to take off one day a week to work for the township, it's okay with me." He said he'd run the Parts Department those days. Well, we ended up closing anyway, so it didn't matter.

11

Jimmie's Fans—Part Three

Leith Adams: Are the fans from Japan the most devoted?

Marcus Winslow: They're pretty devoted. When Mom was living here, it must've been around 1980 on the anniversary of Jimmie's death, Marylou and I were over here, and we looked out the dining room window. A bus had just pulled up in the barnyard and it was full of Japanese tourists. They were getting out, walking around, and we thought, *Well, what in the world?* We happened to have the doors shut to the house and here came two or three of them looking in the windows of the house. I knew they didn't realize it was a private residence, so we didn't take any offense, but I've always kind of gotten a laugh over it.

I went outside to the carport to see what was going on and this older Japanese woman was at the bus and she came up and she could speak English. I was talking to her and she said, "Are you Markie?" I said, "Yeah," and, oh, she got excited.

"Wait a minute! Wait a minute! I have something I want to show you," and she ran out to the bus and ran back up and she had a magazine with pictures of her in Jimmie's room back in 1957, I think. She had been

here, and this was twenty years later or so, and she had pictures of me with her. I kind of remembered her after she showed me the magazine. Really nice people.

The Japanese are very, very devoted fans, very appreciative of anything you do for them. Usually they want to bring you something, nothing expensive, but a nice gesture like a little hand fan or some incense or just some other thing that is special to them. I like the Japanese. We've also had a lot of people from France and England and Germany. I can't begin to tell you where all the people were from because I don't see them all. A lot don't come up to the house.

LA: Have you ever had any other buses pull into the farmyard?

MW: We had one pull in here, probably during the 50th. I thought when they turned in, *Man, I don't know about pulling in here with that big bus,* because it was a big tour bus. The driver pulled in all right and he let the people out, and they walked around, taking pictures.

I said to him, "You want to lay over to the north as much as you can when you pull out up onto the road." That's one reason we're working on the driveway right now, building it up, because there's such a hump from where the county has repaved the road and repaved the road and repaved the road and now the road is up high and it's a pretty big bump there. It also made a difference whether the bus was backing in or driving out.

The driver was able to drive in, but he tried to back out and he didn't hit it hard enough and the right rear of that bus got caught on the road. The bus was stuck in the middle of the road, blocking it, and traffic couldn't get by. We had to call a wrecker for him and, oh, it was probably a two hour deal. People got back out of the bus because they were tired of sitting in it, and we had to kind of entertain them here for an hour or so.

LA: Were they Americans?

MW: Yeah, they were Americans. The wrecker came and, of course, he couldn't get around the bus, so he had to go all the way around, a mile over to the west and a mile down towards town and then come in a mile back from the other way. Then he had to take all kinds of pictures before he'd hook onto it, in case something got torn up. That way he could show the bottom of the bus was already damaged before he hooked onto it. It just so happened that when he pulled the bus off of that hump, why, most of the bottom of the bus went back down. It wasn't perfect, but it was better than it was when it was sitting on that hump. Stuff like that happens.

LA: Did the Highway Patrol have to come?

MW: Oh, yeah, the police had to come out and block traffic on both ends of the road. It was a mess. I felt sorry for the truck driver. Felt sorry for the bus driver. Felt sorry for the tour guide. She said she was probably going to lose her job and on and on and on, but there wasn't anything I could do about it. I didn't tell her to pull in here in the first place. They just did.

LA: What are some of the other incidents?

MW: One time when Marylou and I were living over in the little house where Phil Zeigler's at now, Mom called and she was frantic. "Someone's trying to get into the house! Someone's trying to get into the house!" We were in bed, so I grabbed my clothes and got in the car and ran over here, and some woman was wandering around.

She was drunk is what it was and she had gone up to the house and was trying to get in. I don't think she realized where she was, but she was definitely trying to get into the house. And then the police came. I had told Marylou to call the police. I don't remember if they arrested her, though I suspect they did, because she was drunk and she was driving.

We've had things like that over the years. I can't think of all of them right off the bat, but we've had some experiences. That's for sure.

LA: Do people show up wanting to see Jimmie's room?

MW: There is always somebody wanting to see Jimmie's room. I have to admit we don't let people into the house like Mom and Dad did. They were so good to everyone and they just couldn't tell anybody no. If someone wanted to see Jimmie's room, they'd take them up to see it. Of course, Marylou and I had two little boys at the time we moved in here. Mom, probably lucky for us, she wanted to take Jimmie's bedroom suite with her up to her house in Fairmount for a spare bedroom.

We took it all up there and so it was with her for three or four years and then we had a good reason not to worry about taking anybody upstairs to Jimmie's bedroom. We could say we had taken the bedroom suite out, but now it's about the same as it used to be. It's not that we've tried to keep it the same just because Jimmie slept there. It just so happens that it was a spare bedroom and it was his room. And when Jimmie left to go back to California, it became my room, and it was my room from then until I got married in 1964. As soon as I moved out, it became Jimmie's room again.

Mom and Dad were good people and they did keep an eye on me. If they told me not to do something, I usually didn't do it. I wasn't one to disobey my parents. In some ways, they were very strict and in other ways, they were very good. I had a good life as a kid. It was a different life. Mainly because of Jimmie's death, it was different.

Bill Burwick, the guy that used to work for us, gave me a jigsaw one year for Christmas. I had a little shop set up in the basement and I'd cut out stuff. More than once on a Sunday, I'd be down there working and I'd glance up and see people's feet walking by the house from the window in the basement.

It got so that every Sunday, Mom would have dinner, and I'd get on a bicycle and I'd ride to Fairmount because I just didn't want to be around. You got tired of answering questions and people wanting to take your picture and this and that. It got so I was just gone every Sunday afternoon on the bike, riding to town, and I'd come back home about five o'clock in the evening and watch Ed Sullivan or Steve Allen.

Steve Allen was here one time. It was a year after Jimmie's death. He wanted to do a little segment on Jimmie, which was real nice. Dad told me, "You take the tractor and show him around the farm," so I did. Steve Allen rode on the tractor and I drove around the farm some. We did a little interview out there by the wall and that board fence going out towards the road. It was a big deal at the time.

I just kind of went along with it, but Steve Allen was pretty famous back then—had a show every Sunday night on TV. He went up to the high school in Fairmount, and the kids all came to the gym and he played the piano and talked to them. He was a very talented person, a pretty good piano player. I think the next Sunday they showed all of that on TV. He was really a nice guy. He sent me a couple of cars and a couple of hand puppets.

There was a feud going on between Ed Sullivan and Steve Allen, because their shows were on at the same time. Ed Sullivan used to always be introducing people in the audience. He'd say, "Well, so and so's here," and they'd get up and he'd acknowledge them and because Steve Allen was coming here to film that piece on Jimmie for his show, Ed Sullivan wanted to outdo him, so he asked Mom and Dad to New York to be on *The Ed Sullivan Show* (1948–1971) the same night. He also showed a clip from *Giant* as a little tribute to Jimmie.

I stayed with one of my friends for a couple days while that was going on, because my friend's parents were concerned. They didn't want us out running around too much because they were afraid I'd get kidnapped. It was funny at the time, but I guess it could have happened.

LA: Did you see Steve Allen's show when it was on TV?

MW: Yeah.

LA: So, you missed your parents on *Ed Sullivan*?

Marcus, age 12, drives Steve Allen around the Winslow Farm during the filming of Allen's tribute to James Dean which aired October 14, 1956.

MW: Well, this place where I stayed had two TVs. They had one on *The Steve Allen Show* (1956–1960) and the other was on *Ed Sullivan*, so I got to see Mom and Dad stand up. It didn't amount to a whole lot, but it seemed like a big deal at the time.

LA: So, you looked from one TV and could see yourself and then you'd look at the other TV and see your mom and dad?

MW: Yeah, but the Ed Sullivan thing only lasted for half a minute or so. He just introduced Mom and Dad, said who they were. But the Steve Allen thing was about fifteen minutes long. It was a pretty good show.

LA: Some rock videos have been made here.

MW: Yeah, *Suedehead* (1988), that Morrissey video was made here.

LA: Were you around when he was filming?

MW: Yeah, but I didn't even know who Morrissey was. I found out he was going to be here, and they wanted to know if I'd work with him and let him drive a tractor. They said it was Morrissey and hell, I didn't know who he was, but I guess he's a pretty big star now.

LA: Who are some of the other people that were known by the public who came here?

MW: Maxwell Caulfield, he's been here. I don't know how well known he is, but he's been here. He was here this last year for the dedication of a little park in Marion to honor Jimmie's birthplace. Did you see that?

LA: I saw the photographs on Facebook and I read Lew Bracker's speech.

MW: I suppose I ought to make more of an effort to remember who some of those people are, but they kind of come and go. I just don't think too much about it. It's nice that people think enough of Jimmie to come here, but I'm not the type of person that's overly impressed with someone just because they happen to be famous. A lot of them are very nice people. I'm sure there have been people come here and go to the cemetery in Fairmount and continued on that we never knew about.

LA: How did the James Dean magazine start? *Deanzine*.

MW: It started through the fan club. There have been two or three fan clubs that have lasted quite a while over the years. James Dean Remembered is the last one, and someone in the fan club decided it would be nice to start a little magazine talking about Jimmie and also some of his fans. Pam Crawford has been in charge for several years. She has done a tremendous job. She has a lot of color pictures in it, plus everything is very well written. You don't see any mistakes.

The first time I met Pam, or that I remember, was when we were in Marfa, Texas, and that would've been 2003. She had just taken over the responsibility of the fan club as president. There may have been *Deanzines* out at the time, but I think she started the magazine about then. She just did a wonderful job. I've never heard anyone say they weren't impressed with the magazine.

LA: I've always heard there were foreign fan clubs.

MW: I think there probably are. Like I say, we have people coming from all over the world, so there have to be some foreign fan clubs. But I'm personally not involved with them. I think James Dean Forever has some foreign members.

LA: On James Dean Days in Fairmount, is Pam involved in the events at all?

MW: No. Pam comes usually every year to the festival, which is almost always the last full weekend in September. About once every seven or eight years, September 30 falls on a Sunday, the festival's last day, and it's also the day there's a memorial service at Back Creek Church. For the last two or three years, Pam has participated in the memorial service, but she doesn't have anything to do with putting on the festival. The Fairmount Museum and the 9th Street Car Club, they organize the festival.

LA: You're involved in that too, right?

MW: Somewhat. I used to be very involved, but I've kind of backed off of most of it, though I can't help but be involved in some ways. I spend quite a bit of time out at the park where the cars are. They usually have fifteen or sixteen hundred cars out there. It's interesting to see them all and see the people. On Saturday, they have a parade and when the parade's over, there's really a gob of people who come down to the park. Every year I think, *Well, I wonder if it'll be this big next year?* It usually is.

LA: Fifteen hundred to sixteen hundred cars? That is a lot of cars.

MW: Yes, it is. Supposedly years and years ago there were more than that. You just kind of have to take people's word for it, but there's really not room in that park to get very many more. It's a big park, but when you start putting vendors selling stuff and cars for sale and show cars and all that, it's not long before a lot of room is taken up. But I have seen that park pretty well full before.

LA: Has it spread outside of the park ever?

MW: No, it has always stayed inside the park. There is a festival uptown in Fairmount, and it has a lot of craft booths and clothing and just everything you can think of. There are food vendors and also a section where there are rides for kids like Ferris Wheels and Merry Go Rounds, but that's all uptown.

Another thing they're doing at the park, there's a big pavilion out there and a year from now, I'm pretty sure, the old Fairmount High School stage will be in there. They just about have the money raised to set it up. They're going to put it in the north end of the pavilion, so the people that entertain will have a permanent stage to perform on. And during the summer, they plan to have concerts in the park and things like that.

LA: The Fairmount High School stage?

MW: Yeah, they saved the stage from the school before it began to fall apart.

LA: Fairmount, thanks to Jimmie, seems to draw a lot of people to it who just want to help out, like Phil who was just here in the Car Barn. Can you talk a little bit about Phil and where he's from?

MW: Phil Zeigler is from York, Pennsylvania, and he's the same age as Jimmie. They were both born in 1931. Phil was in the Navy from around 1950 to '54 or '55. He was a big fan of Jimmie's and he's a car fan, too. Phil says the first time he was here was in 1978 when he brought his daughter just because it was Fairmount and Jimmie's home. Then the next time he was here, in 1985, there was a car show. I think he came every year after that.

Phil's occupation was fitting eyeglasses and he retired in 1995. His mother had passed away and his kids were all out of the house, and he just decided he was going to move to Fairmount. I happened to have a house empty at the time, the one right here on the farm in the spot where Marylou and I first lived. He was thrilled to death when he moved in there in '96.

Phil was here only a month or so when Mrs. Nall passed away. That's how I remember when it was. Phil volunteered at the Museum for years and has always been friendly with all the fans. If someone special comes in, the Museum will get ahold of him and he'll bring them out to the farm and show them around, which they wouldn't see otherwise. He enjoys doing that, and everyone enjoys his company.

Phil is eighty-five and his health is still pretty good. He did have bypass surgery a few years ago at St. Vincent's in Indianapolis. There were some complications for a while, but he finally got it straightened out. He's doing real well now, as far as I know. We think a lot of Phil, and he's going to be missed if something ever happens to him, because he's about the only one who will take people around and show them stuff. He's a real asset to Fairmount and to James Dean.

LA: Other people that have moved here…can you talk about David Loehr?

MW: David is from New York, both Dave and Lenny Prussack. They started coming to Fairmount in the late Seventies, early Eighties. David decided he'd like to start some kind of a display in Fairmount, so he bought a big old house on Main Street. It had been a funeral home originally. When the funeral home closed, it was an accountant's office for a few years.

David bought it, and I thought he paid an awful price for it, but it was a good deal for him because he was comparing it to New York prices. Nevertheless, the longer he was here, the bigger the display got.

David and Lenny's business in New York was making tee shirts. They had a shop where they had sewing machines set up, and that's how they made their living. When they moved here permanent, David spent all his time creating the James Dean Gallery, which displays his collection.

He's very involved with the fans and he gives them a place to hang out during the festival and during the fan club weekend, which is this weekend. It's nothing big. The fans get together and they have a dinner somewhere on Saturday night, and Dave and Lenny have a *Jeopardy* contest and stuff like that. On Sundays they have a cookout, but we usually go to the dinner on Saturday night. We try to be sociable with the fans. I don't care about being there the whole weekend, but one evening is pretty nice. They're all nice people.

At one time David had one of the best James Dean displays ever because he had bought a lot of Jimmie's clothing years ago that had come from the studios. He had a pair of pants and a jacket from *East of Eden* and a pair of blue jeans from *Giant* and a pair of slacks from *Rebel Without a Cause*. Anything that was Jimmie's, he had it. David also had a lot of knickknack stuff, plus he bought things that people claimed were Jimmie's. Some of it was. Some of it wasn't.

Even though David is a wonderful curator, he ended up getting in debt so much, he had to sell his collection to pay the bills. Everybody thought that would be the end of him as far as James Dean was concerned. I think he thought so, too, but as time went on, he decided he was going to take what was left and put it on display. He's also managed to get a few more things over the years.

David can take a showcase and do a good job of laying things out in it, so he still has a nice little display in the Gallery, and he has a huge gift shop. He really keeps up with all the James Dean items coming out, books and things like that.

Like I say, he's awfully good to the fans. He and Lenny both are good to the fans. Lenny is the one who really does the work. He still makes a lot of clothes. He goes to a lot of yard sales and picks up things and turns around and sells them on the internet. He does well enough that they can afford to live here.

LA: I saw the James Dean Museum he built on Interstate 69. Can you talk about that building? His displays in that building were great.

MW: It was a very nice exhibit, but that's how he got in debt. David had a fire one time here in Fairmount. It wasn't a serious fire. An electrical thing in the ceiling caught fire and burned a little spot, but that scared him. It's an old house he's in. He got the idea that he needed to get out of there and get into a modern building, one that couldn't hardly burn.

A doctor here in Fairmount was also a developer. He owned a big piece of ground over by Gas City, and they ended up putting a Cracker Barrel on it and a Best Western Hotel behind it. I think he has an investment in that, too. They also built a big medical facility, clear on the back part of the land and also some other restaurants.

I don't know if David went to him or if he went to David, but they got together, and this guy was going to build David this elaborate building. It was a beautiful building. A lot of people tried to tell David, said to him, "You know it's going to be different. You're going over there and you'll have overhead there whereas here all you have to do is get up in the morning and go downstairs and you're at work. And when you go over there, it's not going to be the same."

Well, he knew it. He knew it, but I think he thought every car that went down Interstate 69 was going to stop. That wasn't the case. David is such a fan of Jimmie's that he doesn't see reality sometimes. And once you visit a museum, unless you're really, really dedicated, you're probably not going to come back for a while. If you've seen it once, you've seen it.

Unfortunately, he got in big financial trouble and got way behind with the doctor on his payments for the building, and the doctor finally took the building back. It's too bad that nice building is just sitting there, but that's what happened. To pay what he owed, David contacted auction companies and he ended up letting Heritage Auctions in Dallas sell all the stuff. He got pretty big money out of some of it, but I don't think he has any of it left.

LA: I was impressed with his museum. What did you think about the layout?

MW: Oh, I thought it was a very nice layout. He is just good at setting up exhibits, but I didn't like it because it was in Gas City. Gas City was not Jimmie's home. David has always been here in Fairmount, and then he was pulling out of Fairmount and going to Gas City.

I had a few things I'd loaned him and I said, "My stuff is not going to Gas City." I took them out and put them in the Historical Museum as he was cleaning out the house. I wasn't very happy at all about him going over there. But I took the attitude, it is his stuff, and if that's what he wants to do with it, I shouldn't make a huge effort to stop him. But I felt pretty sure in my own mind that financially it would never pay out.

He got over there and had big utility bills and either had to pay rent or make building payments, I'm not sure which—depends on who you listen to—and he just couldn't meet the overhead, which is too bad because when he sold all that stuff, he sold it all at once. If he could have sold a little at a time, I think it would have brought a lot more, but he had to put everything on the market all at once. He had to get the money raised. So that's what happened to David's museum. He still has a nice display up in the Gallery. I've never heard anyone say they didn't like it.

LA: How did the James Dean Birthplace site in Marion start?

MW: Marion tore the house down where Jimmie was born probably back in the 1960s or '70s. At that time Jimmie's popularity had kind of died down, and the people running the City of Marion didn't think anything about it. The house wasn't very attractive, and so they tore it down.

As time went on, people there began to realize they shouldn't have torn it down, because tourism was becoming a big thing. For years and years and years, they talked about building some kind of a memorial in Marion where that house sat. David Loehr got involved and he helped design it and, again, he did a wonderful job.

There was one guy in Marion who financed most of it. He's a pretty wealthy guy. They had this big monument built. It has a couple of pictures of Jimmie on it and his history, and there are several benches to sit on. Trees are planted around it. It's a nice little park. There's not a lot there, but still it recognizes the spot where Jimmie was born. I think there's a picture of the house on the monument. It's very well done, very good taste.

Marion had a grand opening last year on September 30 after we were done with the memorial at the Back Creek Church. Most of the people went to Marion, and a few people got up and talked. It was very well attended. I think everybody enjoyed it very much. It will be there forever. It's something that probably a hundred years from now, you go to Marion and you'll still be able to see that big granite memorial.

LA: Who spoke at the memorial besides Lew Bracker?

MW: I think the mayor of Marion spoke and a girl who had something to do with the memorial. She was part of the group that promotes Marion. They talked me into getting up and saying a little. There were four or five speakers. It was very nice. They had

bleachers out on the street for people to sit on to watch it. David had a lot to do with it. I'm sure of that.

LA: So, you make speeches pretty often now?

MW: No oftener than I have to. (*laughs*) Occasionally I feel kind of forced into it. I don't like to. I don't like to get up in front of people, but I have occasionally gotten up and talked. I always feel kind of uneasy, but I think when it's all said and done, I do all right.

LA: Were you nervous that first time you had to make a speech?

MW: I'm sure I was. I'm still nervous when I have to make one, but I try to think of something to say that I haven't said before. I make notes and then try to do it without looking at my notes, although I keep them as a tool to fall back on. I've noticed a lot of people get up and read almost the whole thing. Some of them will read it, and then they'll look out at the audience and talk a little, and then they'll get back down to their speech.

That's fine. But I try to get it in order, so that I can get up there and say what I want to say and maybe not have to look at my papers at all. Occasionally I do. I'm definitely not a good speechwriter, but there are cases where I feel like I have to say something. At the fan club supper, they always want me to get up and speak. It gets kind of old because it's the same thing every year, but I do it.

Talking about people from outside Fairmount coming in to help, a guy who participated in the memorial service, for thirty years probably, is Terry Nichols. When he came to town, he went under the name of "Nicky Bazooka" and he had a motorcycle that he always rode ahead of the people who walked from the church down to the cemetery.

He always put a big flower display on Jimmie's grave. He was a colorful character. Hardly anyone knew who he was. I did, but most people didn't. They had no idea where he was from because he'd just go by this name "Nicky Bazooka." One year somebody asked him, "Where are you from, Nicky?" He said, "Well, I'm from everywhere."

Unfortunately, he developed cancer and passed away about two years ago. It was about a month before the festival, and I really wondered how the memorial service was going to go over without him because he'd been there for years, ever since we started having it. I had never gotten up and said anything at the memorial service before, but I did that day. I felt I owed it to him to get up and talk about him.

His wife had told me they were wanting to raise some money to put a bench in their hometown with his name on it, so I encouraged people to donate money for that. That's one of the few times I've spoken, but I wanted to that day. No one

twisted my arm. It was something I wanted to do. I felt I owed it to Terry. He'd always been good to me and he'd been good to the fans. Everybody enjoyed him, so I felt I'd be remiss if I didn't get up and say something.

LA: Did they raise enough money for that bench?

MW: I think so. He lived a ways from here. The last time I sent his wife a Christmas card, I asked her if they'd gotten enough money raised for Terry's bench and if they didn't, I would try to help some more. I never heard anything back from her, so I don't know for sure. I'd like to think they did, but you never know without going and checking yourself.

LA: In your speech, did you tell everybody his real name?

MW: By that time, by him passing away, there were a lot of articles in the papers about him. People knew pretty much who he was. Yeah, I think I mentioned his real name was Terry Nichols. Terry sacrificed a lot to come here every year. Even I didn't realize it for a long time.

On his motorcycle, Terry Lee Nichols, aka Nicky Bazooka, led the procession following the annual James Dean Memorial service at the Back Creek Church to Park Cemetery where he would lay flowers on Jimmie's grave and then mysteriously disappear down the road as mourners watched.

He lived seventy or eighty miles from here. He had this motorcycle and this black leather jacket and motorcycle pants he wore and boots and a cap. It was kind of a motorcycle cap. He worked for a racing team part of the time, and I know there was more than one year when they were in California racing and he took off for three or four days to come all the way back to Indiana just to be Nicky Bazooka in Jimmie's Memorial Service. Then he'd leave and go back to work.

He was a big fan of Jimmie's. He really respected Jimmie, and that's the reason he did it, but he sacrificed quite a bit to be able to do that. He left his motorcycle to me in his will. I appreciated having it, but I didn't have anywhere to show it off.

I asked David if he would like to display it, and he said he would, so we drained all the fuel out of it and prepared it for the Gallery. David built a little platform to put it on and we took it up there and I gave David the uniform Terry had. I think it's on display, too. It's kind of a memorial to Terry.

I felt he deserved it. The Historical Museum is full of our regular James Dean things and doesn't have anywhere to display Nicky's motorcycle or his gear. Also, I don't think the Museum had the feeling for Nicky Bazooka that David had because David and Nicky were involved in a lot of activities together.

I haven't been up to the Gallery for a year and a half, so I should go see what it looks like. I saw it shortly after we'd taken the motorcycle up. We stopped and looked at it.

Terry kept it pretty secret who he was and that he came here on the 30th and did the ride. I don't think he ever made much money as a mechanic. He spent all his time running around, horsing around with motorcycles and fixing motorcycles for people for nothing.

He could tell you motorcycle stories and stories about people who had cycles all day long. It's just what he enjoyed doing. His life was cars and motorcycles, but he never mixed up Nicky Bazooka with his life. He always kept that separate.

After Terry got sick, I really started taking a serious interest in him. Phil and I went down to visit him at least two or three times, maybe more, when he had cancer and he was recuperating at home. We knew he wasn't going to survive. It's hard to go visit someone you know when they're like that, but you gotta do what you gotta do, and he appreciated us coming.

The last time we were there, his wife came home and we told her we'd be back before very long. It was probably a month later, I called him and she said, "Well, he's not doing very good." I said, "Do you think we better not come?" She said, "I think it'd probably be better if he didn't have any company." It wasn't long after when he passed away. I really didn't want to see him in the final stages anyway.

We went to his funeral and we went out to the cemetery after the funeral where they buried him. I've never been back to that town since. Crawfordsville is the name of the town. He didn't live in Crawfordsville, but in a town right outside of it. He did a lot, I felt, in memory of Jimmie, and I think he felt pretty close to Jimmie.

LA: Out of all of the people that came to James Dean Days when he was here on the 30th, how many do you think knew who he was?

MW: Maybe half a dozen people because everyone knew he didn't want anybody to know, so we didn't tell anybody. Somebody was always wanting to know, saying, "Do you know who that is?" I always said, "No, I don't know him."

LA: Sitting here with you today and having two separate groups come into the Car Barn to see you, really, to see you, and this one girl was in tears, can you talk a little bit about that? I mean, Jimmie Dean died in 1955. He made three films, and here's a nineteen-year-old girl in tears meeting you.

MW: Believe it or not, it happens fairly often. It's about always girls, but he has fans that are only fourteen- or fifteen- or sixteen-years-old. Obviously, this girl has been a fan for a while, and it is kind of touching. They came all the way from Louisville. Louisville's not out of this world, but I suppose it's about a five- or six-hour drive.

People come to Fairmount just because of Jimmie, and they go to the grave and they go up to the Gallery and up to the Museum and a lot of them come out here. I don't meet them all, but they'll come out here and turn around and take pictures; something we've always let them do. If they feel strong enough about Jimmie to come here, I feel that's the least we can let them do. They take pictures of the house and the buildings and stuff. It is pretty touching, really, when you see a little girl like that. How old did she say she was?

LA: Nineteen.

MW: Nineteen. Here Jimmie has been gone sixty years, and she's so devoted to him. It's amazing and it happens quite often. Today's not an exception. We get an awful lot of people like that who drive to Fairmount just because of Jimmie.

It's too bad they can't see more while they're here, but you can only do what you can do. If they get to see the Gallery and the Museum both and go by the grave and go through Fairmount and come out here and see the farm, that means a lot to them. It especially means a lot to them when they get to come to the farm and talk to someone. That is something most of them don't expect, you know?

LA: And the group before that was from Canada.

MW: Yeah, they were from Windsor, Ontario. That's a pretty good drive, too, probably even farther than Louisville. I have a lot of people I admire, but I've never had anybody who I've wanted to drive several hundred miles just to see their birthplace or to see where they were raised or see a museum or anything on them.

It's hard for me to absorb all this about Jimmie, the way people are so fascinated with him. I know they are. It's not like I'm naive or anything, but I just never had anybody I admired so much that I'd drive hundreds of miles to see something.

I'm probably in the minority on that. There are a lot of people that will go see someone's birthplace or their hometown or whatever they can see of them. It's great they do that, but I've just never been that way. Of course, I admire Jimmie, but I'm already here. (*laughs*)

LA: You've always said it's hard to separate the actor and the characters he plays and the kid that you knew.

MW: I know a lot of these fans are fans because of the characters he played, because they never knew him. It makes it a little different. But they all want to know him. They all want to know everything you can tell about him. He's been gone sixty years, and I can remember the funeral. And I can remember ten years later and thirty years later and now all of the sudden here it is sixty years later, and it's still going on.

12

Work—Part Two

Marcus Winslow: All of us lost all the money we'd invested. Norman and Dave had invested a lot of money, and the family had to sell off farm ground to pay the bills. When it was all over, we didn't owe Massey Ferguson anything, I'll say that. We paid every penny we owed them.

When I started there, they promised me I'd get "x" amount of salary and I'd get a certain percent of all the parts we sold, which would be enough to make a yearly payment on the loan to pay the interest. I got my salary, but only the first year did I get anything for the parts we sold.

I probably lost $15,000 on the deal, a lot of money back then. It's still a lot of money as far as I'm concerned, but back then it was really a lot, but not so much that you couldn't pay it back if you had a good income.

I got it paid back two or three years after they closed, but closing up was a harrowing experience too. Since they weren't selling anything, they weren't making any money, and so they weren't paying their bills to Massey Ferguson and Massey Ferguson put them on C.O.D. which meant "cash on delivery." Every time I needed a part for somebody, we had to pay C.O.D. for it.

That meant if the part sold for $20 and our cost was $14, we had to pay $20 for it. The $6 we would have made on the sale went to Massey Ferguson for the outstanding bill. That's tough when you have salaries and electricity bills and everything to pay, but we got 'er done. Like I say, we didn't owe Massey anything when it was over. It sure cost those two brothers a lot of money—or the estate of one of the brothers.

Norm's estate and Dave probably lost a hundred acres of farmland over it, maybe more. After we closed, the ground was sold to pay their debts. They really lost a lot. Since then, land has gone from a couple thousand dollars an acre to $10,000 an acre. If they still had that ground, they'd be worth a lot of money now.

Leith Adams: So, what did you do after that?

MW: I was a Township Trustee and also worked on repair projects at the farm, but I also bought a building in Fairmount. The American Legion had been in this place, but they built a new building on the east side of Fairmount on State Route 26. When they moved out, the owner was going to fix it up, inside and out, so he could sell it to the school district for offices, but he only fixed the outside. For whatever reason, he never worked on the inside, and the school district lost interest. The building sat empty for over a year and that's why it was such a good price.

By that time, I'd finished up all the repair projects around the farm and I wanted to keep Buttons working, the guy helping me. I hated to lose such a good worker. Thurlow Knight was his name. But as a kid, his mother said he was cute as a button, and that's the name that stuck with him. He lived right north of here half a mile, the next property beyond Phil's house. He was strong as a bull, but never had a steady job until he came and worked for me. He had a lot of stories to tell.

I bought the building and Buttons and I started doing interior work on it. We tore out the floor with a Bobcat and poured new cement. Then we went to work on the insulation and put in a new ceiling and before long, we had a place to store and show the car collection. There was a Laundromat next door, and so I bought that, thinking it would be a good investment, but it was another money-losing deal.

There was a time when Laundromats were pretty popular. They might still be in big cities, but around here, it got to the point where you could buy a new washer and dryer at Sears Roebuck or just about any store and make payments on it every month and your payment wouldn't be more than what it cost you to go to the Laundromat. If you spend a pocketful of quarters washing clothes every week, it adds up. Business just gradually got a little less and a little less.

Matter of fact, I was having to take money out of my own pocket just to pay the expenses. I sort of hated to close it up, but I thought, *This is stupid. I'm not making any money anyway and now I'm thinking about spending $25,000 to $30,000 on new machinery that won't bring in any more customers.*

I finally closed it. As soon as I shut it down, the lady who runs the library came over and said they were wanting to buy a building or build a new one, because they were just in an old house. She asked if I would be interested in selling my building to them. I said I would think about it and I thought, *It would be pretty nice. If I have to sell the place, I can't think of anything I would rather have in here than the library.* The way the economy was going, if I held onto that building for a while, there might not be anybody around to buy it again.

She said they were applying for a grant to update the library. We talked again, and she said they could have somebody appraise it if I wanted them to. I said that would be all right. This guy appraised both buildings, the Laundromat, plus the building where I had the cars. He appraised it at a little over $200,000. I didn't think the buildings were worth that. Might have been in a big city, but not in Fairmount. Anyway, the library said they couldn't pay that much, so I asked what they could pay; and they said they could pay whatever the grant paid, so I said I'd let them have it.

I had to wait a year or two to get the money. They didn't have it right then, because they applied for a grant. After they finally paid me, that's when I built the building here at the farm where Coy's office is and turned this equipment building into the Car Barn, a showroom for my cars and stuff. I miss that building up in town because I worked hard on it and put a lot of thought into it. But if I had a buyer who wanted it and they were willing to pay me a pretty fair price, I thought I'd better get rid of it and that's what I did.

That's when I brought all my cars out here. These tractors, I couldn't have gotten them in up there. Coy is interested in tractors and started restoring them and started bringing them over here. I bought that old fire truck and this car building gave me a place to put it. It's worked out a lot better than the building in town.

LA: You mentioned you had an accident where you got a metal chip in your eye. How did that happen?

MW: I was getting some drywall work done in the house and the guy doing it, finished all the work he could until some mud dried. He came out to the barn. I forget who was working there, maybe it was Buttons. We were trying to get a bearing cup off of a tractor axle. The bearings were gone and there wasn't anything other than the cup still pressed onto the axle. We were trying to get it off.

He was using a hammer and a chisel to try to drive it off, and I walked up there and this guy that'd been doing the drywall work said, "Let me see if I can't get that off." He picked up the hammer and the chisel and he hit on it once or twice, and I felt something fly by my face. I thought, *This might not be a good place to be standing,* and I was just getting ready to move when something hit me in the eye.

A few seconds later I could see blood, so I said, "Well, I've got to go up to the house and see what this looks like." I went up there and I spread my eye open and I could just see my eye all tore off, kind of hanging there. I thought, *Oh, shit!* Right then, I felt like I had probably lost my eyeball.

Coy ran me over to the hospital. They took me into the Emergency Room and laid me down, and this doctor came in and looked at it. He shook his head and said, "You don't belong here. You belong down at St. Vincent's in Indianapolis," so they made arrangements for me to go down there.

All the way down, I was kind of holding my eye open because the lid would push in on it when I'd close it. I got down there and the doctor wanted to know what happened. I said, "I think a piece of metal just hit my eye at a glance, kind of cut across the front of it." He said they were going to have to X-ray it to find out. They took me into X-ray, and he said, "That piece of steel went clear to the back of your eyeball." I said, "Do you think you can save my eyeball?" And he said, "I don't know. We'll try."

I was scared to death I was going to wake up out of the anesthesia and I wouldn't have an eyeball there. Well, it was there and I was very, very, very fortunate. I had a good doctor and he got that steel out and sewed up the eye back in there. Then they sewed up the front of my eye.

They say your eye is one of the fastest things that heals on your body, if it gets injured. I was in St. Vincent's three nights. The doctor said, "Well, we had to take the lens out of your eye. Maybe later on you can get a contact lens and put on it. Can't tell yet. If it doesn't get infected, you'll probably be able to save your eyeball, but if it gets infected, you might have to have it taken out."

I was really scared, because I didn't want my eyeball taken out. I already knew I was blind in it. They sent me to a place called Cornell Consultants, and I found out one doctor does the front of your eye and another doctor does the back. The one I went to just did the front. The doctor at Cornell said, "They sure did a good job of sewing your eye." He wanted to know who had done it, and I told him.

"After a few months," he said, "let's try to put a contact lens on it." They made a contact lens and put it on there and it did help. I can close my right eye and I can see stuff, but there's a big scar here, a big blurry spot, so I can't see good enough to drive with just that one eye. If something happened to my good eye, I could probably see to get to the house, but I can't really see things very well out of it.

I was having to go back every two or three months for an examination. Now I go back every six months, but after the first examination or maybe the second, they said I had a detached retina. That's when your retina comes loose in the back of your eye.

I don't know how they did it, but they went inside my eye and sewed it all back together. Then they put a bubble inside of my eye and that bubble naturally always floats to the top.

What they wanted me to do was lay with my face down for ten days to two weeks so that the bubble would be pushed up against the top of my eye, which is really the back of my eye, holding everything in place. So, I did that.

Then a couple of years later I was back, and they said I had a detached retina again. They said it was from the trauma of the accident and that I also had a macular hole. It was a major eye operation, and the guy went

back in there and sewed that macular hole up, fixed the detached retina, and it's been all right ever since. That was several years ago.

I've had people tell me they couldn't go through that operation. They couldn't lay face down for ten days or two weeks, but you can if you have to. My theory was that I'd rather be doing this than going to get radiation or chemo treatments for cancer. That was the attitude I had. And I got along pretty good.

Twice I had to do that. The second time, a chiropractor friend of mine in Fairmount had a table and he said, "Why don't you take this table and lay down on it? Put your head in that crack." I told him I didn't want to take his table, but he'd retired and he said, "I want you to take it. Have Coy come in and get it. You can lay on this table."

Well, that's what I did. I got so that I'd either do that or I'd lay on the floor with my hands on my forehead. You just kind of go into a trance after a while. You get to where you'll lay there for an hour or two and then you wake up and pretty soon, you'll go back to sleep again.

13

Bill Burwick & Tuck

Marcus Winslow: We used to have a guy working for us named Bill Burwick, and Bill was like a second father to me. A bull had hit him when he was real small and broke his hip. He was crippled. He was quite a bit shorter in one leg.

There used to be some rocks down at the creek, so you could walk across, but Bill didn't want to walk on those rocks. He's the one who built the bridge. At one time, he had a railing on one side and it was pretty nice. He had to anchor it, because occasionally the water would get clear up to the bridge and try to wash it downstream. It took a lot of work to do it, but he was pretty handy.

Old Bill didn't do any fieldwork, but he loved livestock. Dad let him live in the old house over where Phil's house is now. Bill was really, really good with livestock. He was good with about anything. He wasn't able to do a lot because of his leg and he always walked with a cane and he had one shoe built way up. That's the way they used to do it when people would have a short leg. They'd build their shoe up. I don't know how he lifted up that shoe and carried it, but he did.

Bill helped Dad from the mid-1940s till after Jimmie was killed. That's how I can remember it. Bill was here another year or

two after Jimmie died. I'd say in '57 Bill retired and went to Virginia to live with his son. I don't think he was feeling too good. Bob, Bob Burwick was his son's name. He'd been in World War II and was on the aircraft carrier Wasp when it was sunk by a Japanese submarine. He was in the water for several hours before he got picked up.

Anyway, Bob and his wife had built a new house and they built one room just for Bill, but Bill wasn't too happy down there. I think his son and wife did a lot of feuding around. He wrote me one time and wanted to know if Dad would let him put a trailer back here to live in. Of course, Dad did. We thought he'd probably go south of Fairmount over to our other farm, Grandpa Dean's farm. It had a big barnyard with a couple of barns over there. It would have been a perfect setting for a mobile home.

No, he wanted to put it right here, about where this Car Barn is, so Dad let him. We ran electricity to it and water and sewer and all that. We built a little carport on it for him to park his car under. Then we enclosed the carport and painted the trailer and put in a driveway to get in and out. It's just amazing how much you have to do to get some little thing to work. Dad didn't charge him anything, and Bill was happy to be here. I kind of looked after him

In 1954, Dad had traded in his car, a '49 Ford, for a new Dodge. Bill didn't have a good car and he'd always liked that Ford, so he went to the dealer and bought it. He called it his "Sunday car." He parked it in a garage in Fairmount and got it out on Sundays and picked up his girlfriend and they'd go for a drive and have supper somewhere. That Ford is also the car Jimmie drove to his Senior Prom.

Bill had taken it to Virginia with him and he brought it back and wanted me to have it. Even though Bill was still living, he signed the title over into my name in 1966. He had about quit driving the last year of his life. If he wanted something, I either took him to get it or went and got it for him. I pretty well took care of him for the almost eight years he lived here.

After Bill passed away, he left me his trailer, which wasn't worth anything. I finally gave the trailer away to a neighbor, but it didn't matter what it was worth, it was Bill's home and he wanted me to have it. You used to do stuff like that, that you wouldn't do today. I wouldn't let someone put a house trailer here in the barnyard now, but at the time we didn't think anything about it. We thought it was fine.

Bill was back here from 1961 to 1968. The reason I remember '61 is that's the year Marylou and I graduated from high school. That summer was when I helped him get his trailer set, so he and I were pretty close. He just died of old age. It's hard telling what he had wrong with him, because he wouldn't doctor hardly. He always tried to take care of himself.

I finally went to work at the factory. And Dad came out to Bill's trailer one day, and Bill was standing out back on the deck he had there. Dad asked him how he was and,

oh, he really felt just rotten, so Dad went to the barn and did something out there and came back and thought, *"Well, I'd better check on him."*

Bill had laid down on the bed inside and died. You know, I really hated to lose him, but I knew it was coming because his health was just deteriorating. I used to go out there in the evening a lot and listen to him. He was quite a talker, always talking, big storyteller.

I used to go over to Marion with him to a place owned by Nobe Swoveman. That was also the name up on his garage, Nobe Swoveman. Bill told me stories how the FBI used to have cars, and they'd bring them in there for him to work on. Also, some shady characters would come in and he'd work on their cars, too.

Nobe had an old, old car sitting in the back of the building that he was going to do something with. I don't remember if it was a Maxwell or what. It was an early one, probably before the teens, probably worth a lot of money today, but I remember that car was in his garage.

Bill gave me an old car one time. It was a '36 Dodge, an old four-door, and I used to drive it all over the farm here. We didn't drive it on the road, but I did stuff I'd never think of letting my kids do. Mom and Dad would just say they trusted me and let me go.

I'd drive this car all over the farm with kids, you know. We had little roads going back to the woods. One road came up here behind the house and went down south of the house to an old flowing well that was down there. Kids from town would come out, and we'd all ride around in that car.

We made a board we hooked on behind it. It had an axle on the front with a wheel on each side, but didn't have any wheels on the back and these kids would sit on that board and I'd pull them around with that old Dodge.

Bill Burwick helped Marcus Sr. on the farm and became a father figure to Marcus Jr.

We'd take turns riding on it. I usually drove the car and the kids usually got to ride on the board. But this one kid broke his finger, had his hands underneath it, holding on. I don't remember exactly what happened, but he hit something while his fingers were under there.

We had some big times with that old car. It had an old battery in it, so I'd park the car on the hill up here and whenever I wanted to drive it, I'd put it in gear and take my foot off the brake and let it start down the hill. Then I'd let out on the clutch and that's how I'd start it. I can remember that old car sitting here up on the hill for four or five years. It had to have been an eyesore, but Mom and Dad never thought anything about it. Back then you just kind of let things go, more than you do now.

This well was down by the south pit behind that old cemetery. I think they might have drilled for gas there at one time. They didn't hit any gas, but they hit water and it still flows. Water comes up out of it all the time.

I'd drive down and sometimes we'd stop and go over and get us a drink of water. It was "old school" to me, but the kids weren't used to it. They really thought that was something, going down there and getting to drink out of that flowing well. Even now, someone will ask me, "Is that old flowing well still down there?" "Yeah, it's still there." (*laughs*) I haven't had any water from it for a long time, but it's still there.

Leith Adams: So, Bill would talk about some of the people who brought their cars to Swoveman's garage. Was there an FBI office in Marion?

MW: I couldn't tell you. I don't know. For some reason they brought their cars into that garage to be worked on. There were some,

I guess what you might call gangsters who used to come in there too.

It was down an alley off of Boots Street, half a block of where Myers Drive-In is now and the railroad depot. It's not down an alley anymore because I can drive by on the street and see it, but back when I was a kid, kind of a dead-end alley went down to it. You couldn't see it for the brush and trees and stuff grown up all around, but now you can. The building is still there. Bill thought Nobe Swoveman's was the best place in the world to get anything worked on.

Bill said there were characters hanging around the garage that you wouldn't want to cross. It was kind of a shady-looking place. I always thought it was strange that the FBI brought their cars in and those characters were down there, too. I don't know if any of them were well-known gangsters, but, according to Bill, some pretty mean people were there.

Bill thought Nobe was one of the best mechanics ever. There used to be a restaurant about two blocks away and I remember seeing Nobe Swoveman in there eating. He was always greasy and dirty. He never tried to clean himself up much, but he was a good mechanic. Who has the garage now or whether it's still a public garage, I don't know. It might even be where people store their cars. A house was hooked right onto it. Back where that old car used to sit was a door and if you went through that door, you were in the house. Whether it's still set up that way, I don't know.

One time, Nobe wanted Bill to ride to Indianapolis with him and so he did. They went to get some parts and after they got back to Marion, Bill found out the car they were driving was an FBI car and Bill was upset with him because: "We might have got shot!" (*laughs*)

In 1956, Marcus and his dog, Tuck, enjoy the fresh spring water that flows
from the ground to this day on the Winslow Farm.

Bill really was a second father to me. We went to the circus a couple times when it was in Marion. When I was a kid, he'd always take me with him. We'd go over to Jonesboro to a drugstore there and he'd buy me a Coke with cherry syrup. He got whatever he had to drink too, probably coffee, and he was always buying me peanuts.

A peanut machine was at the drugstore. You never see them anymore, but it was a machine that was glass and it was divided into different sections, probably four different sections. The light bulb inside it kept everything warm. If you wanted peanuts, they'd scoop them out and put them in a bag and the peanuts were always warm.

They had Spanish peanuts which is what I'd always get because they gave you more of those for your money than any of the rest of them, but they also had regular peanuts and cashews and I don't remember what else, but those were the main ones, cashews and Spanish and regular. You'd get a pound of Spanish peanuts for about thirty cents. Now they are over a dollar, probably three or four dollars. That's where I got to eating peanuts.

Bill was quite a character. He was always treating somebody's animals. There used to be a lot of chickens back then, and he'd go out late in the evening. If it gets dark out, you can catch those chickens. When it's daylight, they're hard to catch. He'd go out to the farms after dark and help farmers treat their chickens, whatever they needed. He should have been a veterinarian.

LA: Would you work with Bill?

MW: Not too much. Bill loved working with livestock. Dad had several hogs here at the time and Bill took care of the hogs, and I think he probably helped with the cattle. Dad did most of the cattle, but Bill just loved to do that.

We had this big steel pot in the basement. There are still a couple of them laying around here somewhere, but Bill would put oats in that pot and then he'd put hot water in it and stir it all up. He'd scoop it out and give it to the hogs and, boy, the hogs really went after it. I suppose it helped them gain weight quicker.

I doubt if the veterinarians around here liked him very well because people were always calling him to look at their hogs or cattle if something was wrong with them. He knew as much or more as the vets did if an animal was sick. He'd doctor them some. He had to be careful about what he did because he was unlicensed, but he'd tell them a kind of supplement to get to feed the animals. Dad took care of the livestock some, but he was never as interested in it as much as Bill. I

imagine Dad really missed Bill after he left to live with his son.

Bill probably told me how to treat the animals, but I don't remember what he said now. I know he used to castrate a lot of hogs and cattle. Didn't bother him any. Like I said, he was kind of a second father to me. And I'd say I did a lot for him. When he was living here in the trailer, the role kind of reversed. Instead of him looking after me, I'd have to look after him.

I'd take him to the doctor and I'd take him to the grocery. I used to get so aggravated with him. He'd want to go to the grocery store, so we'd go in and he'd only buy two or three things. Then, well, he'd want to go to a different grocery because they had something on sale. We'd go there and he'd get whatever he could get there that was on sale. Then he might want to go to another one. Of course, I don't think he had much money. Probably all he was living on was Social Security, but he sure did make it last.

I have a .30 caliber carbine rifle that Bob Burwick gave to Bill for me. Since Bob was a career Navy man, he knew how to get ahold of stuff, so he had this carbine rifle and Bill saw it and said it would be perfect for me. It's a nice gun.

I haven't shot it for years and years, but Bill also gave me a bunch of ammunition for it, that old Army ammunition that supposedly had more kick to it than regular ammunition. When Nick Adams came here, he was all interested in that gun, wanting to buy it, but I wouldn't sell it to him. I still have it.

LA: Did you hunt?

MW: I used to target practice, but I never hunted a lot. I remember when Dad and Jimmie used to go out rabbit hunting. They'd shoot a rabbit and bring it up and Mom would fix it. I don't ever remember eating rabbit myself, but I do remember them eating rabbit.

I remember them going out and then coming back. It was always in the winter and cold. They were always all bundled up, but I just never... (pause) ...I got pretty good at shooting at targets. I did shoot a lot of sparrows with a BB gun. Last time Jimmie was home, he bought me a BB gun up here at the Western Auto store. Sparrows are a bird, but they're a trashy bird. I never had any desire to shoot deer or rabbits. I don't know. It just wasn't anything I wanted to do.

As I was growing up, we always had several guns around. Dad had two or three shotguns that have always been here. He had a rifle and old Bill Burwick had a real nice Mossberg rifle that he sold me before he moved away. I still have it. I have a couple of handguns, but I never do shoot them. Dad's brother had a Colt .45, an Army model, 1911 model. It's always been around the house, and I used to shoot it some when I was a kid, but I haven't shot anything for years. I just don't have any desire.

That old carbine probably hasn't been shot since I've been married and that's over fifty years. It's a real nice gun. It's not worn bad and it has a real nice stock on it. Some people want carbines, but I wouldn't sell it just because of the way I got it. I keep it for sentimental reasons, but I have no desire to ever shoot it again.

LA: The reason you didn't eat the rabbit, was it because you liked rabbits?

MW: I don't remember. I was small when Dad and Jimmie would go out and hunt. I don't know why I never ate any at the time. I guess it was just the way I was brought up. I ate chicken and pork and beef, but never had

any desire for any wild animals, wild turkeys or pheasant or rabbits. I don't know. As long as there are other things to eat, I guess I would rather eat that. A lot of my friends, they like lizards and all that stuff. I just don't care for it. I can't stomach it.

Bill Burwick also gave me the first dog I ever had, Tuck. That's the old black and white shepherd dog in the pictures with Jimmie. All the movie magazines put down that Tuck was Jimmie's dog, but it wasn't his. It was mine. Bill bought him and gave him to me. He bought Tuck for himself, but the dog took up with me. He stayed over at the house all the time, so Bill said, "I might as well just give him to you."

Bill had two dogs, two little brothers. He bought those pups at the same time and he named one of them "Nip" and the other "Tuck." (*laughs*) Nip and Tuck. Nip got run over by a school bus when he was fairly small and that left Tuck. Tuck was hit a couple of times by cars, but it didn't kill him. I think Tuck was thirteen when he finally got run over by a car out here.

At one time, we had a big dog that was half German Shepherd and half Saint Bernard. Bob Pulley gave her to us, nice dog. Heidi was her name, but she got hit by a car. This dog we have now would be dead, too, if we didn't have an electric fence out here. I don't know why, but dogs seem to think there's something on the other side of the road that they've got to have. They go over there into that field and when they come back across, they don't pay any attention. They go right out in front of cars.

LA: Would Tuck live in the barn?

MW: Some. I tried to keep him in the house when I could at night, but he usually wanted to go out. He was an outside dog. Sometimes

I would get him to go upstairs and he'd lay there beside my bed on the rug, but it wasn't uncommon to wake up in the morning and he'd gone downstairs and Dad had let him out.

LA: Did you have him when Jimmie was still in the house?

MW: Yep.

LA: So, Jimmie knew him?

MW: Yeah, I think Bill got those two pups in probably 1946 or '47 or somewhere in there. Jimmy was killed in '55, so Tuck was seven or eight years old when Jimmie died. That dog was just like a brother to me. He just wanted to be around me all the time.

That wall going around the house, it used to be you could walk on it from one end to the other. This Tuck would jump up on it and wouldn't let me go all the way around because it started to get high. When you got to the west end, the wall got taller than it was at the east end, and Tuck would jump up and just sit down. I'd pound on him to try to get him to move and tell him to get out of the road, and he wouldn't move. I didn't realize it at the time, but he was doing it so I wouldn't walk down there on that high part. He wouldn't let me go any further.

He was a good dog. He took a liking to me for some reason and, you know, he was my dog. After Jimmie was killed, magazines began writing articles about him saying this dog was Jimmie's old dog. I always took offense at that, because he wasn't Jimmie's dog. (*laughs*) He was my dog. But I got over it, you know.

Jimmie liked animals. When Dennis Stock was here with Jimmie in February of '55, Tuck remembered Jimmie and Jimmie remembered him, so Tuck followed him eve-rywhere he went and Dennis took a lot of pictures. When they got published, under the pictures it said he was Jimmie's dog.

To start with, I kind of didn't like it because it was printed in magazines, "James Dean and his dog" and this and that. Somebody said to me, "Look at it this way. Look at all the attention Tuck's getting that he wouldn't be getting if they knew Tuck was your dog instead of Jimmie's." This was when Tuck was still living, and I said, "Well, yeah, I suppose so."

Then on my fourteenth birthday someone ran over him out here on the road at night. A friend of ours, another local neighbor, came up and said, "I think your dog got hit out here." We went out and he was...of course, he was dead, and that was just like losing a brother. I was just sick over that for quite a while.

I told you he used to come upstairs and sleep on the floor. He never got on the bed or anything, but he'd sleep on the floor by me part of the time. That was back when farm dogs were farm dogs. They'd sleep in the barn or whatever. We let him sleep in the house a lot, just because he was my dog.

The little dog we have now we take to a groomer every two weeks and get his hair cut. He gets a bath and you never did anything like that years ago with your dogs, those old farm dogs, but you still got attached to them.

I built this wooden box to put Tuck in and nailed boards on top of it and I buried him by the pit behind the barn. It was a traumatic experience for me. I've forgotten how I got him out there. I dug the grave myself, buried him and covered it up. Made a cross to put there. I know I was upset.

LA: Were your parents with you when you buried him?

MW: I think Dad asked me if I wanted him to help me, but I said, "No, I'll do it." I did it by myself. He was a good old dog. He was a Shepherd, an English Shepherd, black and white, had a white stripe down his nose. We've had several dogs since then, but I've never had one I liked as well as him. That's just life.

LA: Would Tuck do chores with you?

MW: He'd go out with me. You had to watch him, because he wanted to run after the cattle and nip at their legs. They'd kick at him. He had a big bump on his nose where a cow had kicked him, but, yeah, he'd do anything. He'd jump in the truck with you and ride around. After Jimmie died, well, then of course, people came here taking pictures and they'd want to take pictures of Tuck. Bill Burwick really got wound up when they started putting in magazines that Tuck was Jimmie's dog.

LA: You said Tuck would be swimming on Jimmie's back.

MW: He'd swim over and put his legs up on top of Jimmie. I don't know what he was trying to do, but he'd push Jimmie under the water and (laughs)...

LA: So, this would have been when Jimmie was sixteen or seventeen?

MW: Yeah, it would have been not too long before Jimmie went back to California. I heard Dad and other people talking about it. I don't remember actually seeing it. I might have, Tuck swimming up to Jimmie and kind of jumping on Jimmie's back and Jimmie trying to get him away.

LA: Tuck sounds pretty special.

MW: He was. He was a special dog.

LA: Since he'd been Bill's dog, would he go to Bill all the time, too?

MW: He got so he did. He'd go back and forth some. Of course, that's probably how he got killed. He'd go out on the road, running down the side ditch, but, yeah, he'd go over and see Bill in his house around the corner, but he spent most of his time over here.

Like I say, he was an outside dog. He'd come in the house occasionally, if I tried to get him in, but you couldn't count on him being there every night. If he had something else he wanted to do, why he'd do it.

James Dean: Wary.

14

The Photographers, Photographs & Movie Magazines

Marcus Winslow: We became acquainted with another guy who claimed to know Jimmie in New York and he got to be real good friends of ours, but we figured out before he died that he really didn't know Jimmie. One thing I've noticed about Jimmie, I really think he had a lot of people he was acquainted with, but they didn't mingle together. I mean he had friends that dealt with cars and race cars, but they didn't know any of the friends that he acted with and vice versa.

He had certain little groups he was acquainted with, but they didn't know people in the other groups. I always thought that was kind of strange, but that's the way it was. Maybe that's common in show business. I don't know.

Leith Adams: It seems like with him, he was interested in so many different things. He wanted to learn how to play the piano, so Leonard Rosenman taught him how to play the piano. Next thing you know, he has Leonard Rosenman working on *East of Eden.*

Then Lew Bracker was a car man, so he knew the car people, but then again Roy Schatt and Dennis Stock were photographers and Jimmie learned photography and became friends with almost every photographer that ever took pictures of him. Sid Avery talked about how he loaned Jimmie his camera on *Giant,* so Jimmie was taking pictures of Elizabeth Taylor on the set in Texas.

MW: Oh, was that his camera?

LA: That was Sid Avery's camera. I think Jimmie was learning so much about everything there was to learn that there was no way those people could ever mix.

MW: Yeah, he seemed to be very anxious to learn everything he could. Like you say, he had Roy Schatt in New York and Frank Worth in California and Sid Avery and Sanford Roth. I've always felt very fortunate that Jimmie had his life captured on camera as much as he did. Roy Schatt got a lot of his New York life, and Dennis Stock got some of his New York life and a lot of shots of his apartment there that no one else ever did, that I know of.

Also, Dennis Stock took a lot of photos here in Fairmount, at the high school and uptown in Fairmount and out here on the farm. One or two photographers did a lot of shots on the set of *Giant* and, of course, Sanford Roth was with him the day he was killed. I've always thought there was kind of a reason for everything, you know.

An artist sees things a lot of people don't see. They have an eye for it and a good photographer or a professional photographer, they're like an artist too. Some of them who got acquainted with Jimmie saw something in him a lot of people didn't see. And Jimmie never took a bad picture that I've ever seen. He was very photogenic and apparently knew when he was being photographed, too. He kind of played to the camera. People saw it on the screen. Fans definitely saw something special on the screen.

LA: You saw the magic up close. He played trains with you and stuff like that.

Jimmie and his friends on the roof of New York's Museum of Modern Art. Leonard Rosenman, composer of the scores for *East of Eden* and *Rebel Without a Cause*, is bottom right.

MW: Yeah.

LA: It's easier now to talk about him, isn't it?

MW: No, it's kind of sad to talk about him. It shouldn't be after sixty years.

LA: Still sad?

MW: Yeah, it's like it was just yesterday. It doesn't seem like it was sixty years ago, but that's the way it is. I feel fortunate I was as close to him as I was.

LA: When Dennis Stock and Jimmie came back, you're not in a lot of photos, but you're in some of the photos.

MW: Oh, yeah. I'm in several of them.

LA: Did Dennis Stock ask you to be in those photos, or was it Jimmie, or do you remember how you ended up in them?

MW: I don't really remember. I imagine Jimmie got me in most of them because when I'd get home from school, a lot of times he'd be here. He and Dennis were going to go to town for something and he'd want to know if I wanted to go with them and I'd say, "Yeah, I'll go," and we'd go to town.

Jimmie helps Marcus assemble his toy car in the Winslow living room.

One time in particular I remember, we were walking down the street and someone hollered at Jimmie and Jimmie turned around and waved at them and Jimmie said, "Who is this?" I knew who it was and I told him. (*laughs*) He'd forgotten who it was. Once he knew who they were, he knew who he was talking to, but he didn't recognize them when they'd seen him.

Mom used to kind of be like that. There'd be some fan here and then they'd come back maybe five years later. They'd come up and start talking to her and she'd say, "Oh, yeah," and then when they'd leave, she'd say, "Who was that?" (*laughs*)

Dennis took three or four pictures of Jimmie and me standing in front of a place downtown called Everett Corn Auctioneer.

"Everett E. Corn" is on the window and "Auctioneer." We were standing there because Bill Beck came by and he knew Jimmie and they were talking.

I remember when some of the pictures were taken, especially the ones here in the house, the dinner Mom fixed and Grandma and Grandpa Dean coming out for it, that's when Jimmie had the tape recorder and tape-recorded Grandpa Dean. That's where I have my fingers over my ears when Jimmie is playing the drums.

There were several photos of us during that time. There is a picture of Jimmie and me and Tuck. Grandpa Dean is in the picture, too. It was taken out here. Jimmy and I and the dog were in one picture and then there were a couple of pictures of just Jimmie and the dog and Grandpa Dean in the background. There's the picture of Jimmie shoving me down the hill. There are one or two pictures that haven't been published much. He and I are pulling that car with a rope, pulling it back up the hill and there are some pictures in the basement where he's going to work on my bicycle.

An old Victrola player was down there and it was an Edison. You cranked it up on the side and then it had big thick records that played on it. Jimmie used to play them some and I did too when I was a kid. He cranked that thing up and played with it a little bit that time when he was home.

Also, he went up to the Western Auto Store in Fairmount and got me a BB gun and he got me a speedometer to put on my bicycle. I've still got the bicycle and I've still got the speedometer and I've still got the BB gun. He bought that red tilt-back chair for Mom and Dad. They had it for years and years until it just finally wore out. Oh, he bought them that telephone stand I put in the Museum.

Mom had an old table she used to have sitting along the wall there in the dining room and that's what the phone was on. Apparently, Jimmie didn't like it or he thought they needed a new one, and he went over to Marion and got them a stand that has a chair built right into it and a little drawer you can pull out and put pencils and stuff in. It still looks like new and it's in the Museum.

There's a rocking chair, must be almost two hundred years old. Dad talked about it being at least a hundred fifty years old and, heck, that was probably fifty years ago. It's been around ever since I can remember. There are pictures of Jimmie sitting in it that Dennis Stock took.

I always liked that rocker. I used to sit in it a lot. When Mom and Dad were still here, I'd put that rocker on the carpet and then stretch my feet out over the register. The furnace was just underneath it, so most of the heat came from that register. I'd sit there a lot.

LA: The photograph Dennis Stock took of you and Jimmie in the living room, what are you playing with in that photo?

MW: It was a little plastic Jaguar. I'd just gotten it for Christmas. Matter of fact, I got two of them. Two different people bought me these little Jaguars. I suppose one didn't know the other was getting me one, but they were neat little cars. They were plastic, but you had to kind of halfway put them together. They had wheels on them and a motor and seats and things in it that could all be taken out pretty easy. The wheels could be taken off. They had a little wrench you used to put it back together. I think the trunk raised up on it, but I do know the hood would raise up.

Jimmie got a kick out of it because he liked sports cars. He mentioned at the time he had bought a new Porsche. He picked up a magazine while he was here. I'm trying to think of the name of it, *Motor Life*, something like that. It had a lot of foreign cars in it and there was an ad for a Porsche Speedster just like the one he had ordered. He showed us the ad, saying, "Here's a car I've got coming." I still have that magazine, too. It's in the Museum.

Dennis Stock, I think the first time he came back after the funeral was before his first book was released. Or no, it would've been his second book. He put out a book right after Jimmie was killed, didn't he?

LA: I don't know.

MW: Or was it just in Japan? There was a book that came out in '56 or '57 in Japan, pretty nice book, a photo book. The first book I remember Dennis coming out with was *Portrait of a Young Man: James Dean* (Kodakowa Shoten, 1956).

In '77 or '78, I was working down the road at the implement dealer, and Mom called and said, "On your way home, stop by. There's somebody here who wants to see you." I had no idea who it was…and I stopped by and it was him. Had a nice visit and he had some gal with him, his girlfriend, I guess. He said he was doing a book on Jimmie, a photo book. He sent us copies of it, *James Dean Revisited* (Chronicle Books, 1978).

They were driving some kind of a little foreign truck like a Datsun with a camper on the back of it. I don't remember if it had dual wheels on the back or if it was just wide single wheels. They stayed here with Mom for a couple days, a couple of nights, at least. That was the first time I'd seen or heard tell of him forever.

He came back after that in '85 and was here a couple days. It was for the festival, plus he was doing some kind of a documentary for somebody in France. And he was back a couple times after that. I know he was here for the 50th, which would have been in 2005.

Mom and Dad may have had contact with Dennis after the funeral, but if they did, I was never aware of it. As I was growing up, I always wondered what happened to that guy who was here with Jimmie in '55 taking pictures. I didn't even know his name at the time.

In '85 Dennis called me and said he was coming to Fairmount and wondered if we could get together. I said, "Yeah, that would be fine." So, he said, "Well, I'm going to be up at the Historical Museum and I'll meet you up there." He told me the time, and we met.

We went around to the backyard and sat down on a bench and we were talking. I'll never forget it. He said, "I haven't been to Fairmount since Jimmie's funeral." And I looked at him and then we talked a little bit more. I said, "You were here just six or seven years ago." "No, no," he said, "I haven't been here since Jimmie's funeral."

I said, "Well, I'm sure you were." I mean I didn't want to argue with him, but I said, "You were driving a little foreign truck of some kind." I told him what it looked like. Of course, he had a different girl with him this time. I said, "You had a little lady with you and you spent a couple nights up there with Mom." "Ooh, yeah," he said, "I had forgotten all about that."

I always thought it was so strange that he had forgotten about something which I thought would've been important. I don't know. I don't know what the problem was, but I never thought any less of him for it. I just thought, *Jeez, you don't even remember being here?* But he did remember it then, and we didn't discuss it anymore.

One of the people working with him, one of the camera people, came walking out from inside the Museum, and he told them, "I was here." He told them it had been six or seven years earlier. He said he'd forgotten all about it. Anyway, he was here three or four times after that. I always got along with Dennis all right.

LA: When you talked to him, did he ever talk about what he learned from Jimmie? Or how Jimmie affected his life? Did he ever mention that to you?

MW: Well, he told me if he'd never met Jimmie, his photography career would still be where it was.

LA: Really?

MW: He was very jealous of Jimmie.

LA: Really?

MW: Oh, yeah. He just didn't understand why these fans were coming here because of Jimmie. He was very rude to his fans. One fan walked by him and had Jimmie's tattoo on his shoulder or on his arm. Dennis saw it and he stopped him and said, "Hey!" he said, "Come here!" He got him on the back and raised his shirt up and looked at it. He said, "You're stupid!" He was very...I don't know what happened to Dennis. Dennis had some things about him that were kind of cruel.

I think Dennis always liked me real well. Dennis went to France when Warner Bros. sent us over there, and he was here for the 50th, but I also think somebody was paying him to do it. He wasn't just doing it on his own. But he was always very friendly to me. I think he respected our family and especially Dad. I got along with him fine, but some of the fans had no use for him whatsoever. He just could never understand fans coming here because of Jimmie. He told me one time, "You know he was strange, a very strange guy." I didn't say anything. I just let him talk.

Dennis never talked much about his own family—the wife he used to have or his kids. He never mentioned his kids or anything. He never talked about his childhood.

LA: Something I never realized, but a newspaper article when the movie *Life* (2015) came out mentioned that Dennis Stock shot stills on *Rebel Without a Cause*.

MW: Yeah, I think he did.

LA: Have you ever seen any of those?

MW: Mm-hmm. Yeah, I think so.

LA: Are they in Dennis's books?

MW: There might be two or three in some of his books. I don't think his books focused much on the Hollywood part of Jimmie, but there are some that have been printed.

The photos Dennis took of Jimmie here at home and in town in Fairmount and at Jimmie's New York apartment...to me those captured Jimmie's life. The photos where he's shooting scenes from *Rebel Without a Cause*, there is nothing uncommon about them. Matter of fact, I think Jimmie also got Dennis Stock listed as a consultant on *Rebel*. That's the way I've heard it.

I mentioned some of the things Dennis Stock said that I didn't agree with, but he took some iconic pictures here. I've even heard other photographers say they think Dennis Stock's pictures are the best ones of Jimmie. I've always been thankful that Dennis, Roy Schatt, Phil Stern, and so many photographers saw something in Jimmie that a lot of people didn't see. They kind of made it a point to follow him around, so his life is pretty well-documented from the time he hit the Warner Bros. lot for *East of Eden* and from then on, and I'm really thankful for that.

LA: Roy Schatt photographed him in Los Angeles, too?

MW: No, in New York. He and Roy got to be good friends, so they say. Jimmie wanted to learn all he could about photography, and Roy showed him how to take pictures and loaned him cameras.

LA: So, the photographs of Jimmie with a camera in New York, they're of him with Roy's cameras?

MW: Probably. I think Jimmie liked Roy awfully well because Roy was willing to take the time to show him some things. I don't know. I don't know how Jimmie packed so much time into such a short life. He became familiar with so many photographers and people in other professions than what he was doing. And he was interested in them. I just don't know how he packed all that into such a short period of time.

LA: Can you talk about when you met Sanford Roth?

MW: I never met him.

LA: Oh, you never did?

MW: Never met Sanford Roth. Never met Beulah Roth. I talked to Beulah Roth on the phone three or four times, but I never did meet her.

LA: Did she try to sell you the photos?

MW: No. One day I got this big box in the mail and I thought, *What in the heck is this?* I opened it up and it was the first book that she had put out on Jimmie. Nice big book, white cover, a tall book and about this wide. It just said, "James Dean" on it. And she sent it to me. Why, I don't know. I don't know if somebody talked to her and told her she ought to send me a copy or what. Anyway, she did. Really a nice book. (*James Dean*, Bahia Verlag, 1984).

I suppose that was in the early Eighties. I was working out on State Road 26, I remember, when I got it. That's how I'm putting two and two together to remember the time. Every now and then, I see one advertised on eBay, a used one. Her phone number must have been in that book or on a card, because I called her and thanked her for it. And she and I talked a couple times after that.

It was Seita Ohnishi, a Japanese guy, who got to her shortly after I became acquainted with her. He offered her, this is what I've been told, $250,000 for the negatives and the copyright. He also got a drawing Jimmie had done that she had somehow gotten. In the pictures of Jimmie taken at Sanford Roth's house, there was a little mannequin and he got that. This mannequin is sitting on a dresser or something and Jimmie is leaning against it, has his arm around it.

Beulah Roth died not too long after the sale. At that time $250,000 was worth a lot more than it is today, but Ohnishi has done two or three books...photo books of Jimmie from the Sanford Roth pictures. I also think he has licensed a lot of them to other people for various projects they were doing.

LA: How did he contact you about the photos?

Man with a camera.
Jimmie poses Martin Landau.

Rebel With a Camera.

MW: He…or probably his representative in San Francisco…emailed Mark Roesler and said Mr. Ohnishi wanted to give me the Sanford Roth photos and negatives. I think his health was deteriorating and he was going to retire, which he did do, and I think he wanted it all to go to Jimmie's family. That's what I think.

LA: Have you gotten the negatives yet he promised you?

MW: No, I don't know what's going on. I can't seem to find out anything. When I was in Japan last time, which has been a year ago this past April, he said, "I'll get everything together and I'll send them to you." He wanted me to have the negatives.

Ohnishi made up a contract. It was his contract. It wasn't ours. And he sent it for me to sign, and I signed it and we sent it back. We were supposed to give Ohnishi a certain percentage of anything we made off the Roth photos…which probably wouldn't have been very much. But, whatever, that's what the contract said. I was supposed to be getting that little mannequin, too, and that picture Jimmie had painted.

And Ohnishi never did send anything. He's already assigned the copyright to me because that's in the contract. I have a contract and CMG (Curtis Management Group) has a contract and he has a contract, and he wrote the contract out. He says he's assigning—I think it was September 30 of last year (2015)— everything over to me. I don't know what the deal is. Nobody can seem to find out. I don't know if he's had second thoughts or if he just can't stand to part with them.

188

Mark Roesler did contact Ohnishi's guy in San Francisco about two months ago to see if we had done something to upset him. He said he didn't think it was anything like that, so I don't know. I can't seem to find out anything.

We had an interpreter when we were in Japan in April last year who has been dealing with Ohnishi's people some. Ohnishi had this great big box. It was full of photos and things from some press organization he'd bought out. I forget what the story was on that, but a lot of nice 8 x 10 photos were in there.

Mark says they're not worth anything, but there may be other things in the box besides photos, I don't know. Photos were the main thing we saw, and Ohnishi wanted me to have those, too. He had all these brainstorms of how we could make revenue off of them. Mark says, since the internet, everything is out there, and the stuff isn't worth anything, but we agreed to take it just to make Ohnishi happy.

It's going to cost over $8,000 just to ship back that box, but we were willing to pay the $8,000. We figured we'd do something with it, even though we really didn't want it, but things have come to a standstill. Mark says, "I'll go over there, if I have to." And I said, "You can't go there and just take them away from him. He has possession of them, even though he signed the rights over to us." I don't want to cause Ohnishi any trouble, so I don't know what's going to happen.

LA: And the only person Mark has talked to is the representative in San Francisco?

MW: See, Ohnishi doesn't speak English, plus he's not at his place anymore, either. He has this bottled water place in Kobe, and we had to take a train about two hours from Tokyo to get there. He may still live in Kobe, but our interpreter said he went to see him this fall about making arrangements to ship

this stuff, and Ohnishi was not at his office anymore. We always met him at his office. It was three or four flights of stairs up from the ground floor. His help told the interpreter Ohnishi retired, but whether he's retired or whether he's sick, I don't know. He's a hard bird to catch or get hold of. Seemed like a nice guy. I don't know what his problem is.

LA: And he's pulled the funding for the memorial up at Cholame?

MW: Well, he hasn't pulled the funding. It's just there hasn't been anything done recently. That was another thing, he was supposed to be giving me the responsibility for the memorial, which I am willing to do. We have looked into getting liability insurance for it, so if someone falls or gets hurt on the property, we're covered, but since he kind of stopped doing what he was supposed to be doing with the photos, we've stopped our part on the memorial. If things go ahead, we'll go ahead and get some insurance on it.

There's a guy that lives within an hour and a half from Cholame who used to go to the memorial a couple times a year and he's agreed to go more often and pick up trash there and also up the road at the wreck site. Lee Raskin seems to think he can get a Porsche Club involved, and they would kind of pick up trash and stuff around the wreck site. He thinks that would be a project for them, but I don't know. Everything has just come to a standstill. I still think we'll get the photos and negatives someday, but what can you do?

LA: Yeah, Ohnishi is a long way away. So, he didn't ship you that box of still photos?

MW: Nope, when he quit talking to us, why, we quit thinking about shipping that stuff back. We didn't want it anyway. When we

Roy Schatt

From the "Torn Sweater" session—James Dean: Legendary.

Roy Schatt

James Dean: Help me.

Roy Schatt

At a party with friends in New York, Jimmie plays his Conga.

Roy Schatt

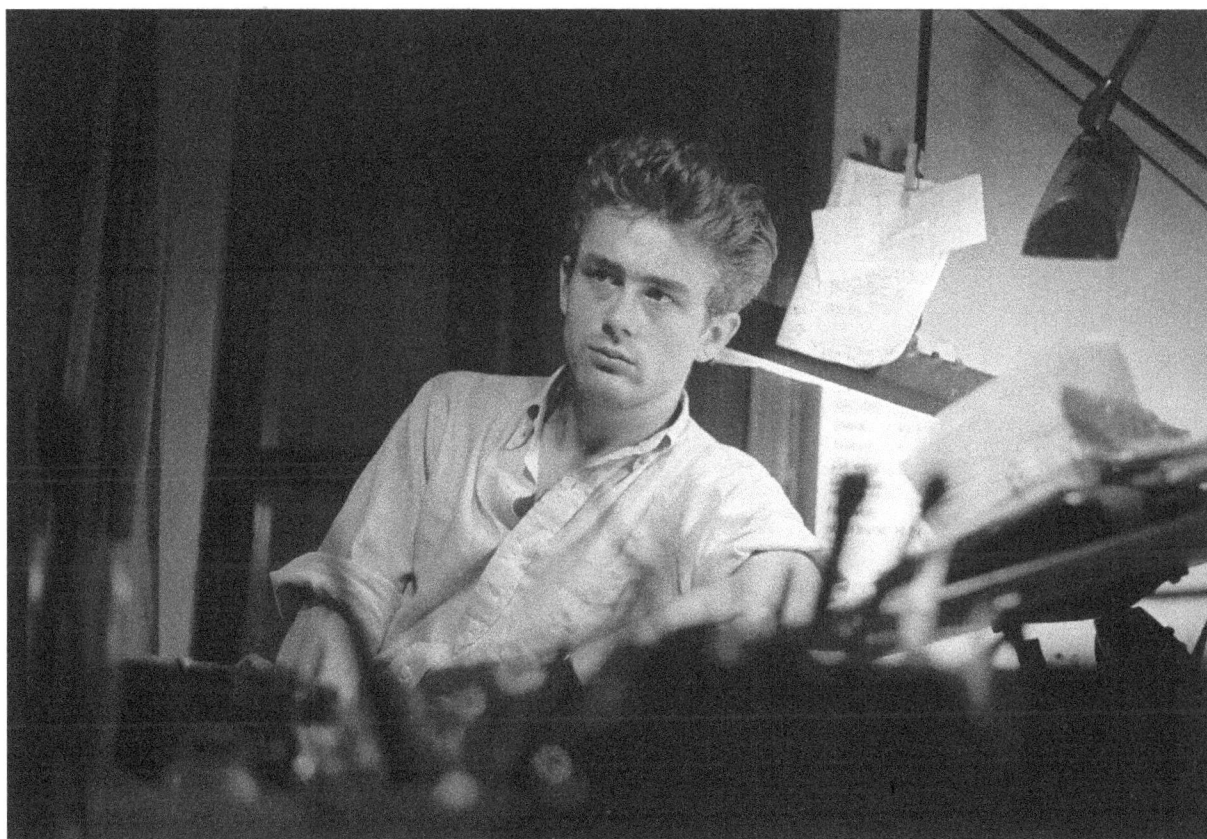

Just a Midwestern kid.

Roy Schatt

Jimmie's New York Exit.

made the deal with him, he wanted to know if we had any objections to a university in Japan keeping some of the pictures, not the negatives or anything, just photos that were made off of some of the negatives.

We said that was fine with us. Now whether the university got to him and talked him out of letting the photos and negatives leave the country, I don't know. Maybe that is what's happening. I still think we'll get them someday, but I'm not as sure as I was a couple months ago.

LA: Can you talk about meeting Ohnishi?

MW: Mark Roesler and I went to Japan to visit him. By the time we got on the train in Tokyo and rode for two or three hours and got off the train in Kobe, it took a day. When we went the first time, Ohnishi had transportation there to pick us up. The second time we took a taxi and had to find the place ourselves, but it wasn't too hard. I recognized some of the area after we got there. And then on the front of the building was "Kobe Water," and I told Mark, "There it is. There's the building."

Across the road from it, he had a business of some kind. On that first visit, one of his helpers took us to see it. I don't know what you'd call it, but in Japan it is common. It was a place for men mostly to sleep overnight. There were kind of little cutouts in a wall where they'd crawl through this wall and back into a bed. I didn't understand it all, but that's what it was. Upstairs there was a big sauna. It was interesting.

We went out for dinner that first night with Ohnishi. He had a cook come all the way from Tokyo to cook us a special meal. I felt bad because I didn't care much for it. It was sushi, and I don't care for raw fish. It wasn't for me, but I gagged some of it down.

He had some other stuff there. Some of it tasted okay, but that raw fish was almost more than I could take.

Anyway, the second time we were there, Mark hired an interpreter who met us outside, and we all went up to the Kobe Water office to meet Mr. Ohnishi. That evening the interpreter invited us to a little club where he and his wife were entertainers. They were singers. That night Mark and I went to McDonald's for supper. The next day we met Mr. Ohnishi again and then took the train back. It was dark by the time we got to Tokyo.

When Mark and I were over there a year ago, he said he wanted to stay in a nice hotel, and I said, "Okay." When we got to it, he said it was the same hotel we had stayed in ten years before when Warner Bros. had the 50th Anniversary.

LA: And Ohnishi put you up there?

MW: No, we paid our own way, all times. Hopefully we'll get something worked out with him someday.

LA: How many Roth pictures are there?

MW: Fourteen hundred, according to Ohnishi. I have photocopies of the contact sheets. He brought me those and gave them to me and that's when he said there were fourteen hundred. Maybe he just decided he doesn't want to part with them. I hardly think it's a matter of him wanting money.

I have confidence we'll eventually get them. If we wanted to go to court, we could show the contract he signed and we could get them. I just wouldn't be interested in doing that unless he died, but according to Mark he's already signed over the copyright.

Ohnishi is different. You can't get around that. I'd like to know what his problem is, but he's gotten honked off about something or else when it comes right down to it, he doesn't want to let go of the photos. I would understand that if he'd just tell us, but he doesn't communicate. Of course, he only speaks Japanese and that doesn't help matters any.

Our interpreter is a heck of a nice guy, and he went back to visit Ohnishi and see about shipping that box. I think he's the one who found out how much it was going to cost to ship. It is a great big box, heavy. You know how heavy paper is. We don't know if he said something to Ohnishi that upset him without realizing it or whether Mark or I… (pause) …I know I never said anything to upset him. I don't know. I don't know. Something's happened. I would never sue him to get those pictures, but they'd be nice to have.

Most of the good ones have been printed time and time again. It's not like these are unknown photos. That stuff is all over the internet. You get on eBay and you can find all kinds of pictures of Jimmie. Now and then you'll see a really unusual one that you don't remember having, but mostly they are common pictures. I sometimes wonder whether there is any value to them as far as money is concerned. Hell, people pirate them and put them on eBay and people print off of there. They may have them for sale, but people like Marlin Wilson print out the images all the time.

What the heck. I may be wrong, but I don't think they're as valuable as they used to be. I used to think if you owned the copyright to this or that, they had to get your permission to use them. Hell, that doesn't mean anything. People just use them and go on. I may have the wrong attitude, but I just don't think the Sanford Roth photos…I'd love to have them just because, but as far as owning the copyright, it doesn't mean a whole lot to me anymore.

LA: Unless someone is doing a watch advertisement or…

MW: Well, yeah, then they'd have to go through CMG anyway. Things have changed a lot. You get on eBay and there's just every picture you can think of on there.

LA: Type in "James Dean" on eBay and all these photos will show up?

MW: Yeah, and most of them are copyrighted, but what can you do? I guess you have to weigh whether letting them do it for nothing outweighs suing them. I don't think they're hardly worth suing over myself. If you had someone put a photo you had copyrighted on an advertisement where it was going out all over the country, then you'd have to sue. I'd say, "Hey, you know you have to pay something for that."

LA: Who are the photographers you have the photos from and own the rights to?

MW: The first one was Roy Schatt, then Frank Worth. He had quite a few.

Then hopefully we'll get Ohnishi's eventually, but, like I say, I used to think the copyrights were really important, which they probably are, but people part with them all the time.

LA: On eBay you can't tell if they're original or copies until you buy them.

MW: They're about all copies. Now and then, you'll see a photo on there that's supposedly an original photo someone took, not a photographer, just a fan somewhere. They are nice to see, but they're not good for commercial use or anything.

LA: And this lady in Marfa, Texas, that was the cook who worked on *Giant*, did you ever contact her about her photos?

MW: No, but there is a lady who took some photos and had them copyrighted, probably half a dozen, and I bought those photos years ago. I bought photos from Bob Middleton. He shot the last four photos of Jimmie in Indiana. He took Jimmie and Dennis to the airport when they left, and he took four different photos in downtown Indianapolis of Jimmie. I bought those off of his estate.

It seems when you license to companies now, they pay a fee for the use of the name and then they want you to furnish photos, so they don't have to buy them, so we don't get much out of the photos, if anything.

LA: During 2015, in the Curtis Management report they sent you, had any photos been licensed or was it mostly film clips where CMG was licensing Jimmie's image?

MW: Mostly clips. I don't know of any photos.

LA: Any products?

MW: Yeah, a shaving company was using Jimmie's picture to promote something. There are some others. I can't think right off what they are, but similar to what we're talking about.

LA: Jackets or anything like that?

MW: Four or five years ago, there was a jacket company in New York that did a lot of jackets with Jimmie's photo inside. They made all different styles of jackets. One of the first contracts we ever had was with the Shad Jacket Company. They made an exact duplicate of the black leather jacket Jimmie had.

I took Jimmie's jacket to New York and they laid it out and photographed it. They said they made it originally. Didn't have a name in it, but they said it was their jacket. Apparently, Jimmie had it made special. One Stop Posters did a poster of Jimmie on the motorcycle, so it was either One Stop or Shad that signed the first contract we had. I think the poster may have been first.

Stetson also had a contract with us. They made a bunch of hats, based kind of on *Giant*. They had Jimmie's picture in them. There were some other styles too, but I guess *Giant* is where the idea came from. And there have been oodles and oodles of tee shirts. I don't think there have been any boots, but one or two companies were interested.

LA: You mentioned a new book of Jimmie's photos coming out.

MW: This Charles Quinn is a heck of a nice guy. I like him. He's always fiddling around doing something. He's on this kick about doing something with the photos Jimmie took at Roy Schatt's place in New York. He put them in frames down here at the motorcycle shop and people seemed to really enjoy them.

Now he's wanting to do this coffee table book. He sent me those pages over there. (points to a stack) He called yesterday and wanted to know how I liked it, and I told him I thought it was pretty neat. A lot of photos need to be cleaned up in there. Schatt didn't take very good care of his negatives, and I don't know if Charles can clean them up or not. I don't know much about what you can do, but he said he knew they needed work. I don't think something like that is going to sell and make him any money, but maybe it would. I don't know.

Frank Worth

Jimmie, uncomfortable, attends a premiere with Pier Angeli.

Jimmie fakes a smile with his girlfriend of the moment, Marla English.

Frank Worth

Jimmie with his last girlfriend, Ursula Andress, at a Thalian's Fundraiser.

Frank Worth

Jimmie and Liz enjoy lunch in the cast and crew tent for *Giant*.

Jimmie horses around with Liz Taylor's stand-in.

Frank Worth

Jimmie relaxes in his new house in Sherman Oaks by playing his Conga.

Frank Worth

Jimmie the photographer gets a close-up of his buddy Sammy Davis Jr. at Villa Capri.

LA: So, the photos Jimmie took were included with the Roy Schatt photos you bought?

MW: Yeah. Whether it will interest other people, I don't know. He thinks it will. Nice guy. When he wanted to display those photos, he asked, "What do you think about putting them in the big barn area and letting people come in and see them?" I didn't think I wanted people coming into the barn like that. I didn't know how many there would be or anything.

I thought about the motorcycle shop. "I know one place you might put them. We might have to work on the building." It was because the floor was falling in. We went in down there and… "I can do that," he said. I told him it looked like a hell of a job to me. "Nah, I can tear those out," he said, "I've torn things up worse than this in New York City and remodeled them, and they made rentals out of them." Boy, he jumped in there. He had the floor torn out in about a day or day and a half. There was a guy helping him. He'd called one of his buddies from somewhere, and he drove down and helped him do it.

I was pretty tickled. He got that new floor down, and it's hard telling when I would ever have gotten to it. It needed to be done. You probably didn't notice the new sign on the building, but we restored that sign. It looks better than it ever did.

When David had his problem there at the Gallery and needed to raise some money, he had a lot of pictures. I had a few photos. I don't remember where I got them now. I said to David, "I'll tell you what I'll do. I'll give you $10 for each black and white you have and anytime you want to copy them, you can."

My original plan was to take the very best ones. I brought them all out here and got to looking through them and I thought, *Aww, shoot! I might as well buy all of them*, and that's what I did. There must have been about four hundred of them. I think I paid him around $4,000 and told him he could copy any of them later, if he wanted to. I found out he had negatives for most of them anyway, since he'd already made copies of them.

That's how my photo collection started and then I just collected photos after that. I'd get them here and there. Marlin Wilson gave me a lot. Anytime Marlin came up with a new picture, he'd make me a copy. A lot of times, we'd look at one of his scrapbooks and if there was something I didn't have, I'd take it and copy it with a copy machine. That's how I made all of the scrapbooks I have. I don't know how many there are. I probably have a couple thousand pictures.

LA: You put them all in three-ring binders with sleeves and all that?

MW: Yep, and I used to enjoy going through them and seeing what I had, but I don't anymore. New pictures still interest me, though. If someone shows me a picture I've never seen before, I'm always anxious to get a copy of it. Marlin likes to sit and go through his pictures. I don't know. I just don't do that, but I'm tickled to death to have all the pictures I have. When we bought the Roy Schatt pictures, I think there were almost four hundred there.

LA: Were the negatives with them?

MW: Yeah. I don't have the negatives here, but yeah, we have them.

LA: So, you have the pictures and Mark Roesler has the negatives at CMG?

MW: I had him make pictures off all the negatives. That's how I got those pictures and the same with Frank Worth's photos. I don't remember how many Frank Worth pictures there were, a couple hundred maybe. First off, Curtis Management chose the best pictures and had them cleaned up and then a few years later, we went ahead and had them all cleaned up so CMG is where I have those. And Marlin got copies of that whole collection of Richard Miller photos. Of course, they were Xeroxes made from proof sheets.

I have a lot of photos, a lot of Warner Bros. shots from the movies. I enjoy the candid shots more than the movie shots, but out of all three movies, I enjoy the candid shots from *Giant* more than any of them, maybe because they were the last ones taken of Jimmie. I just like the *Giant* stuff. It's not my favorite movie especially, but I do like the story. Of course, I've been able to get some of the things that were in the movie, too, you know.

LA: Can you talk about how you got James Dean's Warner Bros. legal file?

MW: Oh, I got that at an auction. I don't remember which auction company it was now, but an auction company in Los Angeles sent me a catalog, and they had Jimmie's original contract with Warner Bros. It was one item they had in the auction and the other was a file that had a lot of carbon copies of studio memos and so forth. I remember I won the bid on the contract, which I felt like we should have. I probably paid too much. I paid $16,000 for it, if I remember right.

Those memos, there were a lot of them, but I don't remember what I had to pay for them. I want to say $3,600 dollars, but I also want to say $14,000. I don't know why they both seem to ring a bell. That was years and years ago. I could have told you at one time without question how much it was.

I do know the contract was $16,000, but whatever the legal file was, I was glad to get it. I don't know that the contract is valuable to anyone else as far as the monetary value, but I felt it was important because it was part of the history of Jimmie. The contract has his real signature on it, and I thought it was necessary that we have it. It's in the Museum too. Some of the memos are also in the Museum. As more things come up for display, I've taken out a lot of the memos because I don't think they're as interesting as some other things. They're interesting to me, but to the average fan, I don't know if they are that interesting. I think different people are interested in different things.

LA: We talked about the movie magazines for a little bit. Was there a store in town where you could buy movie magazines?

MW: Yeah, this old lady and her daughter had a newsstand in Fairmount and they sold a lot of magazines. That was before all these other stores had magazines. You could pay your light bill in there or even pay your gas bill. Things aren't that way today, but I'm talking from the mid-Fifties up until probably 1970.

The ladies represented the gas company and the light company. I suppose they got some kind of a percentage for doing that. If you wanted your electricity turned off, that's who you contacted. All they were was a go-between. Of course, they didn't do any repair work.

When Jimmie started being in a few magazines, Dad asked them if any time a magazine came in that had Jimmie in it to save him a copy. That's how he got a lot of movie magazines and stuff. Today, I don't think

Robert Middleton, Jimmie's childhood friend, snapped this shot in Indianapolis at the end of Jimmie's last visit home.

Mom and Dad would like what magazines have become, not that I like it either, but I'm more hardened to that stuff than I used to be.

When magazines started putting out stories saying Jimmie had a death wish and all kinds of crazy things, those stories really hurt Mom and Dad and they finally refused to give interviews. But it wasn't until several years after Jimmie's death when they quit. For years they did give interviews.

I don't know if someone wrote something offensive about them or what, but I know their feelings were hurt over the simplest little thing, if it wasn't the truth. Today that's a common thing. I know their feelings were really hurt over stuff the magazines said.

Some said things about Uncle Winton, that he didn't like Jimmie and that he didn't want Jimmie, which just wasn't true. So, I can sort of see how Winton and Ethel were upset too. I guess that's all water over the dam now.

It used to bother me a lot too. It still does, if it's very offensive. Anymore, I've taken the attitude, you can't control it. You can't control what people write in books and things they say. That's out of our hands, so I just kind of shrug it off and go on.

Joe Hyams came here in about 1990 and he brought Lew Bracker with him and he was going to write a book on Jimmie. I was a little skeptical, I admit, though I didn't have any reason to be. I didn't know him that well, but I just had a gut feeling he couldn't be trusted.

When he was here, Lew Bracker kept having to correct things. He'd make a statement about this or that and Lew would say, "No, that's not the way it was." It was pretty obvious to me that Joe Hyams… something had happened to him. I don't know what. It was like he'd had a stroke and lost part of his memory or something. He just didn't seem to remember anything. I could easily tell his memory wasn't very good on Jimmie. I thought, *Boy, it's hard telling what this book is going to be.*

Well, he put out in a book that Jim DeWeerd had told him when he was in Fairmount for that article for *Redbook* that Jimmie and he had had some kind of sexual relations and so forth. I know that's not true, because Jim DeWeerd was a very highly respected minister here in Fairmount and had he told that to Joe, and it had been printed in a magazine, it would absolutely have ruined his career. I mean things back then were even more taboo than they are today.

He might get by saying something like that happened today, but you're not going to

get by saying something like that happened back in 1949 or '50. I just knew it wasn't true, and when Joe's book came out, a couple of Jimmie's high school friends were really upset because Joe had in the book that Jim DeWeerd would take Jimmie and some of the other boys down to Anderson, I believe it was. I never read the book. I'm just telling you what I've been told. He took the boys down to Anderson to a place to swim, and they all swam in the nude. Bob Pulley was one of them. Bob went with them and he said, "Yeah, we did. We used to swim in the nude all the time." He said, "Nothing ever happened that shouldn't have. That's the way they used to do back then."

Anyway, whatever, I was pretty upset with Joe over some of the stuff he wrote, but what can you do? You can't do anything. I felt bad that Joe, more than being upset over him writing something that wasn't true, I felt bad that he supposedly was a friend of Jimmie's and knew Jimmie and fifty years later, he writes a book about him and has stuff like that in it that is not true.

LA: Did you ever talk to him?

MW: No, but someone else did. I don't remember who it was, but someone else told him I wasn't very happy with it. I don't know what it was now. I don't remember now, but something came up at Curtis Management and they went to Joe Hyams to get information and Joe said, "I wish you'd pass along to Marcus that I helped you out." It was somebody from CMG.

He and Dennis Stock were real thick and Dennis stayed with him when he'd go to Los Angeles. Dennis always took Joe's side on anything. For a long time, I was upset with Joe, but I finally told Dennis, "I don't hate him or anything." I said, "He's the one who has to live with it." It wasn't very long after that, Joe happened to pass away, but I just quit being bitter over that stuff. It'll kill you, if you don't.

LA: Did Dennis ever comment about Joe?

MW: Oh, he thought Joe could walk on water. He'd go on and on about how great Joe was. We got in quite an argument about him. Dennis came to France with us when we went for the Cannes Film Festival. Michael Sheridan and his wife and Dennis and I went to supper together one night and somehow Joe Hyams' name came up and, oh, he just thought Joe Hyams was the greatest thing in the world. He and I just about got into a shouting match over it. He liked Joe. I don't know whether he liked him because he let him stay in his house or what, whatever.

LA: Back to the movie magazines, if your dad had the lady saving any magazine with Jimmie in it, did that continue after Jimmie's death?

MW: It did for a while. I can't honestly say it did forever. I don't remember. It might have for a short time after Jimmie's death at least, but I can't say for sure, maybe a year or two.

LA: Did your dad keep all the magazines that he bought?

MW: Yeah, we just kept them around. It's nothing that we... (pause) ...I imagine if Jimmie was still living, it would have been something they were real proud of, but after Jimmie was killed, they were so hurt over his death that I'm not sure that stuff meant anything to them.

LA: That was when whole issues of magazines were devoted to Jimmie.

MW: Yeah, there were some.

LA: Did your dad have any of those?

MW: I think so.

LA: That meant he at least collected them for a little while after Jimmie's death.

MW: Yeah, they weren't all bad. Some of them were pretty nice. I've read some articles in those magazines that were very complimentary. Like I say, Mom and Dad were offended pretty easily. They were very protective of Jimmie, and if the least little thing was said that they didn't think was right, why they were all in an uproar, in an uproar in the sense that their feelings were hurt. They knew there was nothing they could do about it. It's just the way it was.

Jimmie pushes Marcus in his home made Hell Drivers racecar in February 1955.

15

Farming & the Winslow Farm

Marcus Winslow: I was only about thirteen or fourteen years old when, one evening, these two young men wanted to know if they could go out and swim in that pit pond behind the barn and I said, "Yeah, you can swim in there." One of them was pretty athletically inclined. At least I thought he was. I probably should have said no, but I didn't and so they said, "Let's go out there and swim across the pit."

I wasn't interested in swimming because I wasn't a good swimmer, but they did and I went there with them. It was about nine o'clock at night, dark. They swam across part way and started coming back and this guy I thought was such a good athlete, he started having trouble. I don't know what was wrong, but he just barely made it back across the pit. I thought, *Man, what would have happened if he'd drowned?*

Possibly two people drowned in there. I don't know who the other one was, but one was Dad's brother, Ren. Dad and Ren both used to swim a lot out there and, later, Jimmie swam there. They had some kind of a board set up that stuck out over the water a little ways, and that's what they'd jump off of when they wanted to jump into the water.

I mentioned Tuck and the story I've been told, which I don't much remember, that Jimmie would jump in to swim and Tuck, he'd jump in too and he'd swim up alongside Jimmie and put his feet on Jimmie's back. (*laughs*) Jimmie had a hard time staying above water when that dog was out there.

Dad's brother, Ren...Dad talked about Ren quite a bit. Dad was always interested in sports and they say Ren was athletic. He was very good in track and baseball and so forth. One time Ren was at the pit with someone. I don't know if Dad was there or not, but Ren jumped in the pit to swim and he never came up. That was back in 1927.

One time a guy stopped in when I was working in Fairmount at the implement store. He was selling something, but I got to talking to him, and he was the guy that found Ren. He'd dive down in the water and he found him and pulled him out. Of course, Ren had drowned.

Oren Kelsey lived about a mile south of us, and he'd talk about Ren quite a bit. They were real close friends. He'd come into the shop, too, and every time he came in, he'd start talking about Ren. And if Dad was there, he'd talk to Dad about it. All I could do was listen, because I never knew him.

Your brother, you're going to be close to him, but Dad and Ren must have been pretty close because Dad spoke a lot about him. It was always something positive. He didn't dwell on it or anything, but he must have thought a lot of him. He's buried down at Park Cemetery with Grandpa and Grandma Winslow.

The strangest thing, here a couple of years ago, I was going through papers I found in the house and there was mention of somebody by the name of Opal, Opal Winslow, and they died really young, just a baby, maybe a year old. It said something about their parents were Ancil and Ida Winslow. I thought, *Why, I've never heard tell of that before,* and I asked my sister, "Did you ever hear of Opal Winslow?" She said, "I'd forgotten about it, but now that you mention it, it does seem to me I've heard that name before."

I presumed Opal was a little girl and I wondered if she was buried down there by my Dad's folks and I went to the cemetery and looked and sure enough, there was a stone there, but it was a son and Dad never mentioned him. He died before Dad was born. Dad was born in 1900 and it seems like Opal died in 1897 or 1898, so Dad never knew him, but apparently that was another brother of Dad's. I don't know why he died or anything, but Dad never mentioned him. All the years Dad talked about the family, he never said a word about having a brother who died as a baby, about a year old, a year and a half. O-P-A-L. I just assumed it was a girl. Sounds like a girl's name to me, but it wasn't.

Leith Adams: Then Ren is short for Renfield?

MW: No, that's his name. R-E-N. Ren Winslow. He was a little older than Dad. He must have been closer to the age of this baby that died, maybe a couple of years older. I

always thought that was strange. Dad never mentioned he had a little brother that died, but he never knew him, so maybe that was the reason.

Ren, I think, used to have some track records. I always thought they were state records. I don't know for sure. I never made any attempt to find out, but Ren was really a good athlete. Dad was a good athlete, but apparently Ren was better than Dad. That's what Dad said.

LA: Are there photos of Ren?

MW: Yeah. Ren was taller than Dad, had a longer face. Dad had kind of a round face, sort of like I have. Ren, in pictures, always looked like he was taller. I guess that's the only major tragedy I can think of that ever happened here on the farm.

In the winter kids used to ice skate all the time back here. As far as I know, no one fell through the ice or came close to drowning. Dad was always pretty particular about how thick the ice was before anybody got on it. We'd take a hand drill and drill holes in the ice to see how thick it was. It always had to be three inches thick for Dad. Other people will tell you that's not thick enough, but three inches is what Dad always said and no one ever fell through. It would have been a real tragedy if someone did fall through and couldn't find the hole to get back out. It could happen very easily.

I used to ice skate. Dad used to ice skate. Dad was a good ice skater. He'd done it for years. Jimmie would ice skate out there all the time. Dad had some hockey sticks they used. The kids that didn't have any hockey sticks would just get a limb that was kind of shaped like a hockey stick and use it.

Sometimes I'd take a sled out there and run and jump on it. That sled would really slide on the ice, even if it had a lot of snow on it. Sometimes the pit had snow all over it and you'd have to take a shovel and shovel off a big area to skate on. Other times it'd just be as slick as glass. It was fun to skate back in those days.

I remember looking out our dining room window at the barnyard and we'd have a bunch of cars, maybe fifteen or twenty, on a Sunday afternoon. Kids were back at the pit skating. They'd go clear to the north end and pile up logs and limbs, whatever they could find, and start a fire, so they could skate up to it and get warm. That was just one of the activities before TV came along. Of course, nobody's interested in it now, but they used to be.

A friend, Doug Mann, and I, we tried to skate all the way to Fairmount on the ice... on Back Creek. I don't think we made it, because there were too many places where the ice was soft. Water was seeping through.

As kids, we used to play a lot around the pits and the creek. I guess that's natural. Kids want to play in water. We'd play in the creek, walk up and down the creek. The creek used to have some deep places in it. When I say deep, I mean three to five feet deep and that's pretty deep to be walking in, especially if you're a kid. There are no places in it like that now. It's all pretty even now.

We had a spot just west of the Car Barn here where a couple of logs came out of these two cement foundations and went over the creek. Boards were nailed onto them, so you could walk across there.

The last time the county dredged out the creek, they did away with that bridge and they took those cement walls down. I don't know who put them there. I suppose some of my ancestors must have built them, but it was kind of a bottleneck for the creek. The creek would get narrow where that was and then it widened back out again. We didn't really care that they took them out, but it

eliminated the walk bridge. There hasn't been a walk bridge on it for years and years.

LA: Did you farm with your dad?

MW: Well, I helped him. After Dad died, we rented the farm to my brother-in-law, and he farmed it. As far as me farming it on my own, I never did. I never had time. When I was in the Parts Department, I was busy working there, and that's when the farmers were the busiest. I guess I took my job serious and I just didn't have time to farm. I used to help Dad. I would come here after work and help him out, but I didn't have time to farm on my own.

LA: Living on the farm, did your dad work seven days a week?

MW: Oh, yeah. We always had cattle to feed and every evening you'd gather the eggs. With the hogs, Dad would feed them enough on Saturday to run them through to Monday, but with cattle, you still had to throw hay to them in the winter. Farming, back then especially, was a seven-days-a-week job.

Today, most farmers work hard in the spring, getting the ground ready, planting and spraying, and after the crops get so high, they're pretty well done until fall when they work twelve to twenty hours a day getting the crops in simply because they don't know what the weather is going to do. They try to get the crops in before the weather gets bad.

When I was a kid, we usually were still picking corn at Thanksgiving. If we had a lot of rain, we'd still be picking corn at Christmas. Heck, now they get the corn all in by the first of November. It's just a different world than it used to be.

Now they come in here with big equipment and get the ground ready and plant it and are gone in a day or two. It's just different. If you're not farming a thousand acres today, why, you just about have to have another job somewhere else to supplement your income.

Today you have cab tractors with air conditioners and heaters. When Dad farmed, you sat in the open with maybe a heat houser on the tractor to keep the wind off you. When you went one direction, the heat would blow on you from the motor. When you'd turn around and go back, the cold air blew at you from behind. It was a whole different world then.

LA: What were your first chores on the farm?

MW: I just did whatever needed to be done, probably mowing the yard.

LA: You were about ten then?

MW: I was driving a tractor when I was six. (*laughs*)

LA: By yourself?

MW: Yeah, I might have been driving a tractor even before I drove a lawnmower, but it was just here on the farm, though I wasn't very old when I started driving a tractor on the road.

LA: On the road?

MW: That was when cars didn't drive as fast as today and there weren't as many of them. That's just the way it was. If your dad needed help, you were expected to be there. And if it involved driving a tractor from one farm to another, that's what you were doing.

Dad had an old pickup like this one here in the Car Barn. When I was about fourteen, he sent me to town in it to go to the mill to get a load of feed. I did that without a driver's

license until I was sixteen when I passed my test. I never did get caught.

As long as you were careful and didn't attract a lot of attention, it was pretty safe. If you started racing around town, you'd get into trouble, but I never did do that. I would always take the back road to Fairmount to the mill. Sometimes we'd pull a wagon hauling a load of grain behind the truck. I never did have any problems.

LA: So, you'd take the grain in by yourself?

MW: Yeah, Dad used to farm Grandpa Dean's farm southeast of Fairmount. He'd get a wagonload of corn picked, and I'd take that old Ferguson tractor with the wagonload of corn and I'd bring it here to our farm by myself. That was when you picked corn by the ear, not shelled like it is now.

We had a piece of equipment called an "elevator" set up to unload into, and I'd back the wagon up to the elevator, drop the elevator chute down and start running it, load the corn onto it and unload it into the corn cribs by myself.

When I'd finish, I'd shut the wagon gate, drive the tractor and wagon back over where Dad had another wagonload, and I'd just run it back and forth, back and forth. I did that a lot.

LA: Would your dad ever have Jimmie drive the grain to the elevator?

MW: I don't know if Jimmie ever did or not, but Dad had me do it. I was always cautious. I'm trying to think if Jimmie had died when I was doing that. I might have been twelve or thirteen. I wasn't over thirteen.

LA: Do you remember seeing your buddies at the grain elevator? Were they driving tractors too?

Jimmie with Marcus and his buddies, (l-r) Jack Ratliff, Jim Poe, unknown, Lao Shelton.

MW: There were kids that did, but I ran around mostly with city kids, so they wouldn't be at the elevator. That's just the way it was for the country kids. If you lived on a farm, you worked.

Dad used to have cows, but I never had to milk them. He sold them off when I was real little, probably five-, six-, seven-years old, something like that. Dad milked them, and I assume Jimmie may have helped him. Bill Burwick helped him, too. If you had to milk the cows, you had to be here seven days a week, milking them every morning and every night. I tell you that would get pretty old.

LA: Can you talk some more about your dad farming and how many acres and all that?

MW: On this farm, there are one hundred eighty acres. Dad also rented another hundred acres from his uncle Clinton Winslow, and then he had the fifty-seven acres at Grandpa Dean's. After crops came in, he'd spend the rest of the fall plowing and in the spring, he'd finish what wasn't done. He'd get the ground worked down and then he'd plant it, all three hundred thirty acres, but he didn't have the equipment they have today.

It used to be, after Dad picked all the corn, he'd turn the cattle and the hogs out into the fields and let them clean up whatever the corn pickers left behind. Today the fields don't even have fences around them to keep the livestock in. The fences have all been taken down. It's so expensive to raise crops that the machinery the farmers use don't leave anything in the field, so there isn't anything for livestock to eat anyway.

We're fortunate to have a creek running through the farm, so the cows can get their water from it, and we don't have to water them. Sometimes in the winter, if the water freezes up, we may have to, but as a rule, our cattle just get their water out of the creek. In the summer they can stand in the creek and flip their tails around and get themselves wet. It cools them off. That's not all good because they can get a foot disease from standing in the water, but anyway that's just part of our life.

Dad or anyone else who harvested crops back when whole ears of corn were picked would have to take the crops to the elevator, either to get it ground up for the hogs or just to plain sell it. Dad took it there in a tractor and a wagon, but today's farmers shell their corn with those big combines. They shell it all.

Pretty near all the farmers around here have at least two semi-trucks, like you see going down the highway. That way it doesn't take them long to get the crops out of the field. They'll park their semis with their grain trailers right on the edge of the road because the fields are too soft.

Then they'll go through the field with the combine and when it's full they'll unload into what we call "buggies," big two-wheeled carts. Some are so big they have dual wheels on the back. Anyway, the buggy will drive out of the field to the semi and dump the grain into the trailer, which is built so that the top is open.

When you unload at the elevator, there's a hopper on the bottom of the trailer and it opens up and the grain will all fall to the center and run out. The semis hold, I'd say, eight or nine hundred bushel of grain. It seems odd to see it all when you remember farmers with a little trailer or a wagon to take their grain to town, but that's the way it is anymore.

We take our grain to a town called Matthews about eight to ten miles east of us or down to Summitville which is south four or five miles. There's also a place in Summitville that makes ethanol, but you have to contract with them because they only want it at certain times. If you have storage, you can store it on your own farm and take it in when they're ready for it.

There haven't been any local elevators around Fairmount for ten years probably. They used to grind a lot of feed. Farmers would take their ears of corn in and they'd run it through the grinder. If they were going to use it for feed, then they mixed supplement, maybe oats, in with the corn at the elevator.

Then the farmer would feed it to his livestock, but there isn't any livestock anymore, so elevators just flat out closed down their grinding operations. It's expensive to have the equipment to grind corn. Two things: number one—no one brings in ears of corn anyway, hardly, and number two—the equipment's getting old and worn out.

Very rarely do you see a tractor and a wagon taking grain in anymore. If they do, it's in the great big gravity wagons because the grain is already shelled. And if you harvest soybeans or wheat, why, about all of it gets taken to the mill. Of course, some people do store their soybeans and their corn and wheat and sell it later in the year.

LA: When the price is higher?

MW: When the price is up, yeah.

LA: What if the grain has too much moisture?

MW: If you have a dryer, you need to run it through one and get it dried down. If you take it to the elevator to sell, they'll just dock you so much per point on the moisture. Most farmers have a big grain bin and have a dryer there and if the corn, for example, is not dry enough to store, they'll run it through the dryer and then it comes out dried and goes into the grain bins. If you put it in the bins wet, it will rot.

Every now and then at an elevator, somebody had a log chain or something in their wagon and forgot it was there and dumped it in with the corn and then they'd tear things up. I saw that happen several times, so the elevators now just specialize in selling spray to put on the fields and maybe they have a big special truck they spray with, things like that, but they don't grind feed anymore. They might as well all close up in the winter, because nobody's coming in.

With livestock, used to be there weren't any big feeding floors around. Then you'd hear of someone building a feeding floor to keep their hogs all inside a confined area. The hogs put on weight faster because they weren't in the field walking it off, but these confinement areas are expensive to build and there's an awful lot of odor to them since all that manure has to go down into a pit and they have to pump it out of that pit into a special trailer to take it into the fields and spray it and then you have the neighbors upset because of the smell. It's become quite a battle.

Every time someone builds a feeding floor anymore, the neighbors usually protest. It's gotten so now all the wells and the creeks are being checked for runoff from those things. If you run liquid manure and it gets into the creek, well, you're going to have to pay to have it cleaned. They're real tough on water supplies being contaminated. Back when I was a kid, you didn't have to think of anything like that.

LA: I'm not familiar with farmers using hog manure in the fields. Did they do that when you were a kid?

MW: Well, that's what they had to do with it, put it in manure spreaders and take it out in the field and spread it in the field. There wasn't anything else to do with it.

LA: But when I was a kid, I don't remember the fields smelling.

MW: They don't smell so bad when it's hauled out in a manure spreader because it's fairly dry, but with these new confinement barns, the manure is always wet. They have to suck it out with a big pump into a special trailer or wagon. Then they take it right out into the field and spread it around.

Some farmers now have great big long hoses they hook onto this trailer holding the manure and they'll drag that hose. It might be several hundred feet long and they'll just drag it all over the field and manure will come out of that hose, but, oh, the smell is terrible. They need to get right in there with a chiseled plow and chisel it under. That does kill the smell. Some of them do that, and some of them don't.

LA: Do crops make more money than cows at market?

MW: It's like anything. Some years cattle are fairly high priced and you can make pretty good money off them, and other years they're not. The biggest problem we had here was anyone who wanted to feed out herds of cattle had to buy the cattle and most of the stock came from out west. They'd bring them in big semis. By the time the cattle got here and were unloaded, they were all sick and you'd spend thousands of dollars in veterinary bills keeping them alive. That was a very expensive venture.

And you never know what grain is going to be. Again, farmers today, although they work hard, they don't work like they used to. Once their crops are planted and once the crops come up, like right now, there isn't much to do until you harvest. Sometimes they go out and "side dress" the fields, they call it. They'll spray for weeds or spray more fertilizer on the field, but mostly from spring till fall, a lot of the farmers don't have much to do.

They've gotten used to this and they don't want to mess around with livestock. Some of them claim they make as much selling the grain right out of the field as they do running it through livestock so that's the way they do it.

LA: Let's go back to the combines today. If they shell the corn, do the combines then mulch the cobs?

MW: Yeah, as the cobs go through the combine, it tears them all up and shoots them out the back. You can't even see the pieces on the ground. They're so small.

LA: And that's to re-fertilize the fields?

MW: It helps some, they say. By the time it sits there and rots all winter long, farmers can sometimes go in without a till planter and plant right in the field and not do anything to it. That saves a lot of time and a lot of money in fuel, if you can get by with it. The fields do look a lot better though if they go through with a till planter or a field cultivator.

LA: So, the two fields we saw down the road, the two bean fields, the one on the right had no weeds at all, but the one on the left had weeds. The one on the right, did that farmer plow the field?

MW: No, he didn't plow it.

LA: How does he have less weeds than the…?

MW: Well, he sprayed it. He sprayed for weeds whereas the other guy across the road sprayed some, but he didn't spray enough. That's just his style. He sprays enough to kill the worst of them, but there are always a few more coming up. He doesn't seem to worry about it and when it's all said and done, he may yield just as much as the other guy.

Back when I was young, you didn't have any spray for soybeans and, boy, they'd get to be a mess. What we called "hog weeds" would come up in the fields. You'd have to walk through them with a short pole that had a sharp hook on the end of it to grab onto the weeds and you'd cut them off by hand. Today they don't do that. The combines will run just about anything through them, but if the field has a lot of weeds, you'll get weed seed mixed in with your grain and then you get docked for it.

LA: So, the combines can separate that out?

MW: Yeah, yeah.

LA: What did farmland used to cost and what is it now?

MW: It used to be $2,000–$2,500 an acre was a pretty average price for ground. Now it's $7,500–$10,000 an acre, depending on where the land is.

LA: Are there a lot of corporations coming in?

MW: About all your farms are incorporated now. Farmers incorporate more for protection, I think, than anything.

LA: Tax protection?

MW: No, protection from being sued because of a road accident or something. Incorporating somewhat protects them. Nothing is a hundred percent, but very few farmers anymore don't have some kind of corporation.

LA: What about investment buying?

MW: Yeah, some farms in the past five years have sold to buyers who don't even live around here. They still let local people farm them, but I don't know who these buyers are. I guess that's all right to a certain extent, but if it gets to where they're buying all the ground and farmers can't afford to buy anything, then that's a problem. I don't think it's a big problem yet.

LA: So, farmers can afford $10,000 an acre?

MW: They can't afford it, but a lot of them are paying that. If your neighbor retires or dies and his farm comes up for sale, that will probably be the one time in your life where you'll have the opportunity to buy it. It's one reason the prices go up so high, just to keep someone else from getting that land. Buying ground right close to you, you can't beat it, because moving this big equipment up and down the road is dangerous and it takes a lot of time too. You have to break it down sometimes and haul it on trailers and then put it back together when you get to the field. If you get ahold of land within your area, then you don't have to go out on the roads so much.

LA: So, when you worked in the implement store in the Seventies, what equipment would the average farm have?

MW: All of them had a tractor, a plow and a disc, and maybe a field cultivator and a culipacker, something to break up the dirt clods and pack down the ground. They'd all have combines and something to transport the grain with, usually "gravity wagons," big wagons made out of steel. That's what the equipment was then. We used to sell one of the biggest combines made, and it cost around $40–$45,000. Now you can put half a million dollars into that combine.

LA: Half a million?

MW: Yep. Corn planters and stuff cost tens of thousands of dollars if you add corn heads to go into your combine and grain tables. It's just awful, awful expensive anymore.

LA: How much investment do you need to start out farming four hundred acres, not including the cost of the acreage?

MW: You'd probably get a used tractor and probably a used combine. Used stuff is a lot cheaper than new, but you can also have problems with it. I don't know what it would cost—quarter of a million dollars at least.

LA: You mention the problems with used equipment. Are there still people that can fix those?

MW: Yeah, a lot of the implement dealers that sell certain brands will come out and work on them, but, boy, the parts are expensive.

LA: Now if farmers are driving to some of the grain places around here, do they sell to these grain...are they still called "grain elevators?"

MW: A lot of people still call them elevators, but they're not really. They buy the grain from the farmer, probably for a big grain company. If they're smart enough, they can buy it from the farmers for "*x*" amount of dollars and turn around and sell it right away for a few cents more a bushel. If you have a lot of bushels, that adds up.

LA: Do any farmers drive a hundred miles to sell their grain to get a better deal?

MW: No, they don't usually go that far.

LA: So, they just try and get the best price they can in the area?

MW: Yeah, because it's probably the price it would be anywhere. A lot of people sign a contract with the elevator for "*x*" amount of dollars a bushel for soybeans, for example, and so they know what they're going to get for it. Usually when the harvest season comes around, the price is down. That's just the way it is. Not always, but sometimes.

My farming operation is very minor compared to most others, but I've held grain back and stored it. I don't have any storage here, so right off the bat I have to pay the elevator by the bushel to keep it and then so much a month to store it. Then you have to hope the price will go up enough over the next three or four months to make money on it.

It's a gamble, whether you store it or whether you sell it. We contracted some beans this spring, and the price was pretty good. Prices had been going down some, but they went back up pretty high and that's when we thought, *We'll contract some, and next*

harvest season we'll see. You like to hope you're going to get more for the contracted stuff than what you could've gotten right out of the field, but it's just a chance you take.

LA: On the other end, the buyer is hoping you get less than what the market is going to give?

MW: Mm-hmm, yep. If you contract a certain amount of beans or corn and you don't have enough crops to cover it, then you have to buy grain from somewhere for the shortage.

LA: What happens if you don't deliver the contract?

MW: You have to.

LA: I didn't even think of that part.

MW: Most people don't contract all their grain. They contract maybe half of it, because you never know what the weather is going to do and how much crops you'll have. You hope you have a good crop and you hope you haven't contracted too much.

LA: So last year, when the rains happened and people couldn't get into the fields...?

MW: Yeah, that would have been a bad year to contract.

LA: It is like Las Vegas.

MW: Yeah, it is. It's a risk. If you contract more than you can deliver, you have to work out some kind of a deal with the elevator to buy however many bushels you're lacking. You lose money on every bushel, if that's what happens.

Farming's getting to the point where there just aren't any small farmers anymore. I never thought I'd see this happen, but it did. Everybody that's farming around here now farms fifteen hundred to two thousand acres or more. Some farms even have two or three generations working, and whenever another family member wants to farm, usually they can't just take over where their dad was because there has to be enough income to support more people, so they'll rent more ground.

The little guy can't hardly make it because of the price of machinery. Back in the mid-1970s, you could buy what was the biggest tractor at the time for $10,000–$12,000. That same tractor today costs $110,000–$112,000. Like I said, combines used to cost $40,000; now, by the time you buy the grain table and the corn head and the combine, you might have $500,000 invested.

There was a time, about seven or eight years ago, when farming was really good. Corn was very high. Soybeans were high. And a lot of farmers bought a lot of equipment. Now beans are down. Corn has gone down, but of course the price of equipment hasn't gone down at all.

Fertilizer, seed corn, soybean seed, it's all so expensive. They have to farm a lot of ground to make enough on each acre to keep going. And if they rent ground, they have to be competitive in paying their rent or someone else will take that land. It's a very tough business. Farming has always been pretty competitive, but you have to know what you're doing today to make it and not go broke.

LA: How does renting land work?

MW: Most people pay so much an acre to rent. In other words, the landlord maybe has a couple hundred acres he used to farm, but he's not able to farm it anymore. People may have ground they've inherited and they want to rent it out. Most will rent it at "_x_" amount of dollars per acre and that's the end of it.

I have some ground I rent out and I also have some that my nephew farms, and we farm it on halves. I pay half the fertilizer and the seed bill, and he pays the other half. Then when we sell the grain, he gets half and I get half. I don't know which is the best.

I think most owners like the cash rent, because they know what they're going to get. There is no doubt, and they don't have to pay expenses on the seed and fertilizer. But taxes are going up. I just read the other day where they're trying to get some relief for farmers on taxes because, like I said, land that not too long ago was $2,000 an acre is now $10,000 an acre to purchase. I don't know how anyone can pay those costs and make a living, but they do.

I started buying land back around 1990 and I was paying $1,800 an acre for it. Then I bought some ground for $2,000 an acre. I bought some more and paid $2,100 an acre for that. The last ground I bought, I paid a little over $3,000 an acre. And the only reason I paid $3,000 is the land hooked right onto our farm, and if I didn't buy it then, it'd probably never be available again. There is some land that hooks right onto our farm that I'd loved to have had, but about two years ago it sold for $11,000 an acre.

With farming, and it's always been this way, you can be worth a lot of money, but you don't necessarily have a lot of money. I can't believe the ground I bought for $2,000 an acre is today worth anywhere from $7,000 to $10,000, just depending on how many people bid on it.

The price of land is like anything else. At auction, whoever wants it the worst will keep bidding and bidding and bidding until everybody quits. Owning several acres sounds real good now, but by the time you pay the taxes on it and if you have any buildings on it, well, you have to insure all that, plus you'll need liability insurance. When it's all said and done, there's not the profit you might have thought.

With crops now getting as low as they were a few years ago, and probably staying there for a while, I just don't see how these guys can make it. You have to be willing to be in debt clear up to your neck, something I never had a desire to do. You have to be willing to do that, so I'll probably never own any more ground.

LA: Who paid $11,000? Was he local?

MW: He's a local guy, but he lives closer to Swayze than Fairmount. Actually, two guys bought this ground, three hundred acres or so. One guy bought it all and then turned around and sold part of it to this other guy. I think they planned ahead they were going to do that. Now, they're doing a bunch of ditching and taking out fence rows and that all costs money.

LA: So, they're squeezing more crop acreage out of the land that's there?

MW: Yeah, if you have trees growing in the fence rows, they get bigger and bigger and they hang out over the field, so you'd have to farm out around them. Most farmers won't do that anymore. They just take out the trees and the fences. When I was a lot younger you thought all the big farmers were out west. They had big tractors out there and now we have tractors just as big here.

LA: If a combine costs a half a million dollars, are they renting it out sometimes to try to recuperate some of their costs?

MW: No, not really. If anyone wants or needs help, some farmers, when they get their work

done, might do it to make some extra money or help pay their expenses. But there are also a lot of them that won't do it. Once they get done… well, they're done. And that's one problem.

You have to have good equipment, especially if you farm a lot of rented ground because if your harvesting is not done and you're having a lot of problems getting it in and your neighbor has his all done, the next thing you know your neighbor is knocking on your landlord's door wanting to rent your ground. So, you have to get it in. Gotta get it done. Gotta get the planting done. It's a tough, tough world out there anymore.

LA: Have any of the farm equipment places started renting equipment?

MW: Yeah, a lot of them lease equipment.

LA: But you have to lease it for a whole year?

MW: There might be cases where dealers have a combine and a tractor and they'll lease them for just a year, but most farmers have to lease them for three or four years.

LA: So, no matter what, you have a combine that you use maybe two months out of the year and then for ten months, it's not being used at all?

MW: Yeah, yeah. You would think a couple of farmers would go together and buy and share equipment, but it doesn't seem to work that way.

LA: They all need it at the same time.

MW: Yeah, they all want their own equipment. If there's a farmer that gets hurt or gets sick and can't get his crops in, the other farmers will jump in and help, but as long as you're able to do it, well, you have to do it on your own.

LA: Because if you don't get it in and the weather comes, you're stuck.

MW: Last spring a lot of acres never got planted because it rained so much. It just rained and rained and about the time they were ready to go in and plant, they'd get more rain. I'd never seen that before around here, but a lot of ground didn't get planted. And if they were renting that ground from someone, they still had to pay the rent on it.

LA: It seems to me one of the benefits of owning the land and just taking in the rent is you're not gambling on the weather.

MW: Yeah, that's right.

LA: That always seems to be one of the major problems...quick freeze or rains keeping you out of the fields or rains killing the crops.

MW: The fields can get flooded. That's the reason there has been so much ditching here the last ten years.

The Winslow Barn...2020.

16

The Winslow Farm Legacy

Leith Adams: What do you see happening to your farm down the road?

Marcus Winslow: I don't know. Coy has always wanted to be a farmer. He had a body shop in Fairmount for a few years. The poor kid didn't make any money, because he spent all his time trying to make everything to perfection. He had too many hours wrapped up in everything.

Time after time, I'd be helping him out of one mess or another and finally we both saw it wasn't going to work, so he shut down the body shop and went to work for a Chevrolet dealer selling cars. Boy, he was successful! He sold a lot of cars and a lot of trucks, and I think he made pretty good money. But he kept saying, "I want to help you on the farm."

I didn't feel I had that much for him to do. I had Buttons helping me all the time and I thought, *Hell, I don't have enough for Coy to do.* But my sister and Marylou both said, "You need to make a place for him."

I had to have eye surgery after my eye accident. When I went back two or three years

later because of a detached retina and had to lay face down for ten days or two weeks, Coy came back. I have to give him credit for a lot that's been done around here because I didn't see it, but he saw it. He's done a good job fixing stuff up and repairing things. He's really doing a lot. He is a perfectionist.

LA: What is an average day for Coy out here?

MW: He's liable to be doing anything, absolutely liable to be doing anything. Right now, he's busy trying to get this driveway raised up, so it's more even with the road, and that's been a week-long project. Coy has cattle here on the farm, so he's always busy checking on them or moving them from one field to another. There's something every day you have to do with livestock. And we mow so darn much anymore. When I was a kid, we didn't even mow this barnyard out here. We used to burn it off.

We had an old rotary push mower with steel wheels and a wooden handle on it. I remember it being in the garage and Jimmie getting it out and pushing that thing in the front yard. Dad would do the same thing. I was too little, thank goodness, to have to push it, but I did move it around. It was heavy. That's all we used to do, just mow the front yard up at the house.

Then Dad bought a Bolens Garden Tractor that had two big handles. You walked behind it, and it had this lever you flipped. One lever would make the tractor move and the other one would throw the mower into gear. We started hooking my little wagon behind the tractor, and then I'd put a five gallon can in it and I'd sit on it and I'd drive it. After we did that for a year or two, Dad bought a lawn roller with a seat on it to pull that little garden tractor and, by gosh, I mowed and mowed and mowed and mowed and mowed with that.

Now we're mowing everything around here. We're mowing our side ditches. We're mowing the Back Creek Church property down the road and the parsonage. Next door where Carter's Motorcycle Shop was, we're mowing that too. We're mowing half the yard across the road and now we're mowing down at Dina's (Note: Chuck's daughter's house) and mowing the side ditch all the way. We have a mile on this road where we mow the side ditch, clear from Marker 700 to Marker 800.

Every time fall gets here, I'm always glad to see the grass turning brown and quit growing, but then next spring I look forward to getting on the mower again and mowing. I haven't mowed any this summer. I haven't been able to, but I hope next summer I can

The Winslow Farm...2020.

get back to it. I don't think sitting on the tractor would hurt me. It takes a lot of hours to get everything mowed.

Chuck, our other son, wasn't as interested in the farm. When he was a kid, he didn't want anything to do with the farm, but now he has developed an interest in it and will be working here fulltime. We have a will leaving everything to them equally, but this summer I'm going to have to go against my lawyer's advice and designate who will get what.

Of course, Coy and Chuck will both get equal on James Dean. And I'll try to be as equal as I can on the farm ground, make it so they'll both have about the same income from it. I'll probably leave Coy the house and the buildings here because he stayed here and worked.

I have already given Chuck and his wife their property, their home. We bought a house for them several years ago in Fairmount and tore down a barn, built a nice new two-car garage with a shop on the side of it. He wanted to remodel the kitchen. It needed it, and I thought, *Hell, I can't just keep paying all their bills*. I said, "Why don't Marylou and I just give you this place and you do what you want?" So that's what we did.

Heather and Chuck went to the bank and borrowed money to remodel their kitchen and bathroom and made themselves a really nice home. I'm glad they have it. It's something I don't have to deal with, plus they needed to have something of their own. Anyway, they can't depend on me all their life. Of course, with Coy's house, I've kept it up.

Someday maybe Marylou and I will move into town and let Coy have this place. I'm not sure what we're going to do. Neither of us wants to move to town very bad. We are used to the farm here. I've lived on this farm my whole life. It'd be a big change for me, but I could do it if I had to.

I don't know what the future holds, but we've done the best we can to get things set up so that the two boys will inherit what we have without paying too many taxes. You just never know about that. You think you have things straightened out and the next thing you know, they've come up with this or that and you find you didn't do that good of planning, but we're trying. That's about all I can say. I hope they'll both get enough income to supplement whatever they are doing.

LA: Growing up in the Midwest, I've seen a lot of farms, but there's something about this farm that's different. It's more attractive. It has something to do with the pasture and the pond, also something to do with the house all by itself. It has a lot to do with Dennis Stock's photography when James Dean was here, but it's got something to do with the barn.

MW: I think you're right. I have to admit I've made an effort to not make drastic changes. We built this barn. We built the other barn.

LA: They fit right in.

MW: We didn't just do it on a whim. We did a lot of thinking and went out and looked to see where we might put the buildings. We tried to build them so that they fit in and I think they fit in as good as any buildings could.

I think you're right. The pond and pasture are very attractive to people and the creek going through here. Of course, Coy takes the big tractor out there and mows the pasture maybe once a month. A lot of people wouldn't do that, but he does, so he keeps things pretty neat.

I've tried to keep the house the same, although we did add a sunroom onto the south end of it which, at the time, worried me. We put all new windows in it with spacers to make it look like there were a lot of little windows in the big windows. That's not the way it was when Jimmie was here, but it's what we wanted, my wife and I. She kept emphasizing to me, "This is not a museum. You can't just keep everything the same. This is where you live."

We made a few drastic changes like that, but overall, the house still looks pretty much like it did in Dennis Stock's pictures, except it's in a lot better shape. The same way with the barns, not only because of Jimmie, but I'm just proud of the barns. So many of the old barns on farms have fallen down. They are not practical for modern day farming. You can't get large equipment in them. This big barn over here, we get quite a bit of good out of it, but we'd be better off if it wasn't there and we just had a big pole barn, but I don't want to do that.

LA: The first time I saw the farm, I knew it because I'd seen the photos, but when you look closer, what makes it special is much more than the photographs. It's the way the farm is laid out.

MW: Yeah, it's an unusual layout. It's more of an attractive farm than it is a working farm. We do all we can, but there's no place here to build big silos, if you wanted to store large amounts of grain. I'd have to build them somewhere else because you can't get in and out of here. By fixing the driveway now, that will be a big help, but then the driveway is so narrow, you couldn't get a semi in and out of here.

We have the creek behind us and there are zoning laws about how close you can build to a creek. I like to never got that barn built over there because of the zoning. They didn't want to let me build it. I can't tell you how much money I spent on surveyors and one thing or another. We hauled in about

$10,000 worth of fill. We used fill just to get that land high enough to satisfy them.

LA: So the creek wouldn't flood the barn?

MW: Yeah, there's no way the creek can get in it now. If the creek ever got into that barn, our house would be filled full of water. If I was a farmer and wanted to put up grain bins and have a place to store the combine and all that, I'd have to do it somewhere else. I couldn't do it here, because with the creek behind us, we're pretty well hemmed in. I'm satisfied with what we've been able to do, but we've gone about as far as we can go. I'd like to have another building here for storage, just to store farm implements, if nothing else.

Coy has been baling quite a bit of hay the last year or two. He bought a lot of hay equipment, and we really don't have anywhere to put it. I don't know what we'll do with it this winter. It'll deteriorate if you let it sit outside. It'll rust. And I just don't want to do that, but there's no room in the barn. Coy bought a hay baler and a rake and a hay conditioner to take the moisture out.

He has a friend who has a pole barn that doesn't have too much in it. I imagine he'll work something out with him and put some of it there. It really needs to be here, but I'm not wanting to spend another $50,000–$60,000 for a building. If I did, I'd have to go all through that zoning thing again and probably haul in load after load of fill to get the ground up high enough to satisfy them. It's just a big pain in the rear.

LA: So where would this new barn go?

MW: I'd have to put it back behind this one. Take a fence down and put it back there somewhere and then put a fence around it.

LA: That does get you real close to the creek.

MW: Oh, that would put you almost up to the creek, yeah. I might not be able to get a permit to do it, regardless of how much fill I put in. If I would build a new barn, I'd probably go down the road across from the motorcycle shop, south of the house here, where there's a big huge yard we mow. I'd probably put it down there. It's kind of a pain, but we could put the hay tools and more down there. I don't think I could build another building here.

I've often thought about putting in a garage. Marylou and I are seventy-three years old. I've lived here all my life and I don't even have a garage to put our car and truck in. It would be so nice to be able to go out on a winter morning and get into a vehicle and back it out of a building without having to start it and let it run and clean the snow and ice off the windows and all that stuff. I've thought about building a garage off of the house, but that would also take a lot of planning to get it to fit in, right north of the swimming pool.

I imagine it'd be a big hassle, too, because of the zoning. I think even that house is in a flood zone, which is all guess work. They're just guessing with that flood zone. We never had water get up to the house and we've had some huge floods here, water clear up to where the swimming pool is now, but it never got into the house. When they cleaned out this creek ten or twelve years ago, boy, that really made a difference.

If water does come up, it doesn't stay very long. Before it used to stay up for two, three, maybe four days. It may come up really high, but it'll be gone in a few hours, so we don't have the problem we used to have. We still do have a problem with the zoning people wanting to tell us we can't do this or we can't

do that. It's one of those deals where if you build it and the water gets in, the only people it hurts is us. It's not going to hurt anybody else, but they still don't want to let me do it.

LA: They're afraid the chemicals will get into the creek and then go on downstream.

MW: Could be. Could be. Yeah.

LA: When you had the flood or the water that went up to the pool, did it ever get in the basement?

MW: No.

LA: Never has?

MW: The only water that ever got into the basement seeped into the foundation because we didn't have the gutters cleaned out. The water ran right down the side of the house. That has happened, but as far as the creek ever getting in there, no. If the creek ever got into the house, we'd have a foot of water in this building here.

LA: Yeah, you would. You're low.

MW: We have had some water in here before, not a lot, maybe half inch or an inch.

LA: Through the whole building?

MW: Yeah, and it didn't come from the creek. It came from across the road, down across that barnyard. It couldn't get away fast enough and came right into the building. That's pretty rare when that happens.

LA: Do you sandbag?

MW: No, never have. I suppose in some cases it might help, but we have such a big area that if it starts coming at this place, it's going to come in anyway. Water has only gotten in here twice since we built this building. I like to think it won't happen again, but it might. You just have to go with the flow.

LA: The building has been here six, seven years.

MW: It was built in 1990 or '91, so it's been here for about twenty-five years. We had a wall over there and it was a workshop. And where we're sitting was storage for farm equipment. We've made a lot of changes from when you were here in '96 to crate the motorcycle to ship to California.

LA: Your car exhibit looks great in here. Now this is your book. Is there anything else you want to say about everything?

MW: Oh, I don't know. I could sit here and go on all day long, but it would be boring. I feel I've been gifted very generously. There were several years of my life when I really struggled to get by. Never, never once did I ask my mom and dad for any money, I mean, after I got older, after I got away from home. Marylou and I just always made do on our own and we lived the lifestyle we could afford. And if we did have to borrow some money for something, we'd go to the bank and borrow it. We didn't have to get any co-signers or anything.

And about Fairmount, people look at the Dennis Stock photos and say Fairmount hasn't changed any. A lot of the buildings are still the same, I'll be the first to admit that, but there have been a lot of changes. The big old bank building that Fairmount is so fortunate to have, that building just has architecture on it like you wouldn't believe. The Selby Family has really kept it up over the years, but they sold the bank a while back because they didn't have anyone in the family who wanted to continue.

I don't know what the future holds for Fairmount, but when I was a kid, there were appliance stores and there was Hunt's Furniture Store and there was an antique shop. It was a real antique shop, not a junk shop, and it was right beside the furniture store. Zelman's, it was called. There used to be two drugstores uptown and a nice jewelry store and a Western Auto store and Kesler Ford used to be uptown.

There used to be a place you could take toasters and appliances to and get them worked on. People didn't just throw things away like today. The shop would take things apart and rewire them, so you could use something for years and years. Everything is "throw-away" today. There's nowhere to get anything fixed.

If you had a television, you had to put new tubes in it, maybe one or two a year. Now you buy a new TV and it'll last for years and you never have to do anything to it, so we don't have TV stores anymore. We do have an appliance store that's kind of off the beaten path, but they do pretty good business.

A post office used to be right downtown. Now it's at the edge of downtown, which is better. Across the street from the Laundromat I once owned was a Dodge and Plymouth dealer, but that burned down. There was also a big furniture store there then.

Fairmount is like a lot of towns. It's had some fires that have done a lot of damage. Used to be a restaurant downtown, I can't tell you how many times that restaurant changed hands over the years. There were two barbershops downtown. One shop even had three barbers in it. Now there is only one barber downtown, and he kind of works part time. Things have changed a lot. That's probably true with all little towns. You look at them and you think they look just like they did fifty years ago. Well, they don't really.

LA: But the great thing is you still have a lot of people coming here for the James Dean Festival.

MW: Yeah, we do. We have the Festival here in September, and it has been very successful over the years. I'm glad for Fairmount. It kind of puts the town on the map for one weekend. It's a pretty big deal.

LA: Maybe somehow the next generation of your family can get involved in the James Dean events. Actually, some do seem involved, so the James Dean legacy continues on.

MW: Well, we'll try to do something.

LA: James Dean is iconic, walking down the street in New York City, but even more iconic is James Dean standing on the road here with the house in the background. All of the Dennis Stock's photos have made this farm iconic.

MW: Yeah.

LA: I know I'm talking out of turn, but this should be a state park eventually.

MW: Yeah, never will be though.

LA: Or a working farm, but, I mean, the farm should be protected.

MW: Well, we've tried our best to keep everything looking good, you know. We let the fans walk around and see things and so forth. If you're living here, too, there's sort of a limit to how far you can go, but I think we're pretty relaxed on it.

LA: I think the fans feel that.

Friend of Jimmie's
who was following
in car (sta wagon)
behind him

Bill Hickman
Ho 22301

ask for his billfold
thought a lot of him
however said had
only known him
about a mo. as a
real friend

From Ethel Dean's notebook written after Jimmie's death. The station wagon
Bill Hickman was driving is the car Marcus wishes was in the Car Barn...and Jimmie's wallet
also got away or it would be in the Fairmount Historical Museum.

17

The Car Barn

Leith Adams: You were a junior when you asked out Marylou...so, you could drive then?

Marcus Winslow: Yeah, I went up to the license bureau the day I turned sixteen and got my driver's permit. Then you had to wait thirty days to get your regular license. Thirty days later I was back up there again and tried to pass my driver's test. You had to answer questions and drive with a guy. That would have been in November, and so I probably bought a car in February from Kesler's in Fairmount, a '56 Ford, about like this one sitting here in the Car Barn.

I had told the guy I knew up there, Ralph Riley, I said, "I'd like to have a '56 Ford." One morning before school, I was walking down the sidewalk getting ready to go up the steps and here he pulled up with a '56 Ford. They called it Meadow Mist Green, a real light green and white. It was a car they had just traded for. I said I'd come look at it that evening. I told Dad Kesler's had a car in up there I wanted to look at.

Dad had let me farm Grandma and Grandpa Dean's farm for the last year or two, and I'd saved up enough money to buy the Ford. I think they wanted around $1,200 for

it. That was in 1960, so it was only four years old. It was a pretty decent car, I thought, and I ended up buying it. I really liked that car. It had duel exhaust and I put glass packs on it.

The engine was a 292, a high horse power for that car at the time, but not really all that powerful; 1956 was the only year I can think of when Ford put dual exhausts on an engine that small. Your regular muffler runs quiet so that's why I added the glass packs. The fiberglass packing in them makes a noise I like. Some have a nice, mellow tone to them.

Another guy in Fairmount, Paul Scott, happened to have a car exactly like mine, but he'd repainted it and had the hood and trunk shaved on it. That was a big deal back then. He had just finished the work when a month later, he traded it in for a new Ford over at Gas City. He said to me, "Why don't you go over and see if they will trade you the hood and the trunk?" I thought, *Well, I bet they won't because my hood has some chips in it from where rocks hit it.*

I went to Gas City one morning before school real early and talked to them, and they looked at my car and said, "Yeah, we'll trade you." They'd rather have a car that hadn't been customized because buyers would know some hot-rodder kid owned it. "Yeah, we'll trade you." They wanted to know what time I got out of school, and I told them.

They said, "You be over here at 3:30 or quarter to four and we'll have it ready," so I drove back after school and, sure enough, they had the hood and trunk off. They jerked the hood and trunk off of mine and put that other hood and trunk on and, boy, I was tickled. Paying a body shop, it wasn't cheap to repaint a hood and trunk and fill in the holes and do all that and I got it for nothing. I thought I was on top of the world.

Another friend, Gary Parsons, had a cable assembly with a knob on the end of it and the very next night, we drilled a hole in what they call the "package shelf" by the back window of the car. Then we put that little handle up through there and ran the cable down and hooked it up to the latch on the trunk. If I wanted to get in the trunk, I just pulled that button up.

One time I was down at the park, went to a dance there at the shelter house. It had snowed and sleeted and the streets were pretty slick when we came out, and I bumped into a tree as I went around a curb. It wasn't a big deal, but it did bend the bumper. The insurance company paid for a new, re-chromed bumper, and I left the bumper guards off. I still had that car when Marylou and I got married. We drove it to Niagara Falls and then in '65, I thought it was worn out.

Kesler's got in a '63 Ford Fastback and I knew the guy who had owned it, all red with red leather seats, 390 with a four-speed transmission. I talked to Ralph again, and he ended up trading for the '56 Ford, plus I gave him about $1,800 in cash.

The Fastback was a nice car too. I had that car from '65 to '72 and then late in 1972 I traded that red '63 for a '72 that had been a demonstrator. It was a car the salesmen

had driven for a year with the speedometer unhooked. Because they'd unhooked the speedometer right off the bat, it only showed fourteen miles on it. It still had a new car warranty, but it probably had 10,000 miles on it. That was the closest thing I ever had to a new car at the time, and we had it until around 1984.

Over there, that '49 Ford is the first car in here you could call a "collector car." I told you Bill Burwick was the one who gave me the '49 Ford Jimmie used to drive. Dad bought that brand-new in '49 up here off of Kesler.

Larry Smith lives here in Fairmount. He was a friend of Jimmie's and he told me one time Jimmie was home from New York and they wanted to go to the show, so they jumped in that Ford, heading to Marion, and Jimmie was speed shifting it, going through the gears real fast, and all of a sudden there was a clicking noise in the transmission. Larry said Jimmie was really worried about it because he knew Dad would get after him for doing that and so they parked the car and went to the show.

They came back out expecting it to be clicking and he said it never made a noise after that. Jimmie must have chipped a tooth in the transmission and I assume it finally wore itself enough so it didn't make any noise. As far as I know, the transmission has never been torn down in that car.

It was also Bill Burwick's "Sunday car." He had an old Plymouth he drove and the old '36 Dodge he ended up giving to me. He kept the '49 Ford car just for Sundays and the lady in Fairmount he'd take out for lunch. Matter of fact, he kept that car up in her garage. When he wanted to go somewhere in the Ford, he'd park his Plymouth along the street because the garage was right close to it. He'd get that car out and they'd go wherever they

The '49 Ford that Jimmie drove to the Senior Prom when he was dating Marylou's sister.

wanted to go and he'd park it in there again at night and drive his old Plymouth back out here.

Bill thought this '49 Ford was about the greatest thing there ever was. He took it to Virginia with him and his son used to drive it a little bit to the naval base. When Bill decided he wanted to come back here to live, he brought that Ford with him. I think he was afraid he was going to die or something, so he just put the title in my name. It was in my name for at least two years before he passed away, meaning I've had it since 1966, over fifty years.

It was rusting pretty bad. I'd done some amateur bodywork when it was Bill's. Matter of fact, I was working on it when Bill died, so I painted it. I used to keep it in Bill's carport that was hooked onto his trailer. It

was all enclosed and he had made doors for it so that's where I stored the Ford. I never thought about Jimmie driving it at the time. When Jimmie started getting to be so well known, people would ask about it, and I'd say, "Yeah, he used to drive that car." It was a dark gray back then, so I decided we'd restore it. And we really restored it.

We took all the windows out of it and all the doors out of it and all the upholstery out of it. We took the body clear off the frame and put it on a rotisserie, I guess you'd call it. I found a guy in New York that had a lot of "new old" stock parts for '49, '50, and '51 Fords—unused original parts. I don't know where he got them, but he had quarter panels and he had doors and he had fenders.

I bought new quarter panels for it. I got "new old" rocker panels for it. At that time, he didn't have any "new old" stock floors, but a company was making them, so we put all new floors in it. The trunk was rusting a little bit in the back. We cut that out and put new metal in it. It was really done right. We painted it that kind of dark red color, even though the car was originally gray. I probably should have put it back to gray again, but there weren't any grays out I really liked a lot, so I thought, *I like that dark red. I'm just going to paint it dark red,* so we did.

Terry Most painted it. He had it on that rotisserie and painted the underneath of it and everything red, even inside the fender wells. Once we had the frame painted and done, we set the body block on the frame and built it back up again. It's a good solid car, that's for sure.

A lot of people really enjoy it. Everybody who comes in here who is interested in Jimmie, when you tell them Jimmie used to drive that car, why, they want to get their picture taken with it, which is fine with me. I feel fortunate that Dad traded it in and Bill bought it and I got it from Bill.

Jimmie did drive it to his Senior Prom and he probably drove it to high school a little bit, not too much because at the time it was Mom and Dad's only transportation other than the truck Dad drove. Dad didn't get a truck until 1954, so I'm sure Jimmie didn't drive it too often. Maybe he drove it on dates and stuff, I don't know. Around Fairmount, he usually rode that little Czech motorcycle everywhere. He wanted a motorcycle instead of a car.

When I was a kid, I wanted a car instead of a motorcycle. I liked motorcycles, but I wanted a car first. I never did get a motorcycle until I was forty years old. Anyway, we put all new upholstery in that car, repainted the engine, put new tires on it. It's just about like a new car.

LA: Are there photographs of Jimmie in that car?

MW: No, there aren't. You would think there would be, but there aren't. We have one photograph, about half of the car is in the picture as I remember it. We were over at my sister's for dinner on a Sunday. She had a going-away dinner for Jimmie when Jimmie was heading to California to live with his dad. Joan invited all the family over and there is one picture of that car sitting out at the garage, but Jimmie's not in it.

LA: What about the tractor over there?

MW: The yellow one? Dad bought it new in 1954, a Minneapolis-Moline UB Diesel. Minneapolis-Moline made the UB for years. That was their big tractor, the "U," and it's a diesel. That particular tractor was one of the first diesel farm tractors in Grant County.

Minneapolis-Molines had always been gasoline models. How Dad happened to buy that diesel, I don't know, but it was new when he bought it. And the "B" means the steering wheel is up high like it is. The old "Zs" had a steering shaft that ran down the side of the tractor. You sat down in a seat way low in the back and you caught all the dirt and the dust down there. Well, they came out with this "UB," and you sat up a lot higher on it, so that's where that name came from.

Dad bought it new over in Jonesboro. It's been a good old tractor. Dad put out, let's see, '55 to '65, at least ten or eleven years of crops with it. He did most of the plowing, most of the disking with it. He always planted with another tractor, but this one did all the heavy work.

We have always kept it inside. It has never stayed outside at night, even when we've taken it up to the James Dean Days Car

Marcus Sr.'s tractor that Jimmie drove when he helped on the farm and that Marcus drove too.

Show. It's there with an exhibit of Jimmie's stuff because Dennis Stock took that photo of Jimmie standing in front of it. Jimmie, Dad and Dennis went out into the field here. I don't know what they were doing, but Dennis took some photographs of Jimmie with it.

Then Dennis made me a big picture. I suppose it's two and a half feet by maybe four feet tall. I put that in a frame next to the tractor, so people can see Jimmie right there by it. It's special. In the first place, it was my Dad's tractor, the last big tractor he owned so that means a lot to me, but it just so happens Jimmie was photographed with it so that makes it extra special.

LA: How old were you when you drove that?

MW: I would have been twelve or thirteen. Let's see, Steve Allen was here in '56 and I was driving it then because I took him riding.

LA: Is this the tractor you'd take out on the road to go to the elevator?

MW: Yeah. I used to take it to the mill to grind the feed. Today it doesn't look like a very big tractor compared to the newer ones in here, but it was a big tractor in its time.

LA: The fire truck?

MW: The fire truck is Fairmount Township's truck. The reason I bought it is that truck went into service on January 1, 1970 and that is the day I started at the fire department. I was on the fire department thirty-seven years.

I was figuring how many fire calls a year we averaged and multiplied that against how many years we had that truck and it came to a little over a thousand calls. It only has about 14,000 miles on it.

Fairmount Township bought a new fire truck in 1997, and we sold this one to Fowlerton, which is a neighboring town. They had it for five or six years, but then they decided they'd quit having a fire department and just contract with Fairmount for fire protection, which was a smart idea.

There that truck sat. Fowlerton wanted to sell it. And I knew it was too old for a fire department to want, but it was too new to be an antique. Probably what would have happened is someone would have bought it because it is such a good truck, but they'd have taken the fire equipment off of the back and put a flatbed on it and hauled corn or something with it, and I just hated to see that happen.

It is such a good old truck, so I bought it, and when we tried to get the Fowlerton name off the door, we scratched the doors. So, we ended up repainting the doors and the back side of the cab. Other than that, most of the rest of it is pretty original.

Fowlerton didn't take care of it. They told me it wouldn't pump water anymore. Why? I don't know. Probably the pump needs new seals, but I have never made an effort to get it running or pump water because…why? It's just going to sit. And when it sits like this, the seals dry out and the tank gets rusty.

I don't know what I'll ever do with it. I've thought about cutting a place in the back, so you can step up and get into it. Make a little stairway to go through the center and put seats on the sides, so people could ride in parades. That's just a brainstorm I had.

It's sort of risky. You start hauling people around and someone gets hurt and you have a liability problem, so I probably will never do that. I haven't had it started for three or four years. It's not a very good idea to let something sit like that, but I just don't have any reason to start it.

LA: Does it come out for James Dean Days?

MW: No. I've never had it out. I did think about bringing it out, but we're so busy that time of the year with other things, I just don't have time to work on it, mess with it. I'd have to put license plates on it. I'm not sorry I bought it because I've always loved that truck, but I know you can't do much with it.

LA: So, the Car Barn is built right where Bill Burwick had his trailer?

MW: Bill's trailer would have been just outside the Car Barn on the driveway. Where we are, there was an empty lot we had fenced in. Sometimes we'd put livestock in it to eat the grass, keep it down. It gave Bill something to do, since he liked livestock.

After Bill was gone, Dad wanted a place to put his implements, so he and Carl Pace built an old pole barn where this one's sitting, built it out of used materials. Dad bought the rafters already made. When they finished, it wasn't very pretty, but it served the purpose. They used old wood, some telephone poles, metal off of other buildings. It had three walls with the east end open. Dad got a lot of good out of it. It kept the machinery out of the weather.

But when it rained, water would come down from the barnyard and it was a mess. This place would be covered in mud. When I built this building, I brought in a lot of fill to raise it up; put down a cement floor. It was built as a workshop and for storage, and it wasn't until I sold the Laundromat building to the library that I turned this into the Car Barn.

When you came here in '96 to pack the motorcycle for the Warner Bros. Museum, we crated Jimmie's Triumph in the workshop where we'd work on the tractors. That space was insulated and we could heat it, but the north part wasn't insulated. When we were making the Car Barn, we tore out the partitions and insulated all the walls and then hired someone to blow insulation in the ceiling.

I've often wished Dad could have seen this place after we got rid of that old shed and fixed the other barns up. They were getting pretty run down. Dad just got old and wasn't able to do it. As I get older, I can see I'm beginning to get the same way. You just kind of look the other way a lot of times. It used to be with things, I'd think, *Yeah, I've got to get that fixed.* Now I can look at it and walk by and think, *Well, we'll get it done tomorrow.* I suppose it's just an aging thing.

Jimmie's motorcycle boots and jacket.

18

The James Dean Exhibit at the Fairmount Historical Museum

Marcus Winslow: Around 1975 a group got together to start the Fairmount Historical Museum. It had a lot to do with the high school closing because they didn't want to lose all the trophies and the pictures from the school, so they started a museum. Matter of fact, the Western Auto store on Main Street had a big room upstairs they weren't doing anything with, and they let the group use it at no charge.

When it opened, they had a little display on Jimmie, but it wasn't very long until they realized most of the people coming to the Museum were there because of James Dean. So, Ann Warr, who was President at the time, wrote Uncle Winton wanting to know if they could borrow some of Jimmie's personal effects—trophies, clothing, things like that. Mom and Dad still had everything here at the house from the James Dean Foundation after it closed down in the Fifties, and Uncle Winton sent a letter saying it was okay to display them. Mom also loaned them Jimmie's baby clothes and school papers, and Marvin Carter let them borrow that little Czech motorcycle of Jimmie's.

When the Historical Museum was formed, they were going to raise some money by having a festival. I don't really think, when they first started, their intention was for it to be focused on Jimmie so much, but they did schedule it in September on the anniversary of his death.

The Museum was on Main Street above Western Auto for several years until the house it's in now became available. It was an old house, one of the first in Fairmount, and the Museum bought it. It had been turned into a boarding house and had some apartments in it, so the Museum rented them out for a couple more years until they had enough money and thought they could afford to not rent it. The kitchens and bathrooms were taken out and the walls were re-done. The Museum did the best they could to remodel it with the money they had.

Mrs. Warr was fretting around that it was going to cost them $1,800, as I remember, for a moving van to bring the stuff out of the Museum to the house. I said, "Why don't you wait and let me talk to the Fire Department. Maybe I can get them to take it all and move it." That's what I did. We had a meeting once a month at the Fire Department, and I asked if anyone would be willing to help move the stuff down to the house and everyone said, yeah, they'd help.

We picked a weekend when everybody was off work. A lot of the firemen had pickup trucks, and they all came up there at once and carried the stuff out, loaded it and hauled it down to the old house. They were done in three to four hours. Mrs. Warr couldn't believe they'd gotten it done so quickly, but they did.

As time went on, we displayed more and more on Jimmie. Finally, Mrs. Warr wasn't the president anymore and someone else took charge. I think Gale Hikade was president when we put a lot more stuff in there. He

said, "We're going to take everything from downstairs that has to do with Fairmount and we'll take it upstairs and display it up there. You'll have the whole downstairs for James Dean." So, I bought a bunch more showcases and, I'm not bragging, but all those showcases, I bought them, paid for them and they have a pretty nice display now.

Leith Adams: What's your favorite part of the James Dean Exhibit?

MW: I enjoy it all. I think that Triumph motorcycle is really nice, but there are a lot of important things in there—his contract with Warner Bros. and a lot of personal effects, tape recorders, and clothing. It's all important if you're interested in Jimmie's life,

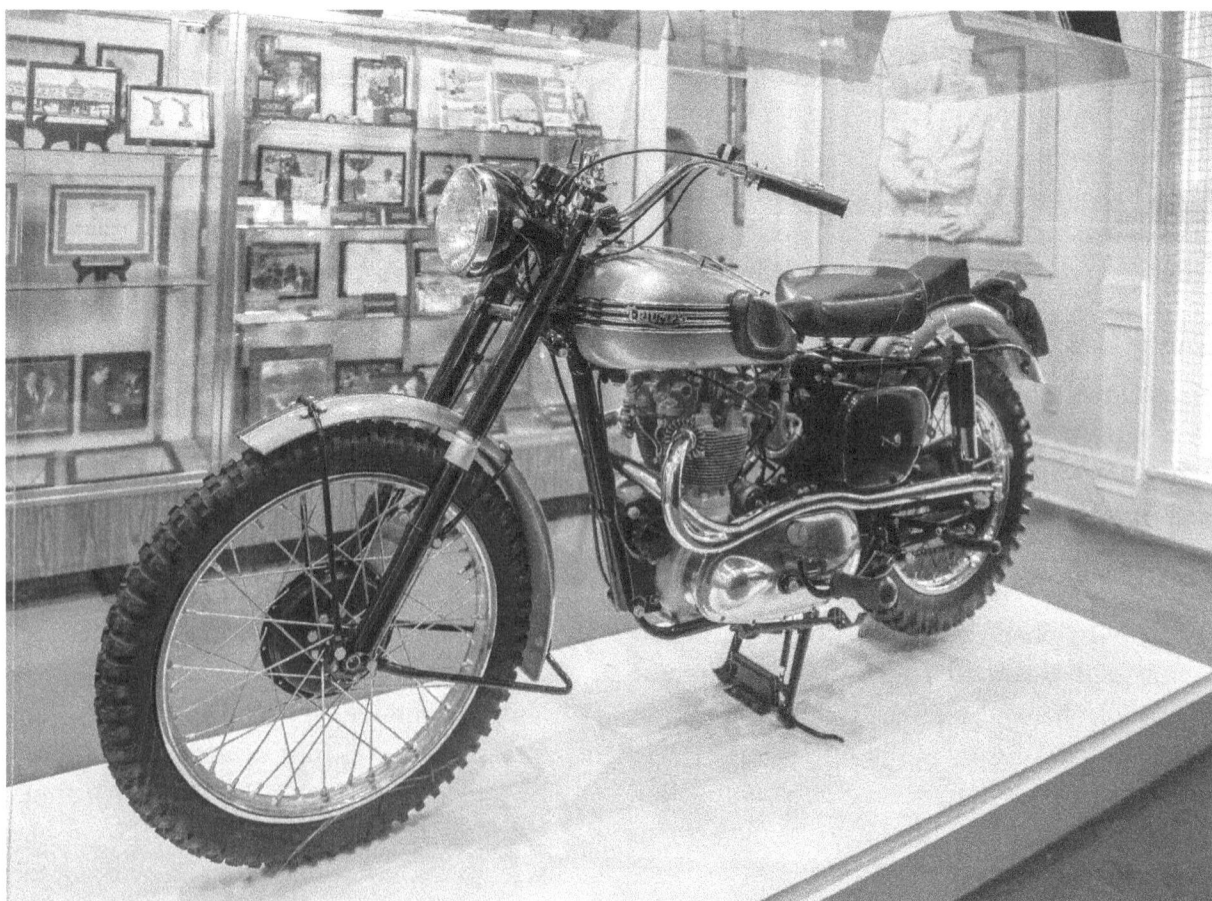

Jimmie's Triumph Trophy 500 motorcycle that Jack Warner banned from Warner Bros.

so I guess there really isn't one thing that I wanted to see more than anything else, other than the fact that the motorcycle is probably worth the most.

LA: It's pretty impressive.

MW: It was in tough shape when we got it. It didn't look like that. It looked like a chopper bike, had the wrong wheels on it and the wrong fork on the front. It was really, really torn up. Charlie Bridenfield up in Michigan helped me a lot. He ran down the parts. Then he'd send them here and Coy would paint them and we'd take everything back up to Michigan and Charlie would put it together.

Someone up there overhauled the engine. We never have started it, but it would start if you wanted to work with it a while. It has all new wiring. The fuel systems are all dry. If you wanted to spend a little time tinkering with it, tuning it up, it'd run. I don't really have any desire to start it because it's in that nice display case Warner Bros. gave me and it's too much trouble to get it out.

LA: Have you had it out of the case since it came back from California?

MW: Yeah, we took it to Independence, Missouri to the Harry Truman Museum. They wanted to exhibit it for a couple months. And then the Gerald Ford Museum in Grand Rapids, Michigan, wanted to know if they could exhibit it there. We also had it at the Indiana State Museum in Indianapolis for about six months in an exhibit over the winter. Matter of fact, Jimmie's black leather jacket is down there right now.

Some guy wanted to take pictures of the Triumph one time for an article or something, but I told him it was just too hard to get out of the case. He asked what it would cost to

get it out, and I said, "If you want to donate $500 to the fire department in Fairmount, I'll get some of the guys down here to help lift it." He said, "Okay," so that's what we did.

As a rule, I don't take it out of there. It's pretty secure and of course we have it bolted down. You have to unbolt it and that showcase is really heavy. It'd be a lot of protection for it if the house ever caught on fire

There are a lot of personal things in the Museum that mean a lot to me. There's a sheet of paper where Jimmie has written a lot of phone numbers. That I think is pretty important for knowing about his life. From Dennis Stock's photos, you can tell what he had in his New York apartment and all that is in a showcase.

At the Museum

LA: So, we're now in Fairmount at the Museum, looking at a display case at the start of the James Dean Exhibit. What's the significance of this little motorcycle?

MW: This is Jimmie's Czech motorcycle. The year on it is supposed to be 1947, but it could be a '46. Jimmie's might be older than what they thought it was. Dad bought this brand-new for Jimmie from Carter Motors, which was the Indian motorcycle shop located in the old schoolhouse a quarter of a mile south of our house. Jimmie used to go down there and loaf a lot. I think Marvin Carter opened it up in 1940, about the time Jimmie came to live with Mom and Dad.

The story I've always heard is that Indian didn't make a little bitty bike for the dealers to sell. Indians were mostly bigger bikes, so a lot of Indian dealers used to handle this size. A "Czech 125," I believe that's what they called it: one hundred twenty-five cc's, made in Czechoslovakia. Nice little cycle.

This bike has looked like this for so long, I'd hate to change it now. It's not restored, but Marvin did repaint it, part of it at least, the tanks and the chain guard and so forth when he had it back in his shop in the mid-Fifties on the trade-in.

That yellow paint isn't original. Marvin picked out that yellow. The rest of the cycle is black. At one time, the seat was changed. I don't know if Jimmie did that or if it was changed before he got it. Anyway, people enjoy seeing it in this un-restored state.

Carter Motors got back Jimmie's bike when Jimmie had Dad and Mom put it in the trunk of their '49 Ford and bring it with them to Fairmount. Apparently, Marvin Carter sold it again and then within two or three years, after Jimmie was killed, it came back to the shop for another trade-in. Marvin recognized it as being Jimmie's old bike, so he kept it. He'd only sold a couple of Czech motorbikes.

When the James Dean Foundation started up in the mid-Fifties, Marvin let them exhibit this bike, and when it closed, he asked Dad to take it. Dad said he had a place in the basement he could store it, and it was in our basement for twenty-three years or so.

I had an old BSA motorcycle I'd restored and repainted, and Marvin was pretty impressed with it. He said, "Why don't you get that Czech cycle of Jimmie's and bring it down to the shop sometime and we'll tear it back apart." He said, "I'll get it running and you can repaint it, and it'll just be yours and mine." I said I would, but he died before any of that happened.

Mildred, Marvin's widow, gave me the cycle and when the Historical Museum opened, I thought, *Well, I'll bring that up here rather than keep it sitting in the basement where people can't see it. People will enjoy it, I think.*

In the same showcase are a couple of Jimmie's Fairmount High sweaters, athletic sweaters, that's what they are. This one is baseball and the other one is basketball. If you were on a team, you got a sweater and a big *F* letter you sewed onto it. They are still like new. He apparently enjoyed them because they went to California with him and they were there when he died.

Jimmie's dad had them packed up with the stuff from California. Then we have some photos in the showcase also. One of them is a picture of Jimmie on this motorcycle. He's parked uptown on it.

In this display case across from the Czech, I was in the attic one day looking for something and I ran onto a cardboard box that said, "Jimmie's Baby Clothes." His baby clothes were in that cardboard box in the attic. Those two pictures in the background are kind of silhouettes. I don't know what you call them exactly, but in the Forties and Fifties, they used to hang on walls in houses and in bedrooms. Those two always hung in my bedroom or in Jimmie's bedroom.

That trophy up there, Jimmie won it, "National Forensic League Meets," while he was a senior at Fairmount High School. Mom always had that sitting in our hallway between the dining room and the living room in the bookcase. Anytime Mrs. Nall would come to see us, she'd walk by it and she'd say, "I was supposed to have that." I don't know if Jimmie told her one time, she could have it or not, but we never did give it to her. I think more than anything, she just wanted it.

There are a lot of ribbons here, pole vaulting and low hurdle, high hurdles. There's a mile relay, half-mile, and shot put, more high hurdles, broad jump. Jimmie was a very good athlete, and these are all ribbons he won from sports meets. A few of them are blue ribbons. Some are red ribbons. Some are white. They're either 1948 or 1949, it looks to me like.

LA: The blue one back there?

MW: Yeah, there's one back here. "First Place Dramatic Dramatization District Tournament." It says. "National Forensic League 1949." So, he did pretty good with his debating. What's this one over here say?

LA: "Sixteenth Annual High School Debaters Conference and Legislative Assembly, Purdue University, December 3rd 1948." Oh, here is the Colorado ribbon.

MW: Is it?

LA: "Contestant National Speech Tournament, April 29–30, 1949." April, and he graduated in '49 so that was his senior year. It looks like he's written something, "Extemporaneous." That's the speech he made, so it's "off the cuff." I think that's what it means.

MW: Evidently those ribbons meant a lot to him because he packed them up and took them to California with him. This other stuff we had at home, notebooks and schoolwork that he's done. Here's a picture of a grasshopper he drew, probably for a biology class. There's a lot of biology stuff in there. He liked to use his initials. Here's one where he's written "JBD."

LA: So, he drew that?

MW: Yeah, he drew those. And here are some more Fairmount *F* letters that were just loose. I put them in there.

LA: Looks like another baseball *F* up there.

MW: Yep, yep. It's a baseball letter. He played baseball and basketball and was on the track team. There's his high school diploma. This is the Bible the Back Creek Church gave him when he graduated. His name is imprinted on it.

He has some report cards. He was an average student, not exceptional or at the top of the class, but he certainly wasn't towards the bottom either. Then there are several drawings he did in high school, either charcoal drawings or pencil drawings. Some were taken out of notebooks and some of them are framed. They're just plain pictures that he painted and had hanging on the walls of the bedroom. He's got a squirrel down there. It's kind of nice, this one right here. All this stuff is high school stuff. He was pretty talented.

LA: The photographs of his bedroom, when were the photographs taken?

MW: The late Fifties after Jimmie died. A fan became acquainted with Mom and Dad, and he was a pretty good photographer. He wanted to know if he could take pictures of the bedroom and he did and sent copies to Mom and Dad. People can get an idea of what his bedroom furniture was. It was made out of maple. Mom and Dad had gotten it not long before Jimmie came to live with them. I don't know whether they bought it for themselves or bought it thinking he was coming, but Jimmie always liked it. I guess he asked them if he could have that bedroom suite, and they said, "Yes." Then when Jimmie left, well, then I went into his room. It's the same bedroom suite I always had and it's in very good shape, no scratches or anything on it.

LA: Where is it now?

MW: It's still up in the room. The room looks just like it always did. It's not that we tried to preserve it because of Jimmie, but there's no reason to change it. With just about any house, there are only two or three different ways you can put a bed in a room. When I was in there, every couple years we'd turn the bed around and put the head in a different place, just to be different. I imagine Jimmie did, too.

LA: The statue of Jimmie to the right of this case?

MW: Kenneth Kendall wanted to put a monument at Griffith Observatory for Jimmie because it was where *Rebel Without a Cause* was made. He had meetings with the people at the Observatory, and they agreed to let him do something. They wanted to see what it was going to look like, so he made this. It looks like cement, but it's not. It's plywood with some kind of a plaster on it. The bust on top is the same bust at the Observatory, though the one at Griffith is bronze.

The Observatory was able to take this model and move it around because it isn't

Kenneth Kendall's test statue used to place his monument to Jimmie at the Griffith Observatory in Los Angeles.

heavy. That's how they determined where to place the statue. I'm pretty proud of this because it's an exact replica of the one in Griffith Park and also of the one we have here in Fairmount at James Dean Memorial Park right on Main Street. It's the same exact design for the base and also for the head, so I feel fortunate to have this one here.

I got it at an auction. Kenneth Kendall and David Loehr used to be pretty close and Kenneth either gave it to David or loaned it, depends who you talk to. David had this for several years in the Gallery, and I always admired it very much. Then, when David had to sell everything, this statue went to Heritage Auctions in Dallas, Texas.

I was interested in the bust and the base it sat on. It brought $8,000 or $8,500, something like that. I bid on it, but I backed off. I didn't want to pay that much. It sold to someone in New Jersey. Then I got word that it was coming back to Heritage. I was talking to Doug at the auction house, and he told me the guy who bought it claimed the bust was damaged and he was sending it back.

I asked how much Heritage wanted for it and he said he didn't know because he wasn't sure what it looked like. He said, "I'll tell you what, just as soon as it gets back, I'll take some pictures of it and I'll send them to you and we'll see if we can work something out on it." So, he did send me some pictures.

What had happened was, Kendall had taken one of the old busts and it sat on this heavy steel ring. Then it had a shaft that went up into the head. Kenneth had taken one of those rings and made a neck around it for the bust, a neck and a shoulder on one side made out of something like clay. It did look a lot better than the old ones, but it was fragile because of the clay. Well, there were places on the neck where it wasn't very thick and somehow, in shipping, it got bumped and it busted into a hundred pieces.

Doug said, "I think you could glue it back together." I asked, "Well, what are you going to want for it?" And he says, "I'll have to talk to somebody higher up than me. I'll call you back and tell you." He did and he said, "They want $5,000 for it. If you want it, we'll sell it to you for $5,000, and we'll ship it to you and we'll pay the shipping."

I told him it seemed like an awful lot for something that was damaged and he said, "I know it. If it was up to me, I'd give it to you, but it's not my decision. If you don't buy it, we have a place we'll take it to and get it repaired." Then he said they would just put it back up for sale, and I said I'd take it. I wanted it. I didn't mind paying $5,000 for it, but I didn't like having to pay $8,000 or $8,500, whatever it brought at the auction.

Coy and I took this bust and stood it up on this ring Kenneth had made and some of the pieces were big enough that you could put them back, so you could get the shape of it. I got some Super Glue and glued those pieces together, and they were really tight. Then I took the little pieces and started fitting them around. I got most of them back in somewhere. I don't think I got them all because there were still some holes here and there.

Coy and I sanded it down, the neck part, kind of got it smooth on the outside, and then we turned it upside down and I had Coy take some of this fiberglass cloth. You mix up a resin and you put it on this cloth. It's how they patch car bodies, so we put that on the inside of the neck. We coated that all over the inside, and we let it get good and dry and then he made another coat of that resin and put it in there. That made it stronger than it ever was.

Then we turned it back over and where there were holes, he took body filler and filled them in. Once we had it all filled in, we sanded it and masked off the top part of the bust that wasn't damaged.

Before we glued all of the neck, Coy and I had taken a piece to an automotive paint store in Marion where they could match the colors. They took a photo of it with one of those machines that can take that picture and match any color perfectly, and that's what they did. We told them we didn't want it real glossy, so they put some kind of a flattener in the paint.

Coy had a miniature spray gun and he took that gun and that's when we masked off the whole top part of the bust. He just fogged the paint on it real careful and painted it all the way around, giving it two or three coats. When we took the masking paper off from the top, you absolutely could not tell anything ever had been done to it. It's almost a perfect match. If you saw it before and saw it now, you wouldn't believe it was the same statue, because the neck had broken into a hundred pieces.

That head is the one the mold was taken from to make the bronze for Griffith Observatory and for the park here in

Fairmount, so I guess you could say that head has been around.

The ironic thing was, when I got it, we took the lid off and on the other side was the name of the guy Heritage had shipped it to the first time and it was somebody I knew real well. It also had the guy's phone number on there and an address in New Jersey. I knew the guy, but I would have sworn he had moved to Florida. I thought maybe he'd moved back to New Jersey because that's where he was from originally.

I called the phone number and left a message on the machine saying who I was and said I was calling him about that bust he bought at the auction in Dallas. Two or three weeks later, he called me back. It turned out the phone number was his brother's and so was the address. His brother had bid on it for him because my friend didn't know how to bid on the internet.

He told me, "When I got that box, I started opening it and I could see it had broken up in pieces." He said, "I was real careful and I took all the pieces out and put them in plastic bags." He had a casting made of it, had a mold made. And then the guy that made the mold supposedly made the bottom right on it.

I said, "Well, Kenneth Kendall is dead, so maybe it won't matter so much, but I sure wouldn't be making any more of those for anyone." And he said, "Oh, I won't." Anyway, he had one made out of bronze and he was telling me how beautiful it was and everything.

About a year later that fellow came to the car show in Fairmount, he and his wife. He said, "I have something I want to show you," so I went over to his van and he opened up the side door and pulled a cover off and there was another bust. It was not bronze. It was gold, just beautiful. He said, "That's yours." "Well,

what do you want for it?" "Nothing. I had it made for you." I said, "You can't do that." And he said, "I can. I've already done it."

He and his wife came down to the church for the memorial service and somebody was outside taking pictures and I said, "Hey, take a picture of the four of us together," so they took a couple of pictures and when I got them, they turned out so nice, I took a check of Jimmie's and had it mounted inside a frame and had it matted with this picture of us and sent it to him. He was just flabbergasted. He's a really strong fan, but he's not a nut. He has common sense. He just couldn't believe it. I felt I had to do something for that bust. He comes here about every year.

I think Kenneth was pretty proud of his bust and the pedestal. It's not an exact copy of Jimmie's face, but kind of a caricature. That's what I call it. Kenneth might not call it that, but I do. Some of the features are kind of extreme on it, but I think it's pretty neat.

The big dedication was at Griffith Observatory in California in 1988 because Bob Pulley from Fairmount, a friend of Jimmie's, went out to it and, of course, Kenneth was there and Frank Mazzola and a few of the fans.

LA: Do you have photographs of that event?

MW: Bob took photos and he gave some to me. I don't know where they are right this second, but I have some.

LA: Now, we were talking about the napkins that have Jimmie's doodles on them.

MW: Yeah, Chuck Sachs of the Scriptorium contacted me and said he had several photos Jack Simmons claimed were taken by Jimmie. They were pretty nice photos. He offered them to me for $1,000, and so I ended up buying them. I never did do anything with them, but I have them.

Chuck also had all these napkins that this ex-policeman was going to put in an auction. I'm not trying to defend Jimmie especially, but Jimmie never dreamed anyone would save all that stuff. Supposedly every time Jimmie drew something, Jack Simmons picked it up and put it in his pocket because Jimmie was just going to throw it away. It was a nervous thing Jimmie did while he would be talking with his friends at Googie's Coffee Shop.

The drawings were kind of odd. I don't remember what all of them were now, but there were several. Three or four of them could have been offensive to somebody. The people selling them recognized we owned the copyright and if we would agree to let them sell the others in an auction, they'd give me the ones that could be offensive. We said, "Okay."

This is also the guy who called me, the guy who had this big, huge, five- or six-feet tall painting that Jimmie supposedly had done, although it wasn't signed. Simmons claimed Jimmie had painted it at Warner Bros. Studio and it was there when Jimmie died and the studio crated it up, and somehow Simmons picked it up and just kept it.

Uncle Winton didn't know anything about it. I don't know whether it's Jimmie's work or not. This guy sent me a picture of it. I could probably find it, if you wanted to see it. I can't even remember what it was now. I mean there was nothing wrong with it, but it didn't look to me like something Jimmie would paint.

I've forgotten the guy's name now, but Simmons had a whole bunch of stuff packed away that he claimed was Jimmie's. There weren't the cameras or anything like that, but Simmons told him Jimmie had done that

big painting. I don't know whether he had or not. He might have, I don't know, but how do I know if I wasn't there?

LA: So, you didn't buy any of the doodles at all? They did go up for auction.

MW: Yeah, they did sell them. They brought, I suppose, an average of $1,500 apiece. Some brought more and some brought a little less. They weren't signed or anything. You just had to look at them and, as far as I was concerned, you just had to assume that Jimmie did them. He probably did, but he might not have. I don't know. I never authenticated.

LA: So now we are in the room next to the entrance foyer. The display case to the right seems to be a mix of things.

MW: It is. We have a menu from the Villa Capri. Shortly before Jimmie died, he was there and a little girl wanted his autograph, so Jimmie took a Villa Capri menu and wrote his name on it and wrote her name on it too.

Matter of fact, the daughter of the fellow who owned the Villa Capri called me one time and said she understood I had a menu from Villa Capri. I said I did and she said, "Well, would you sell it?" I told her I didn't want to part with it because Jimmie had signed it, but I said I'd make her a copy, so I did. I took it over to Marion to a print shop. They printed the front and then they opened it up and printed the insides.

She wanted it because of her folks, but also to get an idea what the prices used to be. My interest in it is because it was Jimmie's favorite restaurant. Some fan had put it in the auction, and I bought it.

The owner's daughter had never seen it. I had it all laminated and sent it to her and she was tickled to death with it. She has a pizza place in Farmers Market. If I ever get to California again, I want to stop in to see her. She owes me a pizza. (*laughs*)

LA: And then the autographed Junior Class play program?

MW: I found out the female classmates kept a lot of stuff, but the boys didn't pay much attention to what they had. I bought it off of one of Jimmie's classmates, one of the girls. It's the Junior Class play Jimmie was in and all the cast signed that program. Eddie Van Ness. Jerry Brown. Joanne Roth. Jim Dean. What is the play? *Our Hearts Were Young and Gay?*

LA: Yeah, and directed by Adeline Nall Brookshire. Ethel Thomas?

MW: I think that's who the program came from, Ethel Thomas.

LA: Crowell Veder, Wilma Jean Underwood, Jerry Jones, Ranson…?

MW: Hanson Leach?

LA: Yeah, that may be it.

MW: Some of those people are still around.

LA: Do you remember them from when you were a young kid?

MW: I just remember them from seeing them at school. There used to be a furniture store up here called Hunt's Furniture. One of the girls worked in there and Jimmie used to go in to see her and I'd be with him. I remember them from things like that.

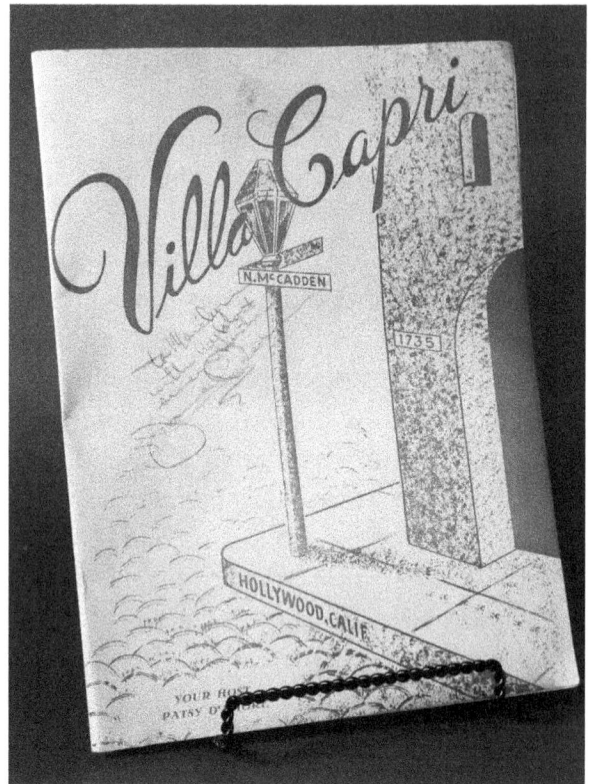

An autographed menu from Villa Capri, Jimmie's favorite Los Angeles restaurant.

LA: So that was after graduation?

MW: It was his senior year.

LA: Then there's this letter to your mom and dad. Can I read it?

MW: Sure. Sure.

LA: "Dear, Mom and Mark, Pleased to hear you liked the show. I got so many wonderful encouraging letters from home. I have a very small part as a bellboy on *CBS Studio One* this Monday…" That's the one where he hams it up in the elevator and John Forsythe gets really upset.

MW: Yeah.

LA: "I have a lead opposite Lloyd Nolan on *Martin Kane, Private Eye* March 6th 10-10:30 NBC. My check for the last show has been delayed a week. Could you help me out for a while? About $10 should do it. When my check comes, I'll send it right back. Love, Jim."

And this is from the Young Men's Christian Association, the YMCA. At "5 West 63rd Street, New York 23, New York." So, this would've been '52?

MW: Probably, yeah. He did over thirty television shows and most of those shows were all live, so you had to be correct when you were saying your lines. Eventually it got so the station in California could film them off a tv screen and show this kinescope three hours after we saw it here in Fairmount. A lot of the shows were thrown away, but most of Jimmie's TV shows have finally been found and have been restored. There are two or three, I guess, they still can't find.

That bracelet there, that's just something he used to wear. I've seen pictures of him with that on. Next is a sheet of paper where Jimmie wrote down a lot of phone numbers, names and phone numbers, and he's done some doodles on the page, too. He liked to doodle. He was always drawing some little thing on paper. You can probably see some famous names there.

LA: "Liz Taylor, Competition Motors," where he bought his cars. "Colter and Grey."

MW: They were his accountants for his paychecks and stuff.

LA: "Lew Bracker. Marla English," an actress. "Bruce Kessler," not sure who Bruce Kessler is.

MW: He was a race car driver. Matter of fact, Bruce Kessler may have come by the accident right after it happened. It seems to me that's what I've been told. They were on their way to Salinas to the sports car race. This one road is the main road most of them would travel from Los Angeles to Salinas. I think he's one of them that came by right after the accident.

LA: Did he ever come back here?

MW: No, I never talked to him. Lee Raskin knows him. He's talked to him before. Apparently, it was pretty late in his life when he wrote all that out. It's just a spare piece of paper, it looks like.

LA: Yeah, probably kept it right by the phone. This came with...?

MW: Uncle Winton's stuff. Uncle Winton had kept it.

LA: And then this silver cup?

MW: Yeah, Jim DeWeerd, the minister here in Fairmount, he influenced Jimmie quite a bit. He had that and he used to serve Jimmie Coca-Cola in it.

LA: It says, "The Lord is My Shepherd—I Shall Not Want." How do you know he served Coca-Cola in it?

MW: Jim DeWeerd said that.

LA: Oh, and he gave it to you, to the family?

MW: I think I got that when I got the clay sculpture Jimmie made, the one called "Self." Jim DeWeerd's wife told me about the cup.

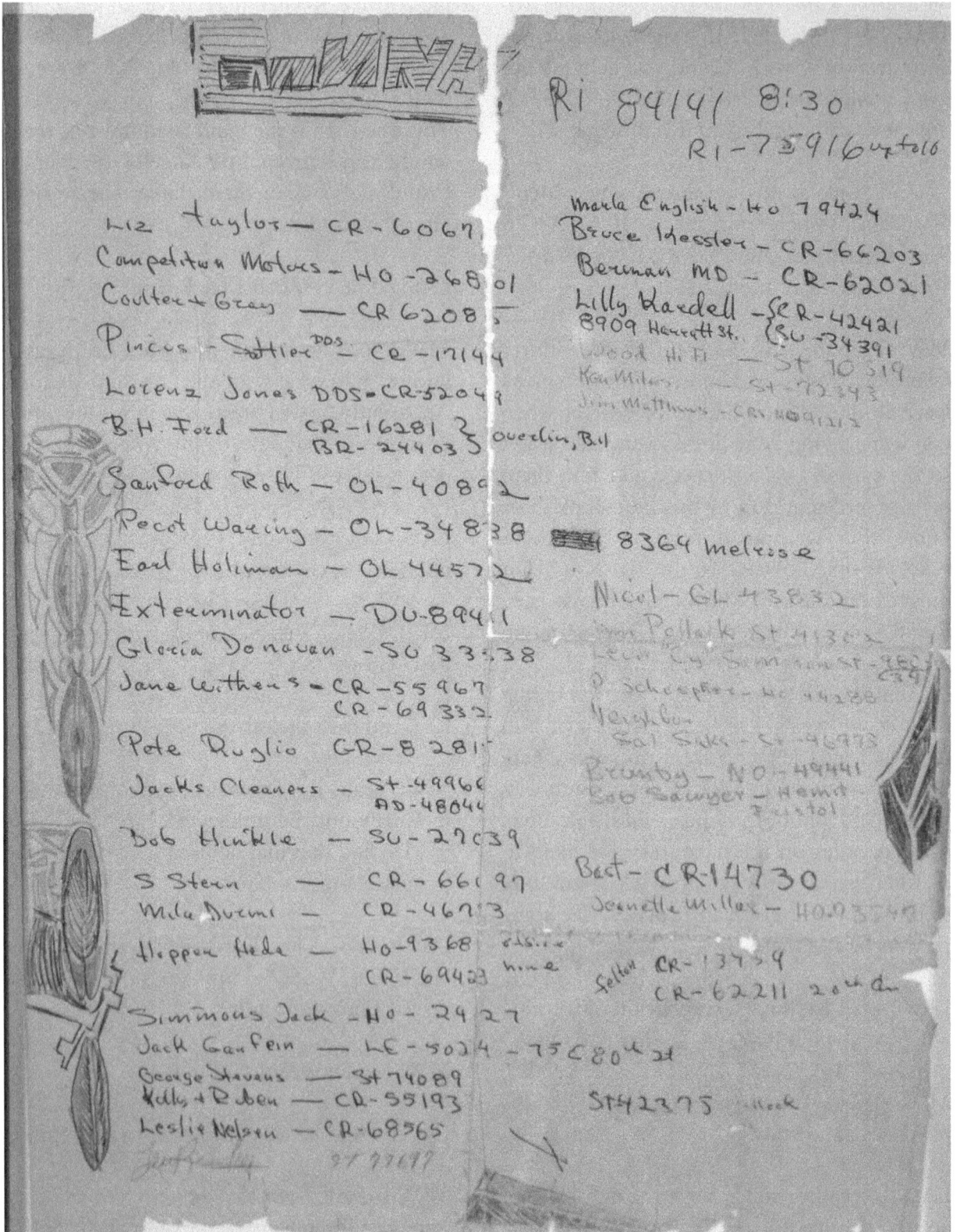

Jimmie's handwritten phone list circa *Giant*.

I told you a little about how I got it. That is another interesting story. I didn't even know James DeWeerd's wife lived around here. She lived at a place called Kendallville. This guy, I don't even remember his name, but just to tell you how much nerve people have, he wanted to talk to James DeWeerd's wife and he found out she lived in Kendallville and he went over there and visited with her. He found out she still had the little clay sculpture Jimmie made and he tried to get it off of her, but she wouldn't sell it. He was a friend of David Loehr's and he wanted to get it for David. It is a good thing he didn't, because David would have had to auction it.

Anyway, she said, "No." She didn't want to part with it to him. Then this guy said, "But would you sell it to a member of the family?" And she said, "Yeah, I probably would." He came and told me he'd talked to her and that she wouldn't sell it to him, but he wanted to know if I would be interested in it. I said, "Yeah." I don't think it was important to her monetarily. She just wanted to know it was going to the right place, and so I went up and visited with her.

This guy had even said she wouldn't put a price on it, but whatever she got for it, she was going to give to this Children's Home down in Kentucky. She said she and Jim both had been down there several times because they didn't have any children. I don't know how they got hooked up with this place, but she said, "Whatever you want to give, it will be given to the Children's Home," and she told me the name of it. Matter of fact, I think when I made out the check, I made it out to the Children's Home.

The sculpture was up in a china cupboard. Because they didn't have any children, no one had been playing with it. That thing was still soft. You could still crush it, if you wanted to, or put a fingernail mark in it. The deal with this guy for finding it was that if I ever

displayed it, I'd let the Gallery display it, so I said, "Okay." I thought that was better than not having it, so I didn't display it. I had it up at the house here. I put it in a china cupboard and I bought one of these glass display globes to put down over it, had a little base at the bottom. I did that to keep dust off.

That other cup? It's something Jimmie always had sitting on his dresser. What do they call it, a whiskey flask?

LA: It says "First Shot of Whiskey...Say When!"

MW: Yeah, but he never drank anything like that out of it. He got it somewhere and I remember as a kid, it always sat there on his dresser, something that Jimmie had.

LA: And your parents let him have it? It has a figure of a guy and a girl, stick figures, drinking martinis.

MW: Yeah.

LA: Here's a pay stub for $210. It's a W-2 form and doesn't say the date on it, but it's 1951, so that's the W-2 form for 1951. Jerry Fairbanks Agency must've been who he was working for, so that would've been the commercial.

MW: Probably the Pepsi commercial.

LA: Yeah, and then Ted's Auto Park.

MW: Well, he used to work at a parking lot.

LA: In California?

MW: Mm-hmm.

LA: So that must be his W-2. Maybe that was his pay for a week?

Jimmie's sculpture, "Self," created during high school.

MW: Could be.

LA: "$41.50." Yeah, $41.50 for forty-one and a half hours. He was getting a dollar an hour. And then a paystub from 20th Century Fox. That's probably for *Fixed Bayonets* (1951), which was a Korean War film released by Fox. And then Foote, Cone and Belding for "Alias James Doe" (*Alias Jane Doe*, radio drama, 1951). What about these little figures here in the case?

MW: Jimmie made a little film of bullfighter characters, and those are what he used: miniature bulls and Mexican people and bullfighters. He kind of set up a scene and he'd evidently click the camera and then he'd move them a little. Then he'd click it again. Then he'd move them again. We have the original film from it and those characters are kind of going around in circles. It only lasts twelve to fifteen seconds, but it is kind of interesting.

That other thing is a rock. Jimmie's dad had it. He said Jimmie picked it up on the beach at Santa Monica, and he just always kept it, so I displayed it. I thought maybe it would be something people would be interested in. Then some letters up there you can see that Jimmie wrote. One of them is to Mr. DeWeerd.

LA: From the same YMCA, in New York. How long do you think he lived there?

MW: I don't really know for sure. It's hard to say because he may have taken the stationery and written it from somewhere else, but he did stay at the YMCA for a while.

LA: "Folks to Remember." This is his address book from 1950.

MW: That's another address book from shortly after he went back to California from

Fairmount. I displayed that page because it has Bob Pulley's name on it. He was a classmate and good friend of Jimmie's, so I displayed that page even though there are some other ones I could have displayed.

LA: Then, a pencil drawing of a "James Dean Transport" truck heading to Hollywood.

MW: I think that's pretty significant. See it's a semi-trailer with an arrow on it pointing to Hollywood, isn't it?

LA: Yeah.

MW: It's pretty obvious Jimmie had ideas young in his life. It's also something Uncle Winton had in a box.

LA: So that would've been in California?

MW: Mm-hmm. That was in California.

LA: Then a bongo drum?

MW: Jimmie liked bongo drums for some reason, but that's what you call a Conga drum there. He has a set of black Conga drums.

LA: You're right. It's a Conga drum.

MW: It has a picture on the side of it, drawn in pencil, if you look close. It may be on the back where you can't see it. I'm not sure. It's odd looking. Whether he drew it or it was on there when he got it, I don't know. It kind of looks like a dancer. I don't know if he did that or if someone else did it, but there are pictures of him playing that drum.

LA: Oh, the drawing looks like Eartha Kitt.

MW: Really?

LA: She's African American. I don't think he drew it, though. I mean, it doesn't look like his drawing.

MW: Could be. I don't know where he got the drum. There are some pictures of him playing those drums, so I assume he got this in New York.

And then this sweater here is from Santa Monica Junior College. Jimmie's dad used to wear that sweater around. I happened to look at it one day for some reason and it said, "Dean." "Dean" was sewed in the back of it and Uncle Winton said, "Well, that was Jimmie's." Jimmie used to have that patch on it, but Winton took the patch off and he just wore it. Took good care of it. I mean, it still looks like new, so I put the patch back on it to display it.

LA: He kept the patch?

MW: Mm-hmm.

LA: That's great. Boy, if Santa Monica College only knew that this was here, I think they'd be blown away.

MW: Jimmie did this paper in Agriculture class in high school. He wrote about farmers and he dedicated it to my dad. I think it says there that it's dedicated to Marcus Winslow.

LA: "I dedicate this book for Marcus Winslow, good farmer and a true and understanding parent. Jim Dean." Your dad was like his dad.

MW: Yeah, he was. And that shirt, Martin Sheen donated that shirt to the Museum. Martin Sheen wore it in *Blind Ambition* (1979) and Jimmie wore it in *East of Eden*.

When Cole Reeves took over as President of the Museum, he got with me and said he'd kind

Jimmie's Conga drum, bull horns and matador cape.

of like to update things. I told him it sounded like a good idea, so he took a showcase that used to be natural wood and painted it all white. Then we put that mannequin of Jimmie wearing those clothes in there and put this sign that says, "Marfa is proud of George Stevens' *Giant*" on the back wall.

There are some photos of those signs around town in Marfa. I think Marfa made the signs up. Anyway, someone put them around Marfa when they were making *Giant*. It is a very rare piece. A friend of mine bought it off of a person who lived in Marfa. It has just a little bit of water damage on it,

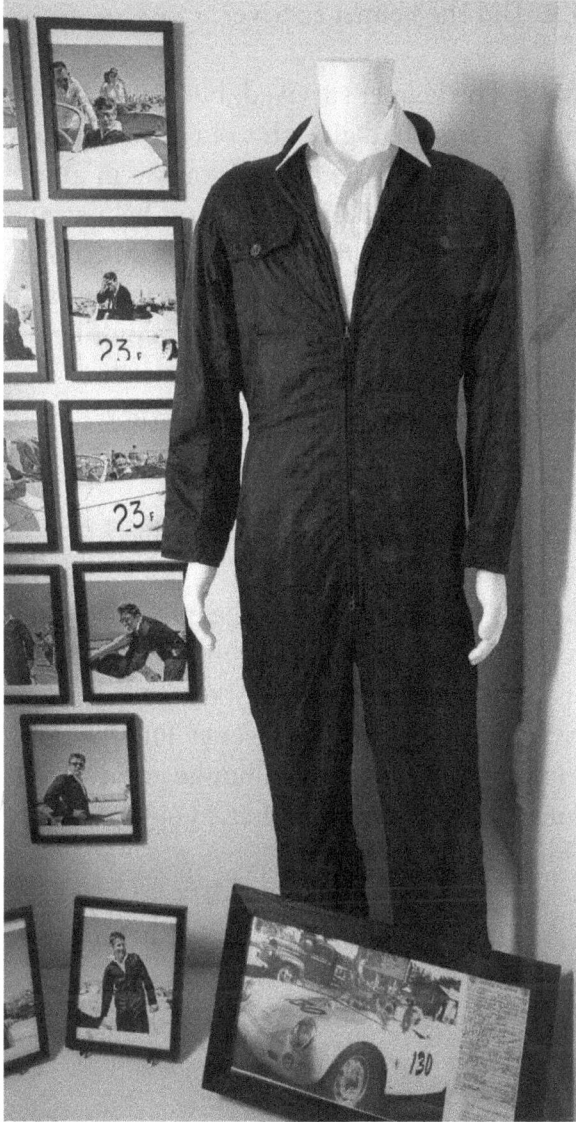

Jimmie's racing uniform.

but these are not around, so it's possible that is the only one left.

We put everything in the case and I said, "Where's that other showcase?" Cole said it was at the warehouse and asked if I wanted to use it too, and I said we might as well. He got it and we painted it all white and put the racing uniform in that one. Several of Jimmie's racing pictures are in with it.

LA: And then this drawing?

MW: That was just something Jimmie had, something he had drawn, a coffee pot with a towel hanging in the background. It's more or less an art object, I'd say, but it's interesting. He did a good job of it.

LA: And the board it is on? Does the board have any significance?

MW: Yeah, that was Jimmie's drawing board. Jimmie's dad gave me that very shortly after Jimmie died because I used to draw a lot. He thought I might want it. I never used it much. It takes up a lot of room, but it is adjustable. You can lay it down flat or straighten it up, whatever you want to do.

Jimmie apparently bought it just before he died because it's like new. It doesn't have any rub marks or paint or anything on it. I appreciated getting it. It's something I always kept. Then when we set it up in the Museum, I thought it would be nice to put some drawings on it. If I ever display his other one, I'll put some on that one, too.

LA: Did Winton drive this board back from California?

MW: I don't remember him bringing it back. I think he broke it down and shipped it back. It has little wing nuts, so it can be folded down pretty small. I won't say he didn't drive it back, but he probably just shipped it to me, also that black leather jacket of Jimmie's. Winton gave me that at a very young age. I felt it was something to be preserved, so only occasionally I'd let someone try it on, just to give them a thrill, but as far as taking it out and wearing it, I never did.

LA: Where is that jacket?

MW: I loaned it to the Indiana State Museum. It has the big black fur collar around it and two little Triumph pins on the front of it. It was here in the Fairmount Museum for a long time.

LA: Then the black jumpsuit over here.

MW: The black jumpsuit, again Jimmie's dad kept that. For a long time, it just hung on a hanger here in one of the showcases and about two years ago, Cole Reeves and I got a mannequin and put the jumpsuit on it. That's what Jimmie wore when he raced. Today the drivers wear fireproof jackets and fireproof clothes. I don't think this one is fireproofed. It's just an all-black driving uniform.

Those photos there were taken by one guy. His daughter gave me a copy of all his pictures and almost all are of Jimmie's Porsches. The 1500 Super Speedster he had. He participated in a few races with it

LA: Is that the car Lew Bracker bought?

MW: Yeah, that's the car Lew bought. Lew had it for a while. Of course, Lew didn't think it would ever be anything to save, so he traded it back in and it got lost. Nobody knows where it's at, but it was a pretty fast car. It had the super engine in it and Jimmie had a special exhaust system put on it. He was pretty successful in it in the short time he raced.

LA: He must have had a suitcase packed to go to Salinas.

MW: Yeah, he probably did.

LA: So, this racing suit would have been in that suitcase.

MW: Yeah, that and the helmet and whatever he wore.

LA: Did the helmet survive?

MW: The helmet survived, but it was brand-new. Jimmie had given his old helmet to Lew Bracker. That's the helmet you see in all the pictures. He had bought a new helmet and was going to wear it at the race in Salinas, but he never got there. The estate sold that helmet to someone, but I don't know whatever happened to it. The sales list has a woman's name by it, but Jimmie never wore it.

LA: So, Winton sold the new helmet?

MW: Yeah and they sold the motorcycle and a 1955 Ford station wagon. Those are all listed as being sold by the estate. Lew Bracker, over the years, lost the helmet Jimmie wore. He wishes he still had it, but he got divorced once and with this and that...you know how things get lost.

LA: The list Winton made of all the things he got from Jimmie's apartment in New York, do you have the originals of that list?

MW: I have the list, yeah.

LA: And it was done by...?

MW: I don't know who actually did it. They wrote down everything Jimmie had on a sheet of paper for inventory. The government required that list because he died. He even had a box or a bag of dirty clothes from New York, so they listed everything, all the books and records Jimmie had. There's nothing of great value, I think. It was just personal effects of his. I mean everything's of value now because Jimmie used to own them, but at the time it wasn't anything of any value.

LA: Then the photograph down here in the case is Jimmie in the Spyder?

MW: Yeah, that's him and Rolf Wutherich who was the Porsche mechanic with Jimmie when he was killed. Rolf was hurt pretty bad. He had serious hip problems and it seems like he had a broken leg and more. He was hurt pretty bad, but he did survive. I think he eventually died in Germany in a car accident.

LA: In a car accident?

MW: Yeah, as ironic as that sounds.

LA: Did he ever have contact with your mom and dad?

MW: No. Matter of fact, he sued the estate after the estate was settled, but he waited too long to file his lawsuit. The court threw it out, didn't even have a trial. He tried to sue for damages, physical damages and so forth. Like I say, he was hurt pretty bad. He was in the hospital for quite a while.

I think Jimmie's insurance paid for his hospitalization, but he was going to try to get some of that insurance policy that Jimmie had...for suffering. I

understand that, but he did wait too long. There was some kind of a period where he had to file a lawsuit, but he didn't file it in time, so he lost out.

LA: And the ticket to the right of the photograph?

MW: That's a copy of Jimmie's speeding ticket from that day, the one the Highway Patrol had. It was their copy and they let people make copies of it. Jimmie's original ticket, I don't know whatever happened to it. It may have been lost in the accident or something.

LA: And what's the story on the ticket?

MW: Well, he got a speeding ticket on the way to the race. Jimmie was stopped and Bill Hickman got stopped behind him. He was driving Jimmie's station wagon, pulling a trailer. At the time there was a law that if you were pulling a trailer, you had to go ten miles per hour slower than the speed limit and Bill was running up close to the speed limit. I forget how fast Jimmie was going, something like sixty in a fifty-mile zone. He wasn't speeding excessively, but he was speeding and the police officer

Jimmie's unfinished sculpture and his sculpting tools.

wrote him a ticket. When they wrote tickets, there used to be two or three copies, one underneath the other. That's what that one is. The word "deceased" is written on it.

Over in this case along the east wall, down on the bottom shelf is a bust Jimmie was working on at an art studio in Los Angeles. It's not completed, but after Jimmie died, the guy from the art studio contacted Jimmie's dad and told him he ought to take that bust and have it fired. If he hadn't done that, it would have stayed soft and so that's what he did. There's a picture of Jimmie carving that bust and right there, we also have the tools Jimmie was using to make it.

LA: Is the photographer...?

MW: I think the photographer that took the picture was Sanford Roth. The name of the art studio, I'm not sure what it was. Those are the tools he used. Then the other thing is a coffee pot, Jimmie's. That's the one I told you about when Marylou and I were visiting Jimmie's dad and stepmother in Florida. It was sitting on the counter in the kitchen. Marylou could tell it was old, but she didn't think too much about it.

She made a comment about the coffee pot and Ethel said, "Yeah, that was Jimmie's. One of the last things he bought was a new coffee pot." They'd been using it for years and years, but they quit using it. They asked us, "Would you like to have it?" Well, of course, you know, if they didn't want it, well, we wanted it, so there it is, supposedly one of the last things he purchased.

The next thing there is the actual contract between Jimmie and the guy who owned the house he was living in. This fellow managed the Villa Capri or something, but that's the agreement for Jimmie to lease that house off of him.

It looked like a log house, but I don't think it was. That was the impression you got. It was kind of a western-style house with a little front porch. Not a very big house, but something Jimmie was proud of. Sherman Oaks is where it was.

LA: Here's another letter to your mom and dad and a photograph of your mom and dad.

MW: That photo was taken not too long before Dad passed away. I think the Marion paper wanted to do an article on Jimmie, so Mom and Dad agreed to go along with it, and that's a colored photo taken by the newspaper, pretty nice photo out in front of the house.

LA: What did your dad die of?

MW: He died at age seventy-five. He had an artery in his bowels that deteriorated and there was nothing they could do with it. He more or less bled to death. Today they might have been able to take out part of the intestines, but they weren't able to then. That was in 1976.

LA: ...and then Jimmie's mom's driver's license?

MW: Yeah, that's something Jimmie's dad had. Apparently, he'd saved her driver's license, so I put it in a little thing here and put it on display. It's about the only thing we have that was actually hers.

LA: ...and then a lot of photos of her?

MW: A lot of photos of her, yeah. She was a very attractive young lady, they say. She died at twenty-nine of cancer, but these pictures are of her and one with Jimmie from 1931 over there in the corner. That would have been taken here in Indiana before they went to California.

Next is a picture of the train called "The Challenger." That's the train that brought Jimmie and Grandma Dean and Jimmie's mother's body back here to Indiana. They rode on the train and Jimmie wanted some kind of a souvenir, so the train people gave him that cup and saucer there that says "The Challenger" on it.

LA: Is that a menu?

MW: I think it's a brochure that describes The Challenger. Maybe it's a calendar for the train. That picture there was taken at the railroad station when they came into Marion with Jimmie's mother.

LA: What's the book that's in front?

MW: That is the book people signed for Jimmie's mother's funeral. People who came would sign it. It's kind of interesting.

LA: ...and who's the cowgirl on the top shelf?

MW: That's Mrs. Nall. It was taken at one of the festivals here in Fairmount. She was out in front playing with that rock lasso like Jimmie had in *Giant*, and someone took those pictures and put them in that frame. Those other things are more letters Jimmie wrote. One of them in

particular he wrote to me, and I made copies of it and have it displayed here. It's a pretty significant letter.

That next one is a drawing Jimmie did of an orchid. After one of the high school plays, the cast members all bought Mrs. Nall an orchid and they gave it to her. After class, Jimmie wanted to know if he could take that orchid for a little bit and she said, "Yeah,"

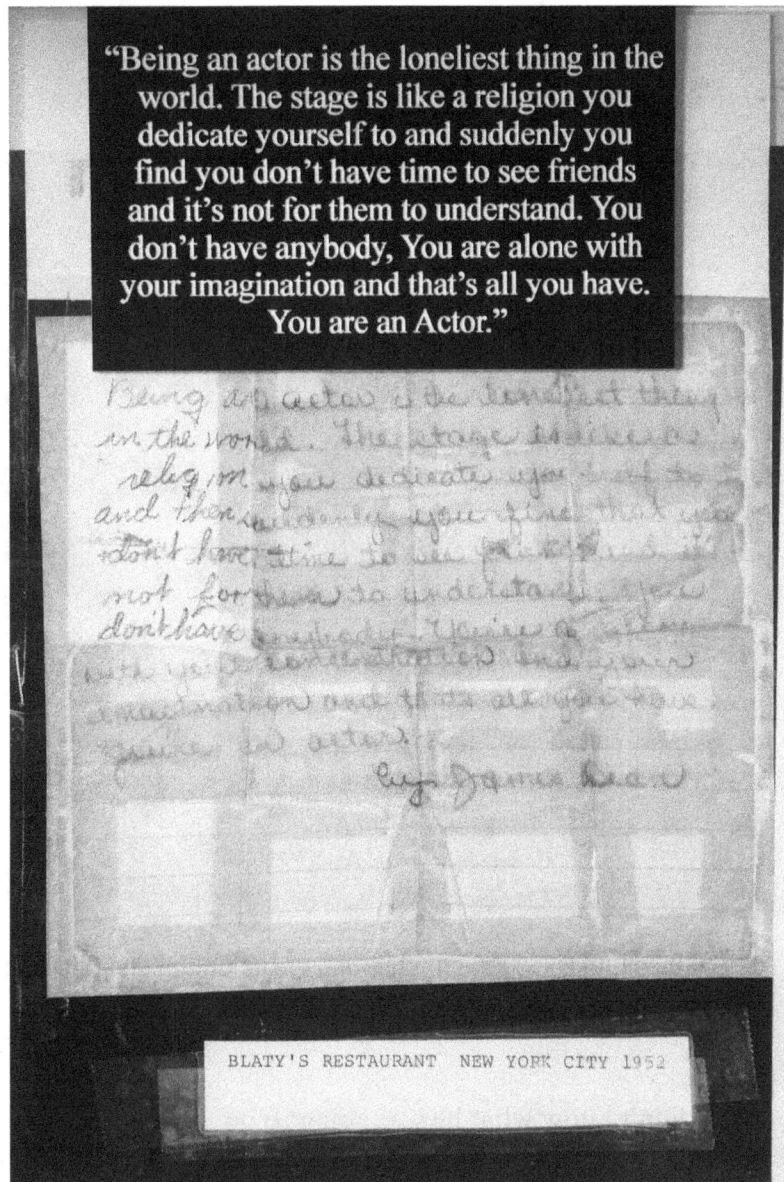

"Being an actor is the loneliest thing in the world. The stage is like a religion you dedicate yourself to and suddenly you find you don't have time to see friends and it's not for them to understand. You don't have anybody, You are alone with your imagination and that's all you have. You are an Actor."

BLATY'S RESTAURANT NEW YORK CITY 1952

Jimmie's handwritten statement on what it means to be an actor.

"Her Pride," Jimmie's legendary painting of the orchid given to Adeline Nall by her drama students. He told her when he gave her the painting that the orchid would now live forever.

but she didn't know what he was going to do with it. He went down to the art classroom and painted it and gave it to her and said it was something she could keep forever. He did that when he was probably a senior in high school. Pretty good painting.

LA: Yeah, it is. "Memories—Ye Muscle Men!" This must be a high school book that you would just take around and get people to sign.

MW: I think so, probably for a dance or something.

LA: In the back, it's signed by "Bud Cox—Number 9, Jim Grindle—7, '49" and on and on.

Then something Jimmie wrote on a napkin. "Being an actor is the loneliest thing in the world. The stage is like a religion you dedicate yourself to and suddenly you find you don't have time to see friends and it's not for them to understand. You don't have anybody. You are alone with your imagination and that's all you have. You are an actor."

MW: Sounds like he took that pretty serious. That bullfighting cape and horns, those were hanging on the wall in the New York apartment. When he was home last time, he had the cape with him. He'd rattle it around and try to get you to run at him. He got a big kick out of playing bullfighter. He seemed to take fighting bulls pretty serious. I don't think he ever did fight a bull, but whether he would have or not, I don't know.

LA: What's in the scrapbook?

MW: It's just some odds and ends. Does that say "Hudson Pope" on it?

LA: It says, "James Dean's Personal Scrapbook, poems, newspaper articles, and quotations from the Bible."

MW: Hudson Pope gave that to me and said it used to be Jimmie's. That's the guy who invited Mom and Dad and me to Canada. I don't know for sure the history behind it, but he became friends with Nick Adams and I think that's how he got it. There are a couple of doodles that kind of look like Jimmie's, so I thought it must be authentic.

Here in the next room is a life mask. If you look on the wall at this picture taken by Sanford Roth, there's a life mask of Jimmie in the background. Well, when Jimmie died,

Warner Bros. gave that life mask to Jimmie's dad. Then Kenneth Kendall got ahold of Jimmie's dad and wanted to know if he could borrow it and make a mold, so he could make a life mask. He said he'd never do anything with it. It was only for himself, but he did make others. This one here is all painted and it's pretty spooky-looking. It looks very real. Kenneth put eyes in it and painted the eyelashes and it's very realistic.

We put Jimmie's Triumph over in the next room and we put most of Jimmie's racing things all together in the cases along the wall. We have four trophies here from when he won some races. It tells on each trophy where the race was and what position he was in and so forth. I think they're all either First or Second Place positions.

Here's the valve out of Jimmie's Speedster that broke. That's what put him out of the last race. He gave that valve to Uncle Winton and Winton always saved it. Back here is a pit pass. If you look in this picture right above, you can see a pit pass hanging on his shirt.

These passes, I bought them out of collections. They weren't Jimmie's, but they are pit passes for the races he participated in. And here's his California Sports Car Club badge. You'd put it in your wallet like you would your driver's license to show for identification.

Over here are some of the things Jimmie wrote shortly before he died. One of them I think is very interesting. He's drawn a picture of a Porsche up there. Take a look at the front of the car. That's the Spyder. He's written under it, "Karl Orr—James Dean Motors." He has an address down there and from what I understand, Jimmie wanted to open up a Volkswagen and Porsche dealership.

This Karl Orr was going to be his partner and the address down below it here, "928 N. Fairfax," that's the machine shop that built the trailer Jimmie had Bill Hickman pulling when he had the accident. Jimmie borrowed that trailer while Karl Orr was making a trailer for him. Back in 1955, you couldn't just go anywhere and buy a trailer like you can today. You had to have one made up.

On this other thing, Jimmie made notes about who might go with him to the Salinas race. One of them says, "Karl," which would've been Karl Orr, and "Nolan" which would've been my uncle, Charles Nolan, and "Dad" which, of course, would've been Uncle Winton and "Bill Hickman" who did go with Jimmie, following in the car behind him. And "Rolf," he's the mechanic who rode with him to the race. Then he has some notes about the race, some things for him to do.

This little toy car, the summer Jimmie died, a friend of his by the name of Whitey Rust went to California and visited him and Jimmie gave Whitey this little car to give to me. It's very detailed. It winds up on the side. I never played with it, always had it sitting up on a shelf. That's the reason it still looks so good.

That magazine it's sitting on, it's the magazine you see in the Dennis Stock picture of Jimmie and me on the floor. That magazine is down there with us and it had a full page advertisement about a Porsche Speedster. It told the price and everything about it. I remember Jimmie showing it to us and saying he had one ordered just like it. I think it came in the same month he visited here. February.

This is a letter from Jimmie's doctor saying he was physically fit to race. I guess you had to have that to show the race officials before they'd let you enter, so it says that he's physically in good condition. These other things are photos of him racing. Here's a copy of an insurance policy receipt for the Speedster. It doesn't give the serial number, but it says something about the Porsche Speedster.

LA: Lew Bracker sold insurance. Did he sell that policy?

MW: Yeah, he sold that policy to Jimmie.

LA: He didn't sell the life insurance, did he?

MW: I think he might have.

LA: Oh, he sold both life insurance and car insurance?

MW: I think so. I'm not one hundred per cent sure, but Lew told me Jimmie said, "Well, I don't know whose name to put down for beneficiary." He told Lew, "Just put your name down." And Lew said, "I can't do that," so he put down Jimmie's dad's name. He was the closest relative at the time.

That other display case has his nominations for the Oscars© for Best Actor in *East of Eden* and Best Actor in *Giant*. We also have the nomination for *Giant* as the Best Picture for that year. It wasn't Jimmie's, but the other two were. I bought that Best Picture nomination in an auction. Henry Ginsberg was the producer and his estate had an auction and sold a bunch of stuff and I thought that was very important, that certificate for an Oscar©.

LA: And then the wooden Academy Award© up there?

MW: It's from Germany. I think Jimmie's fan club there may have made it up. Mom had it sitting on a shelf ever since I can remember. It's kind of neat. It's just like an American Oscar© except it is carved out of wood. Then there are a couple of other awards, three or four he won over the years.

LA: And the boots?

MW: Those were Jimmie's boots. I call them "motorcycle boots." In the picture to the left, you can see the soles are worn out. I have a lot of pictures of him wearing those boots. You can't tell it, if you're not looking closely, because his pant legs come down over the boots, so you can't see them, but if you look real good at the picture, you can see that this is the style of boot he has on. He used to wear them with blue jeans and he'd wear them with a suit or anything. He just loved those boots.

LA: Then that monkey that's up on the...?

MW: Okay, it doesn't belong to me. A person loaned that to me to display. On the set of *Rebel*, they had several of those little monkeys just in case one got lost or something and that's supposedly one of them. They said they couldn't really say one hundred per cent that the monkey was in *Rebel*, but it was one that was on the set at least. One of the gang members got it and put it in a memorabilia auction. That's where this person got it.

LA: Do you know which one of the gang members?

MW: It may tell up there. I'm not sure.

LA: Oh, yeah. Steffi Sidney.

MW: Okay, yeah, so I guess you have to go along with what she says.

LA: Yeah, I believe her...and then the knife?

MW: Those knives were given to Uncle Winton by Warner Bros. They're prop knives, and I'm pretty sure they used them in *Rebel* to practice the fight. They're not sharp like a real knife, but they look like a real knife. Warner Bros had "Rebel Without a Cause" painted on each one of the blades. They're just something to display, but they're kind of nice.

LA: This miniature windmill with Jimmie sitting on top? Where did it come from?

MW: I made it, made it from the exact wood off of the windmill in Texas that Jimmie sits on top of in the movie. This guy from Texas came in here one day and we were talking. He said his family lived in Michigan and the next time he came through he'd bring me something. I didn't figure he would, but a year or two later, here he comes.

The guy went out to the ranch where the Little Reata was. The windmill was beginning to fall down pretty bad. He said it had really deteriorated. He got ahold of the ladder and jerked it off, the two sides of it. I think he brought one of the step boards, but the rest of them, he said, were all rotten and had fallen off. The two sides of the ladder were cut in half, so he could haul it in his little Chevy S-10 pickup truck. He brought me that and he brought some other boards he picked up off the ground.

I forget that guy's name. I have it written down up at the house in my address book, but he lived in Texas within a couple hours of Marfa. He'd been to the Marfa area several times before. At first, I thought, *What the heck am I going to do with them?* But I was glad to have them, you know.

We had a doll of Jimmie in a cowboy outfit like he wore in *Giant*, and I took this doll and I measured the height and I looked at a photograph of Jimmie where he's standing up on the side of that windmill and that's how I figured out the height of the windmill, taking the doll and the picture and trying to scale it down. That's how I ended up scaling the windmill.

Marcus's model of the windmill in *Giant* from which Jett Rink surveys his inherited ranch, Little Reata.
It is made of wood from the original windmill.

I didn't cut that ladder up, but I took part of the windmill boards, not nearly all that he brought, and I cut them up with my table saw, running them through a planer and made them into clean boards again and I made this miniature windmill which is about three foot tall. I made a little place up there and put the doll of Jimmie as a cowboy sitting just like he does in the movie.

I kept it at the farm for quite a while. Then I thought, *Well, I wonder if that would fit inside one of those showcases at the Museum.* It just barely fit in there. It was almost too wide, but it did go. And it's pretty tall. Had to take all of the shelves out on one section to set it in there.

These two posts in the case, if you look at that picture, you can see the two posts and Jimmie has his hand on them. The rock is right there on the ground. The guy from Texas brought those also. Those two posts and the rock were still there. Pulled them out of the ground. Pulled the rock out of the ground down by where Jimmie's foot was. Brought them all up here and gave them to me.

For a long time, I had them in the barn, didn't know what the heck I was going to do with them. When I decided to display the windmill, I thought, *Let's see if I can do something with those,* and they're now sitting inside this showcase and I think it's a pretty nice little exhibit, especially since the windmill is made out of wood from the original windmill. I don't think it would mean as much if it wasn't.

The Museum says people are really taken by the fact that I still have the posts (*laughs*) and the rock and everything. I always thought that was real nice of the guy to bring that stuff. He called here about six months ago. It was the first time I'd talked to him in three or four years. I didn't even know who he was at first until he started talking about that stuff.

I said, "The next time you come through, I'll have to show you that windmill I made out of everything."

I wouldn't have had the nerve to carry that stuff away, but it was just falling apart. It's not like he took something somebody wanted because if they'd wanted it or cared, they'd have done more to protect the place. Probably whoever owns the land isn't even the same person that owned it when the movie was made. I don't think they care what happens to the stuff.

LA: And the red shirt, red and white?

MW: Supposedly it's one of Jimmie's favorite shirts. There's a picture of him wearing it. Ethel always claimed it was one of Jimmie's favorite shirts. For years and years, we had it displayed, but not very well. It was kind of folded up. When we started doing all this work with mannequins and putting up new captions, we got several mannequins to put clothing on, and it looks a lot better on a mannequin than just laying in a display case.

LA: ...and the rifle that's up there?

MW: That rifle was brand-new. It's the one I told you about...the one Jimmie used hunting jackrabbits with Bob Hinkle when he was making *Giant.*

Here is a program they gave out at the premiere of *Giant.* It tells about all the different actors and the characters they play. Also, in this case are some parts of the original Reata house in Marfa.

LA: Is that stuff you picked up?

MW: Yeah, I picked this up when we were there in 2003. If you look at those real close, you can see the molding looks like the window frames. The story is that after the movie was made, they left the house there because it was just a three-sided façade. The people who owned the ranch took all the windows out and sold those to someone and then a big storm came along and blew the house down. It is too bad it's still not standing. It would really be interesting if it was, but it's not.

LA: Then the ropes in the display case…?

MW: One of the ropes, according to Bob Hinkle, is the actual rope he made for Jimmie that he used to flip and tie into a knot. A "rock lariat" is what Bob calls it. The other rope is the one in the behind-the-scenes photos where Jimmie tied up Elizabeth Taylor. I got those off of Bob.

LA: And in the center of the room is the motorcycle?

MW: Yeah, the motorcycle, I'm pretty proud of that. It's the '55 Triumph Jimmie used to own. We have several pictures of him riding it. We got all the parts together for it. Coy painted it kind of a grayish blue and I think it's pretty close to the original Triumph color. It has a black stripe on the front and back fenders. There's a little luggage rack on top of the tank and the seat on the back is turned around.

It's supposed to be turned the other way so that the high part is towards the front and it would be sitting flat, see? In *The Wild One* (1953) with Marlon Brando, they turned theirs around, so we think it's the reason Jimmie turned that one around. Whatever it originally was, that's the way he had it. It's a nice bike, very nice restoration. There's a decal on here from Evans' Triumph Motorcycle Sales and so it's a very nice thing to have.

LA: Is that the place he bought it?

MW: That's where he bought it. What does that say on there, something "Evans?"

LA: "Ted Evans."

MW: One time we were in California, and we stopped in that dealership and Ted Evans' son worked there. Ted Evans was still living, but he wasn't there at the time. His son told us what his dad said about the time Jimmie bought that cycle. I think since then Mr. Evans passed away and the dealership is not Triumph anymore, but we felt fortunate to even talk to the son.

Mr. Evans said when Jimmie bought it, evidently, he had made *East of Eden*. He told Ted Evans, "I'm gonna be famous someday if you want to take my picture on this motorcycle." Ted Evans just kind of laughed it off. He had a lot of people coming in there blowing off. Then when it turned out Jimmie was famous, he said he wished he had taken some pictures of him, but he didn't.

LA: Can you tell the story about how the Triumph was found?

MW: Well, I had seen Jimmie's estate papers and it listed all the things he had. On the list was a '55 Triumph motorcycle. I talked to Uncle Winton about it, and he said it was there at his house for a while, but he knew he wasn't ever going to ride it, so he just decided to sell it. This was while the estate was still being settled, so the motorcycle was listed in the estate papers and the serial number was listed, too.

I mentioned it one time to my friend, Charlie Bridenfield. I told you Charlie is a fan of Jimmie's and he and his brother, Bill, would come down here a couple of times a year from Michigan, and we became good friends. Anyway, Charlie said, "Well, I know someone who might be able to see if that bike still exists." I said, "All right," but I didn't think they'd ever find it.

Charlie called me one day, "Hey, I found that motorcycle." They had run it through the California DMV. I said, "You're kidding." And he said, "No," and told me whose name was on the title and that according to the paper, he'd had it a long time. When Charlie contacted the listed owner, the guy had given the motorcycle to someone else, traded it for a gun, and he didn't want to tell Charlie where the new owner was. Charlie finally figured maybe this guy was running from the law for some reason. He told me, "I can't go any further, so I've done all I can do. Why don't you see if Mark Roesler and Curtis Management have anybody that can find it?"

Mark put me in touch with a private detective from Indianapolis, and I gave him all the information. I didn't hear anything for six months or so and then one day the detective called Mark and said he'd found it. I don't know how he found it, but he did. The detective was up in Minnesota and not very long after Mark talked to him, I got a phone call that he was on his way back from Minnesota with the motorcycle. He'd been up there in his own vehicle, a Bronco, and he got it and was bringing it back. That was in 1988, I would say.

It wasn't much to see. I think he only paid like $500 for the cycle, but the whole bill was over $8,000 for him running it down. At the time, it seemed like an awful lot of money, but I paid it and didn't argue with him. The guy who had it was tickled to death to find someone that wanted to buy it.

You know, it's probably a very valuable cycle now, but it was in tough shape. A lot of the parts were gone. Someone had made a chopper-type bike out of it. It had the wrong fuel tank on it and the wrong fenders and the wrong seat. It didn't look anything like it does now.

I have to give Charlie credit. He made a lot of phone calls to Triumph collectors. He was very particular and he got all the right "new old" stock he could find and what "new old" stock he couldn't find, we painted them and made them look brand-new. It's really a showpiece.

Charlie found someone that had a tank. It might've been a "new old" stock fuel tank, if I remember right. The seat...he found the seat for it and it was "new old" stock. He found a new front fender and the rear fender is used. He had a hard time even coming up with a used one, but we finally found enough parts to put it together. This was before the internet. Today you could probably get on the internet and find all kinds of listings for Triumph motorcycle parts, but back then they were hard to find.

When Jimmie had it, he put special handlebars on it. He wanted them lower than the ones Triumph had on it. A company by the name of Fleener made Jimmie's handlebars and we found one set of Fleener handlebars for that Triumph. They were on another bike and were dented where a U-bolt had been tightened up around the center, so we got it and Coy fixed it, ground it down and had it re-chromed.

Charlie found all new cables for the clutch and the brake and he took the engine and had it overhauled, the engine and transmission. I had a ton of money in just the parts when we got it done. The parts shipped here first and when we were finished with them, we'd drive them up to Michigan to Charlie to put it together, probably two or three trips it took.

Coy is a good painter and he repainted everything. He used a Chrysler blue, kind of a silver blue color, for the tank and fenders. He painted the frame and all the little pieces black. You look at something like that and you don't think about how many pieces are on it, but when you take it apart and take every single piece off of it, you have a whole bunch of parts. Coy painted every one of those parts.

LA: And the serial number is still the same?

MW: Oh, yeah. That's the right serial number. Yep. Thank goodness for serial numbers. You know, we got the title and had it put in our name. I never have started it. Didn't really want to because those old motorcycles, Indians and all of them, were prone to leak a lot. We did put engine oil in it and kicked it over a few times, and then drained the engine oil out.

LA: Except for what leaked on the Warner Bros. Museum floor.

MW: Yeah, that's right. They were prone to leak. It didn't leak up here in the Historical Museum, but I kind of think maybe hauling that motorcycle in an airplane out to California, the different air temperatures, may have done something to it. It's not leaking now, or at least I don't think it is.

I was really proud of that cycle. I felt it was an accomplishment to find it after forty years. It's a pretty good accomplishment because so many motorcycles just get scrapped out. You're always seeing an old motorcycle in a barn that someone quit riding and they just shoved it over in the corner and there it sits. The same thing could have happened to that cycle.

We found it because the guy registered it and had plates for it at one time and it was still on the Department of Motor Vehicles' list. How? I don't know, because we've tried to find the station wagon Jimmie had. For

years we've looked for that. I hired the same detective to search for it. Can't find it. Can't find any information on it. I mean we found out the serial number and all, but we can't find anybody who owned it. We have even checked a lot of out of state numbers, and it hasn't shown up.

LA: Did the private detective say where the Triumph was physically when he saw it? Was it in a barn?

MW: I don't know. He got ahold of the guy and the guy said he'd sell it. To be honest about it, I'm sure the guy didn't know it was James Dean's old motorcycle, but I don't feel bad about that because it was a piece of junk when we got it. It was nothing and no one else would have ever restored it.

LA: So, you saw it on the inventory that was made after Jimmie had died?

MW: Yeah, mm-hmm.

LA: When did you see that inventory?

MW: I don't know. Uncle Winton was living here in the little house. He'd come back from Florida when we found that list. I think it was from someone who had gone to the courthouse and printed it out. I don't think I had seen Uncle Winton's inventory list at that time.

LA: So, you put the Triumph right into the Historical Museum?

MW: No, we left it with Charlie for a couple of years to cheer up his brother. Bill had Lou Gehrig's disease and it made him happy to be there in the room with the cycle. We did bring it down to the car show, but we always took it back up to Michigan. It was the least we could do. Finally, one time when it was here, I told Charlie, "I think we'll put it in the Museum now," so this is where it is.

Charlie and Bill just became good friends. They'd rent a cottage on Lake Michigan in the summer right on the water. Marylou and I would go up and spend a week with them. We'd walk down steps and just sit out there by the lake and sometimes go out on it. There'd be boat races. We just really had a wonderful time with them.

They wouldn't let us pay for anything, so we'd bring food, to contribute, but we didn't even have to do that. They always came down here three or four times a year, and Coy and Chuck even got to be good friends with them. They talked cars all the time. Charlie was always buying cars and fixing them up and he'd bring them down, even stored a couple for a while at the Laundromat building.

One year around Christmas time they were here and it was really warm. They were playing football outside and I noticed Bill was limping. He said he thought it was a planter's wart and he'd have it looked at when he got back home. Well, it turned out it was Lou Gehrig's disease. Then their father contracted it and he didn't last long. Charlie had a touch of it, too, but he's been taking medicines and natural stuff and they've done him a lot of good. He married a girl from Southern Indiana, and they moved to Northern California so that's where he lives now.

When Charlie first was working on the Triumph, his brother could read, watch TV, and things. I don't remember how he was when Charlie finished, but the Triumph was in his bedroom for him to look at. One time I had a '65 BSA motorcycle Charlie liked and I sold it to him, and he restored it. That was also in Bill's bedroom. When they needed

money, I bought it back. It's a beautiful bike, maroon and a lot of chrome.

LA: Let's move to the case on the south wall.

MW: This up here is a little statue of Napoleon Bonaparte and Jimmie used to call him "Nappy." Actually, it was Jimmie's dad's statue. I asked Uncle Winton about it one time and he said he and Ethel bought a guy out, bought everything he had, all his furniture and everything and that was in the house and they just kept it. Then Jimmie took a liking to this statue, and it's in the background there in that one photo of Jimmie's house in California, sitting on a table.

Those composer statues, where Jimmie got those, I don't know. He might've gotten them in Marion somewhere because when he was home last time in '55, I remember he had them and he wrapped them up in bathroom tissue. I was really surprised when Uncle Winton showed me Jimmie's stuff and there were those statues.

It's amazing how many little things he kept of Jimmie's. Those cowboy boots, I don't think he wore them in *Giant*, but he wore them on the set of *Giant* because in the photo right there, he's got those boots on. Then there's a letter up there he wrote to Mr. DuBois, who was the school superintendent, about his plans for his life. I think everyone had to write one. That was his.

Over here's a shaving kit and Jimmie had his initials on it, "JBD" in gold letters. I think it's kind of neat. Here's Jimmie's watch and a picture of him wearing it. Uncle Winton said the band wasn't on it when Jimmie died. Jimmie took the band off and used to leave it lying on his dresser to tell what time it was.

A little gold locket Jimmie had that opens and closes. It has his initials on the front of it and inside are two pictures of Pier Angeli who Jimmie thought a lot of. Pier Angeli gave him that locket from what I understand. That's what Jimmie's dad told me.

LA: What's the red book here?

MW: That's a Bible. We were told Pier Angeli gave it to Jimmie, but there's no name on it, so it may not be. I think I've mentioned that we now think the girl in New York, Barbara Glenn, may have given it to him because the handwriting matches up with quite a bit of the letters from Erie, Pennsylvania. We found out Barbara Glenn lived in Erie, Pennsylvania, so it may be that she wrote them. We have several letters in that handwriting and none of them are signed.

This is a watercolor Jimmie did of a bullfight which I think is very, very good. It's a bullfighter and a bull and he signed it down in the corner, "James Dean." It's very impressive.

There's what Jimmie used to record Grandpa Dean the last time he was home. You can see how big that thing is. You had to carry it here on your shirt or if you had a big pocket in a coat, you put that recorder in there and then that wristwatch is the microphone. You'd wear the wristwatch and you'd have your hand laying on the table and anyone talking would think it's just a wristwatch, but really, it's a recorder. The tape went in this other little box that you had to carry in your pocket or clip on your shirt or something.

This was the tape recorder we thought for years and years had been stolen, but we found out Bob Hinkle had it. Bob said it was Jimmie's recorder and Jimmie had brought it over to Bob's house to practice lines for *Giant*. And then he died and Bob just had it there. It wasn't anything of great value. I guess he used to have some tapes on it of

Jimmie talking in *Giant* and so forth, but Bob said he gave the tapes to Warner Bros. to try to dub back in some of the stuff Jimmie said during that last scene in *Giant* where he gets drunk and falls over the table. Rumor has it that Nick Adams finished dubbing in some of the words. I don't know if that's true or not, but that's what they say.

These up here are what I call, "Miniatures." They're little miniature paintings of Jimmie that Kenneth Kendall did.

LA: He did all of those?

MW: Yeah, Kenneth Kendall did all of them. Aren't they good?

LA: Yeah.

MW: There are eighteen of them. They're very, very good paintings. I bought those also at David Loehr's auction, but they weren't in that frame. They were just loose. David hated to see them go, I think.

Here we have a script from *Rebel Without a Cause* and that script originally belonged to Nicholas Ray's secretary. It's signed by all the cast members and a lot of them wrote her a note. There's where Jimmie wrote his name.

LA: "To the most unselfish…"

MW: Then this is an Oscar© that has some controversy about it. Supposedly it was stolen from someone. It hadn't ever been presented to anybody because there's no serial number on it. Maybe the company that made it had it on display, but the story is Jack Simmons and Maila Nurmi gave that to Jimmie. They thought he deserved an Oscar©. There are some pictures of it in a movie magazine from back in the Fifties. That's the story. They stole it and gave it to Jimmie.

270

THIS AGREEMENT, made and entered into this _____7_____

day of March, 1954, by and

BETWEEN

WARNER BROS. PICTURES, INC.,
a Delaware corporation, hereinafter referred to as the
"PRODUCER,"

AND

JAMES DEAN
hereinafter referred to as the
"ARTIST,"

W I T N E S S E T H:

For and in consideration of the mutual covenants and
agreements hereinafter contained and set forth, the parties hereto
have agreed and do hereby agree as follows, to wit:

1. The Producer hereby employs and engages the Artist
to render his exclusive services, except as in paragraph 26A(1) and
(2) set forth, as herein required, for and during the term of this
agreement, and the Artist hereby accepts such employment and agrees
to perform and keep all of the duties, obligations and agreements
assumed or entered into by him hereunder, and agrees to perform sole-
ly and exclusively for and as requested by the Producer.

2. The Artist agrees: To comply promptly and faithfully
with all requirements, directions or requests, and with all rules and
regulations made by Producer in connection with the conduct of its
business; to act, pose, sing, speak or otherwise appear and perform
as an actor in such roles and in such photoplays and other productions
or assignments as Producer may designate; to perform and render his
services conscientiously and to the full limit of his ability and as
requested by Producer at all times; to perform and render such services
whenever and wherever and as often as Producer may request or deem
necessary or convenient; but there shall be no obligation on Producer

-1-

Page One of a signed and initialled copy of James Dean's first Warner Bros. contract.
Each page is initialled to show Jimmie read and understood the terms of the contract.

When *Giant* was done filming, the cast members gave each other different little gifts and so Jimmie had an inscription to Bob Hinkle put on that Oscar because Bob helped him learn how to talk like a Texan and taught him some of the lingo a lot of the Texan people said. Jimmie gave it to him and the cast gave Jimmie a stuffed armadillo.

LA: Has the armadillo shown up?

MW: No, I don't know whatever happened to it.

That script down there was Jimmie's actual script from *Giant*. And then there's a letter from Henry Ginsberg. He wrote on *Giant* stationery to my mom and dad after Jimmie's death. The paper in the background is where Jimmie borrowed a salary advance for $700 from Warner Bros. and that's the note he signed, saying he had to pay it back. Most of the other things here are "in house" Warner Bros. memos from Jimmie's legal file, which I have.

There's an original contract of Jimmie's with Warner Bros. Matter of fact, it is Warner Bros.' original copy. It's several pages long and he signed it. Pretty rare, I would think.

LA: Yeah, the studio sold James Dean's contracts plus his whole legal file when the Warner Bros. Archives donations were made to the University of Southern California and Princeton. They did it to show the collection's value because they knew the IRS would contest Chuck Sachs' appraisal. The only thing Warner Bros. Legal has of Jimmie's is a file of Xerox copies of everything you have here. They don't have any originals.

MW: I'm glad I bought it. There's an *East of Eden* book (Viking Press, 1952) Jimmie signed and gave to his stepmother.

LA: No kidding? Did he write something to her?

MW: Yeah, he did, but you can't see it. It's inside and it says if she would read this book, maybe they'd both learn something.

And then this record obviously came out after his death. Matter of fact, there's that wooden Conga drum on the front of the album. He was recorded playing those Conga drums. I can't tell you who recorded it, but they put it on a record. I have seen a lot of those advertised on eBay. Whether they're original or not, I don't know, but this is an original one here. It says, "Bob Romeo on flute." I heard it one time and it is kind of neat.

LA: Does he talk at all on it?

MW: I don't remember. It was years ago when I heard it.

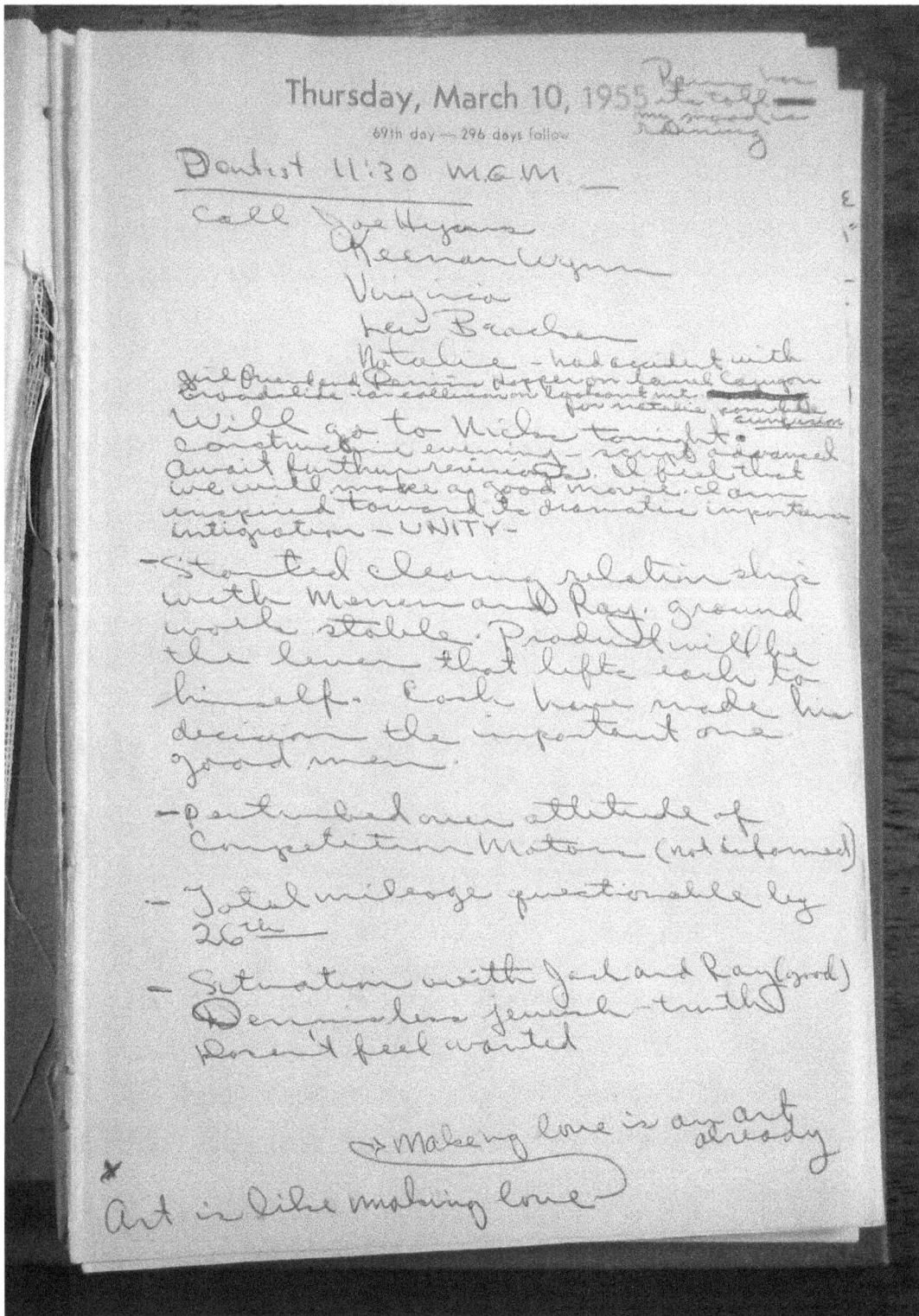

Jimmie's entry in his Daily Reminder documents a car accident Dennis Hopper and Natalie Wood have had, plus a successful script meeting with Nicholas Ray about *Rebel* and comments about Nick's reaction to Jack Simmons ("good") and Dennis Hopper who Nick eventually put in the background due to his relationship with Natalie.

Dear Dad,

I am having trouble with my teeth. I have a few cavities and (whether because of my diet or what) my teeth seem to be getting soft.

front *Back side*

* Left lateral starting to wear away all at once and rather rapidly. The hard enamel coating is worn away, leaving the soft interior.

left *right*

This left bi is violated. No cavity, or decay evident. Seems to be on the inside above gum. (As far as I can observe.)

I have some shows now, and, I think can ~~manage~~ to get back to you. You could make another partial and maybe make an extra. Also investigate the rest of my horrible mouth. I'm kind of worried. I would rather fix them up now than be sorry later. Would it be more costly to come back home and then return to N.Y. City? Or to have the work done here? I could only remain in Calif., long enough to get patched up. Could you look me over Dad? You know how important my teeth are to my craft. What do you think? Please write immediately. Ask questions or whatever. I'm anxious to clear this up. If I come, I want to come about the 19th of this month.

from
Jim

Jimmie sketches the problem with his teeth and sets up a meeting with his dad in Fairmount in September '52.

Afterword

Since Marcus was only twelve when his "older brother" died, the furor that started happening at his home and in his town had to have been incomprehensible to him. People were coming from all over the world to see where Jimmie lived and learned and was nurtured. How could a boy of twelve, living on a farm, handle it all?

It has been quite an honor to work with Marcus on his book, helping him tell his story, and capturing his legacy for his family and for all of the fans still coming to Fairmount and the Winslow Farm to pay tribute to one of the greatest actors to ever hit the silver screen.

Marcus, thanks to his parents, Ortense and Marcus Sr., was able to handle Jimmie's loss... and it was also thanks to the farm itself and thanks to his buddies. Life goes on. Cars. A girl friend who becomes the love of his life. Two sons. Grandchildren. As life went on, interest in James Dean, always an undercurrent of life on the Winslow farm and in Fairmount, exploded in the Seventies when the music and culture of the 1950s was rediscovered.

Winton, James Dean's father, eventually returned to Fairmount, and Marcus became his caregiver. A taciturn, quiet Midwesterner, Winton had been deeply hurt...first by the loss to cancer of Mildred, his wife, Jimmie's mother; then by the loss of his son; then by the scandal magazines writing about him as if he was the model for Raymond Massey's Adam Trask rejecting James Dean in a real life *East of Eden*.

As Dean's popularity grew again, Marcus Winslow was forced to assume the role of his parents, protecting and honoring Jimmie and his memory and making his history available to the multitude of fans coming to Fairmount to pay tribute.

Because of James Dean, Marcus has won and survived scurrilous lawsuits, yet he's also traveled the world, helping others see and understand just how far James Dean had grown from the small-town boy to the internationally acclaimed actor and film star.

Dean was still a work in progress when his life ended. Rhea Burakoff's October 5, 1955 letter to Hedda Hopper, housed at the Margaret Herrick Library in Los Angeles, expresses her feelings for the James Dean she knew:

I'm very grateful for the beautiful eulogy in your column about Jimmy Dean.

I was Mr. Kazan's secretary on *East of Eden* and knew and understood

Jimmy from that moment on. You're right—this boy had a lot of love to give, but perhaps was afraid of being rejected, like so many sensitive people. The birthday scene in *East of Eden*, which was almost unbearable to watch, must have been easy for Jimmy to do. I'll always be haunted by that terrible sob that seemed to come from his soul.

It's too bad that people judge that first deceiving, unimportant layer instead of trying to understand sensitive people—there's a lot of good stuff underneath! Toothy, insincere smiles and glad hands are a dime a dozen.

Thank you again—very much.

James Dean's work in his three Warner Bros. films still inspires and amazes. The stories I heard from studio retirees, plus those of others who knew or worked with Jimmie, paint the picture of a very complex, very talented, human being.

There was Eddie Bockser who was moving props from one stage to another when James Dean almost ran him down with his Triumph Trophy 500 motorcycle; another instance, I feel, where Jimmie would draw out reactions he'd study and file away for possible use in later performances.

There was Bill Schaefer, Jack Warner's assistant since 1935, who grimaced when I mentioned Jimmie's name. "He pissed on the soundstage walls," Bill said, a story Dennis Hopper transposed to Texas during the making of *Giant*, as told in his introduction to *James Dean: Behind the Scene*, saying Dean was sometimes so nervous before a take, he'd have to relieve himself urgently.

Julian Ludwig became friends with Jimmie at the Villa Capri and invited him to a party he was throwing in the Hollywood Hills where he was house sitting, but Jimmie never showed up. As Julian was driving his date home, he glanced over as they were about to leave the estate and there was Jimmie sitting against a tree, his motorcycle parked beside him.

He stopped the car and called to Jimmie, asking him what he was doing. Jimmie said he didn't feel like a party, but he didn't want Julian to think he didn't appreciate the invitation. Julian said that's when he knew how complex Jimmie was.

But then there was Steffi Sidney, one of the gang members in *Rebel*, who at the dedication of a time capsule in Hollywood, said how funny Jimmie was, something his screen image never showed, something her fellow gang members, Beverly Long and Jack Grinnage, confirmed.

Bill Hendricks, another trusted confidante of Jack Warner, said he liked James Dean—the only studio executive to say so. He and Jimmie talked about racing cars, since Bill had raced in his younger days, growing up in Texas. Marine Colonel Bill Hendricks was a publicity man extraordinaire and with his wife created Toys for Tots, based on a doll his wife made. He was also the studio representative who met James Dean when he arrived from New York and showed him his dressing room. He was also who Jack Warner sent to tell Dean he could no longer live in his dressing room, that he had to find an apartment off the lot...and he was also the one who on the evening of September 30, 1955, drove to the theater where Jack Warner was attending a sneak preview, called him up to the manager's office and told him James Dean had been killed in an auto accident. "He turned white. I thought he was having a heart attack," Bill said.

Marcus and I would like to thank Ben Ohmart and BearManor Media for allowing us to publish exactly the book we wanted to see. It is much appreciated.

Marcus and Marylou Winslow at the Winslow farm...2020.

Acknowledgments

Magnum Photos...Michael Schulman...all Dennis Stock photos are © Dennis Stock/ Magnum Photos...Cover, pp. ii, vii, 183, 208, 213.

Marcus Winslow owns © of Roy Schatt, Frank Worth, Robert Middleton, Matt Scott and Winslow Family photos and writings, James Dean's writings, photos, artwork and image.

Kenneth Kendall...Artwork © by Kenneth Kendall Estate 2018

Leith Adams...© p. 77.

Warner Bros. Inc....© James Dean Stamp Day photo...p. 67.

The Theresa Bowman Adams Estate...© WB Museum photo...p. 6

Photographers:

Dennis Stock...Cover, pp. ii, vii, 183, 208, 213.

Winton Dean...pp. 101, 102, 105.

Theresa Bowman Adams...p. 6.

Roy Schatt...pp. 16, 25, 78–81, 86, 87, 180, 182, 187, 188, 190–194.

Frank Worth...pp. 12, 22, 65, 70–75, 90, 122, 125, 140, 143, 198–202, End Page.

Robert Middleton...p. 205.

Matt Scott...p. 4, 117, 130, 132, 147, 222, 224, 233, 235, 238, 240, 244, 248, 250, 252, 254, 255, 257, 259, 260, 264, 271, 277.

Leith Adams...p. 77, 230, 273.

James Dean...p. 25.

Unknown... p. 20, 43, 44, 53, 55, 60, 92, 124, 127, 134, 158, 164, 173, 175.

Thanks To:

Adept Content Solutions: Lori Martinsek, Jason Pankoke, Friederich Schulte, Jorge Cazares

Curtis Management Group: Mark Roesler, Ryan Plukebaum

Guru.com: Transcribers Haley Lovejoy & Madison Taylor

Greenbriar Picture Shows: John McElwee

Advisors: Char Adams, Scott MacQueen, Dave Eisenstark

Marion Public Library: Rhonda Stoffer

Fairmount: Marylou Winslow, Coy Winslow, Chuck Winslow, Bob Pulley, Adeline Nall, Phil Zeigler, David Loehr, Lenny Prussack, Christy Pulley Berry, Dorothy Schultz

Fans: Marlin Wilson, Kip Brown, Susan Bluttman

Actors: Frank Mazzola & the Mazzola Family, Jane Withers, Dennis Hopper, Steffi Sidney, Beverly Long, Jack Grinnage

Filmmakers: Gary Legon & Sarah Dalton Legon, Michael Sheridan, George W. George & Robert Altman, Steve Allen, David Puttnam, Ray Connolly, Kirby Warnock

Warner Bros.: Marisa O'Neil, Robert Daly, Terry Semel, Barry Meyer, Judy Singer, Julie Heath, Patricia Kowalski, Barbara DiBella, Brian Jamieson, Linda Malcolm, Bill Hendricks, Bill Schaefer, Eddie Bockser, Lisa Janney, Julian Ludwig, Ken Taylor, Jules Melillo, Dominick Bruno, Greg Dyro

University of Southern California Cinematic Arts Library: Ned Comstock

Acknowledgments

Warner Bros. Museum Exhibit Design: Ruth Gilliland, Vincent Beggs, James Volkert, WB Property, WB Costumes, WB Special Effects, Cooke's Crating, Curtis Movers & most especially the WB Corporate Archive staff starring Billy Blackburn

Writers: Lew Bracker, David Dalton, George Perry, Liz ('Dizzy') Sheridan, Stewart Stern, Bill Zavatsky, Lainie Kazan, Bob Hinkle, Bruce Levene, Warren Beath

Musical Inspiration: Leonard Rosenman, Dimitri Tiomkin, The Eagles, John Prine, John Mellencamp, Bruce Springsteen, Morrissey, Bob Dylan, Mark Governor

And of course: JAMES DEAN!

Index

Note: an *f* indicates a figure; a *c* indicates mention in a figure caption.

James Dean—Thinker—Little Reata.